# A History of
# Europe
# since 1870

**M. L. R. ISAAC, M.A.**

*Headmaster, Latymer Upper School*

**SECOND EDITION**

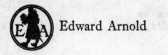

Edward Arnold

© M. L. R. Isaac 1971

First Published 1960
by Edward Arnold (Publishers) Ltd.
25 Hill Street
London, W1X 8LL
Reprinted 1961, 1962,
1963, 1964, 1965, 1966,
1967, 1968, 1969, 1970

**Second Edition 1971**
Reprinted 1972, 1974, 1975

ISBN: 0 7131 1693 5

Printed in Great Britain by
Western Printing Services Ltd., Bristol

# Preface to Second Edition

Many young people demand that their studies should be relevant to contemporary society, or even to the world of tomorrow, and history teachers have gone some way towards meeting this demand by removing the end date from their syllabuses. The first edition of this book, entitled *A History of Europe 1870–1950*, included a number of events up to 1956, and indeed some before 1870. This revised and enlarged edition, entitled *A History of Europe since 1870*, continues the story up to 1971 to meet current needs. Nevertheless, it remains a history text-book rather than a manual of current affairs.

The line between modern history and current affairs is indeterminate but it is not non-existent. Writing recent history or current affairs can be a hazardous business. Single events can alter the whole emphasis of the story. At the time of writing, for instance, the U.S.A. government has unexpectedly changed its policy towards China in a move that was unsuspected even by the U.S. Defence Secretary. Equally, though it seems certain, it is not yet known whether Britain will join the European Community, and if it does, what significant changes this will bring about. At the same time, crises which suddenly hit the headlines at the time of their occurrence can just as quickly disappear from public concern and interest. Vietnam and Northern Ireland can go the way of the Congo, Aden and Biafra as news items.

Current affairs are World affairs, and while it is impossible to study European history in isolation from the rest of the world, this book is concerned primarily with Europe. The history of Europe over the last hundred years, looked at against the broader background, remains an interesting and important study. It provides a sound foundation on which contemporary events can be based and against which they can be assessed. One of the dangers of the present concern with relevance is that contemporary problems may seem unique unless they are placed in a deeper context. The purpose of this edition is to provide Fifth or Sixth Form students, whether they are taking O level or whether they are following a general course, with such a context within a volume of manageable length.

M. L. R. Isaac

# Acknowledgments

We would like to thank the following for their kind permission to reproduce photographs used in this book:

The Radio Times Hulton Picture Library for those of Gambetta, Boulanger, Dreyfus, Moltke, Grey, Lenin, Nicholas II, Rasputin, Kerensky, Trotsky, Masaryk, Stresemann and the Hungarian uprising; Keystone Press Agency Ltd. for those of Tirpitz, Wilson, Pilsudski, Hoover, Atatürk, Mussolini, Chamberlain, Franco, Hitler, Goebbels, Himmler, Churchill, Marshall, Roosevelt, De Gaulle and Macmillan; J. Russell and Sons for that of Disraeli; Putnam and Co. Ltd. for those of Bismarck, The Kaiser, Bethman Hollweg, Edward VII and Schlieffen; The Travellers Club for that of Salisbury; The Imperial War Museum for those of Hindenburg, Kitchener, Foch, Lloyd George, Clemenceau, Poincaré, Stalin and Tito; U.S.I.S. for that of Nixon and Khrushchev; Camera Press for those of Mendès-France, Kennedy, Adenauer, Rippon and Heath; London Express News for that of von Braun; all efforts to trace the owner of the copyright of the photograph of Röhm have been unsuccessful. Cover photographs by courtesy of Radio Times Hulton Picture Library.

# Contents

# Maps

# 1 Economic Changes since 1870

This book is a political history, and as such it is chiefly concerned with the work of politicians and diplomats. But no history of events since 1870 could properly ignore the great technical advances, the expansion of the world's productive power, and the startling improvements in communications, which have accompanied political changes. Indeed, it was in this period that politicians began to realize how much their actions were controlled by economic factors. The First World War, for instance, showed that technical efficiency and manufacturing capacity counted for far more than manpower. Equally, it might be added, economists have come to realize that their ideas must take into account political considerations. It is easier for instance, to carry out a co-ordinated economic policy in a dictatorship than in a democracy. The truth is, as the history of this period abundantly proves, that politics and economics are dependent on each other, and that although it is possible, and certainly necessary, to concentrate on the study of the political, or of the economic, or of the social history of a period by itself, one must remember that the other branches exist. The purpose of this chapter is not to provide a comprehensive economic and social survey of the period. It is simply to emphasize some important points which must be borne in mind when considering the political affairs described in the subsequent chapters.

## INDUSTRIAL DEVELOPMENT

Britain was the first country in the world to reorganize her industries on the factory system, making extensive use of power-driven machinery. The basic stage in this industrial revolution took place roughly between 1760 and 1830, and for the greater part of the 19th century Britain enjoyed an almost unrivalled position as a manufacturing power. Her industrial greatness gave her wealth, and hence strength, and hence enormous political importance in the world.

In 1870 Britain was still by far the greatest industrial nation, though by then a few rivals were just appearing in the field. The basis of industrial expansion was steam-power, and as that depended on coal, some indication of the relative positions of the leading industrial countries may be seen from a comparison of the figures for coal production. In 1870 Britain produced 112 million tons, Germany 34 million, France 13 million, the

U.S.A. 10 million, Austria-Hungary 8½ million and Russia less than 1 million. Britain was then producing nearly four times as much pig-iron as any other country.

In the next forty years, industrialization in a few countries, chief of which by far were Britain, Germany and the U.S.A., proceeded at a very rapid pace, though the pace varied among the different countries, so that by 1914 their relative economic power was very different from that of 1870. By 1914 British coal production had increased to 292 million tons, Germany's to 277 million and the U.S.A.'s to 455 million.

In steel production the picture was even more startling. In 1870 world steel production was negligible, but in the 70's a major technical revolution was brought about by the perfection of processes for the production of cheap steel. The discovery in 1878 by Thomas and Gilchrist of a method of producing steel from phosphoric iron-ore enabled Germany, for instance, to make full use of the deposits she had recently acquired from France in Lorraine, and with their aid to build up a thriving steel industry which was to transform her into a mighty industrial power with staggering rapidity. Cheap and abundant steel enabled more and more industries to become mechanized and it also brought about a revolution in engineering. In 1880 both Britain and the U.S.A. produced rather over a million tons of steel, and Germany produced just over half a million tons. The figures for 1914, in millions of tons, were: Britain, 6·5; Germany, 14; the U.S.A., 32.

By 1914, then, it was the U.S.A. not Britain, which enjoyed overriding manufacturing power. But although from the turn of the century the U.S.A. had been taking much more interest in world affairs than she had hitherto, her strength was by no means fully appreciated in Europe. This was partly because she absorbed so much of her manufactures on the home market that European countries were not, until the eve of the First World War, conscious of the U.S.A. as a troublesome competitor. Germany had, however, rapidly entered the export markets, and her industrial rise was therefore much more quickly noted, particularly in Britain.

In comparison with Britain, Germany and the U.S.A., all other nations were industrial pygmies before 1914. France had made modest industrial beginnings quite early, but was developing slowly. Russia, on the other hand, though her manufacturing power was small (very small, if her size is taken into account), was developing very rapidly.

Between 1914 and 1939 the pace of world industrial expansion was less rapid than it had been in the previous twenty-five years, though it was still impressive. Manufactures rose by between 80 per cent and 90 per cent. Further changes, however, took place in the relative position of the industrial powers. In 1938, the U.S.A., responsible for 32 per cent of the world's manufacturing activity, was still in the lead, but the U.S.S.R. had climbed to second place with 19 per cent while Germany (11 per cent), Britain (9 per cent) and France (5 per cent), lagged well behind. What is more, countries like Japan, Finland, Sweden and India were building up their manufactures rapidly.

## ORGANIZATION OF INDUSTRY

In 1870 most businesses were small-scale family affairs relying for their capital on what money the partners had or could raise privately or from banks. The expansion of mechanization called for much larger capital investment than private firms could normally raise, and it became necessary to tap new sources of capital. Several methods were adopted, including the creation of banks whose chief or sole function was to provide long-term loans to businesses. These were particularly important in Germany, and they were also employed in France and the U.S.A. In Britain, however, and in the U.S.A. the system most favoured was the creation of joint stock companies, to which the general public could subscribe capital in return for a share in the profits. In the 20th century, company organization has spread to most industrial countries.

The joint-stock principle was not a new one, but its development had been hampered by frauds and mishaps which occurred in its early history. In Britain the famous speculative mania known as the South Sea Bubble of 1720 had cost thousands of people their savings, and some their lives. After that, companies could not be formed except by royal charter or act of parliament. Even then, shareholders had unlimited liability, i.e. if the company went bankrupt the shareholders not only lost the value of their shares, but they were also personally liable for the debts incurred by the company. Legislation was, however, introduced in most of the growing industrial countries in the second half of the 19th century to meet the needs of expansion. Limited liability companies, in which the shareholder stood to lose only his investment, were permitted provided that certain safeguards were observed. The companies were required to be registered, to publish the names of their directors, and to publish audited accounts annually. The U.S.A. was the first country to adopt the company system on a large scale. Not until the very end of the century did it become common elsewhere.

Limited liability made possible the creation of very large companies and these increased in number in the late 19th century, and even more rapidly in the 20th. In certain industries production and distribution fell into the hands of fewer and fewer companies. Some combines, like Carnegie's Steel Corporation in the U.S.A., controlled every stage of the manufacture of a given piece of steel, from mining the ore to marketing the finished product. Others, like Rockefeller's Standard Oil Company, were organized horizontally to restrict competition in one particular process—in Rockefeller's case, oil refining. Britain, Germany, and France, as well as the U.S.A., all had examples of big industrial organizations enjoying near-monopolies by 1900, though it was in the inter-war period that the concentration of industry increased most rapidly. France has been slower than other industrial countries to eradicate the small business. On the other hand, combines, or cartels, played a big part in the industrial expansion of Germany. Throughout this period, however, the tendency has been for

industry and commerce to become concentrated into larger units, and for
some of these units to become international. Even in the retail trade, the
same growth has developed from the first chain and department stores of
1900 to the supermarkets of today.

## POPULATION CHANGES

Well over 20 million people emigrated from Europe to the U.S.A.
between 1870 and 1914. Others went to Canada, Australia and New
Zealand. Several million Russians left European Russia to colonize Siberia.
Yet in spite of this enormous movement of peoples to the underpopulated
regions of the world, the total population of Europe increased in these
years from 290 million to 490 million. Britain added some 15 million on to
a population of 31 million. Germany and Russia increased at similar rates.
France, on the other hand, grew by only 3 million from a population of
36 million in 1870. In an age when military strength was still thought of in
terms of manpower, the low birth-rate in France was a matter of great
concern to the nation's leaders.

The growth of population was accompanied by increasing urbanization.
In Germany and Britain the percentage of people living in the towns grew
rapidly. In France the change was less marked, and by 1914 half the
population was still rural. Where industrialization was not greatly felt, as
in eastern Europe, populations remained predominantly rural.

## AGRICULTURE

Hand in hand with industrialization went the development of agriculture. The rapidly expanding industrial populations needed cheap, plentiful
food, and those agricultural areas which were in easy communication with
them introduced new techniques to meet the demand by increased productivity. Land was reclaimed, artificial fertilizers and oil-cake were produced,
and more and better farm machinery was introduced, some of it driven by
steam-power. Stock breeding improved and new methods were discovered
to prevent the spread of disease among crops and animals.

Most industrial countries erected tariffs to protect their home agricul-
tures and they were able to meet much of the new demand by increased
production. Even in Britain, the home of Free Trade, a strong movement
for protection, led by Joseph Chamberlain, arose at the turn of the century.

Nevertheless, as industrialization increased so did the need to import
more food. Production of foodstuffs was thus stimulated in some non-
industrial countries. Denmark, the Netherlands and Switzerland, for
example, specialized in the supply of dairy produce to western Europe.
Costs were cut in Denmark by the formation after 1860 of agricultural co-
operatives through which small farmers were able to enjoy the benefits of
bulk purchasing, transport, and marketing. Grain exports rose from

Hungary, Rumania and Russia, and from 1870 onwards the prairie lands of North America, in rail and sea communication with the big markets of the U.S.A. and Europe, were producing wheat cheaply and abundantly. Prairie conditions and the shortage of labour encouraged the widespread application of highly mechanized farming in America.

As national incomes rose, demand increased also for sugar, tea, and tobacco. Former luxuries like coffee and cocoa, and almost unheard-of tropical fruits like bananas and pineapples, came within the purchasing power of millions. European needs and enterprise expanded the production of these and other goods in distant parts of the world. Places like New Zealand and Australia developed as important food producers, particularly after the introduction of refrigerated vessels. In 1877 the rubber tree was first introduced into Malaya and it began to be planted extensively there in the early years of this century. Food crops were displaced, and Malaya, with the Netherlands East Indies and French Indo-China, rapidly became the chief source of the world's natural rubber supply. At the same time, other parts of south-east Asia were stimulated to supply food for these areas. Agricultural productivity had not increased universally by 1914. Even in Europe, particularly in the east, peasant communities still farmed in their traditional manner. It was not until the late 20's that mechanized farming was introduced into Russia as part of the programme of rapid industrial growth. Other countries of eastern Europe have introduced mechanization, using the Soviet collective farm system, since 1945. One of the many factors which determined where agricultural development took place first was communications.

## COMMUNICATIONS

Neither industry nor agriculture could have expanded with such rapidity without a revolution in communications and transport. Railway building had begun well before 1870. Britain had by then already acquired a reasonably comprehensive system, though its growth in the hands of numerous private, and often competing, companies, had been somewhat haphazard. The great age of railway building in other countries, however, came in the period between 1870 and 1914. Immense mileages of new track were laid and important transcontinental links were made. In 1869 two routes were completed across the U.S.A. from the Atlantic to the Pacific. The Orient Express began to run from Paris to Constantinople in 1888, and the Trans-Siberian Railway was finished in 1904. In Germany, as in France and Belgium, railways were planned as a national system, and they played a great role in unifying the Empire, and also in transforming Germany's geographical position in the middle of Europe from a commercial liability to an asset. She found herself at the hub of inter-European trade routes.

Road transport offered no serious competition to the railways until about 1920. Since then, however, private cars, buses, light delivery vans and heavy goods vehicles have supplied an increasing proportion of the expanding demand for land transport. By 1950 the state of its motor industries could be taken as a reliable indication of the general economic condition of an industrial country, and most railway systems are state-controlled and -subsidized.

The years 1870–1914 saw the change in shipping from wood to iron, and from sail to steam. Technical progress on marine engines in the 1860's cut fuel consumption considerably, and gave immense advantages to the steamship. In 1870 steamships accounted for only $12\frac{1}{2}$ per cent of the total shipping tonnage of the major maritime powers. In 1900 they accounted for 65 per cent. The increasing use of iron, and, later, steel, enabled much larger chips to be built, and furthermore the total tonnage of ships increased.

Between the wars the total shipping tonnage continued to grow, and further changes took place. Oil replaced coal, and shipping became more highly specialized, with the growing demand for oil tankers and refrigerator ships.

Port facilities were extended and improved as the volume of shipping increased, and valuable savings in time and costs made by the completion of the Suez Canal in 1869 and the Panama Canal in 1915. The closure of the Suez Canal following the Arab-Israeli fighting in 1967, encouraged oil companies to build super-tankers to carry crude oil from the Persian Gulf to the European refineries by the Cape route. The advent of these monster vessels, incapable of navigating the Canal, made its reopening less urgent commercially.

Not until after 1945 did air transport seriously challenge shipping. Even then, only passenger transport and mail have been affected to any marked degree. Regular air services began in 1919 and their range was gradually extended. Services began between Britain and India in 1929, between London and Sydney in 1938, and between New York, Southampton and Marseilles in 1939, but it was the Second World War which stimulated the rapid development of air transport. In the 1950's and 1960's air travel competed successfully with other forms of transport. In 1970, the Boeing 747 Jumbo-jet went into service on the Atlantic run to herald the new age of air travel for the masses, while the Anglo-French Concorde promised supersonic travel for the busy, the rich, or the adventurous.

Other forms of communication have played their part in speeding up contact between different parts of the world. In 1866 the first transatlantic cable came into operation. In 1876 the telephone was invented, though it was not used extensively until the 20th century. In 1901 the first wireless signal was transmitted across the Atlantic, and in 1927 a radio telephone service began between London and New York. In the 20's and 30's broadcasting spread over the world, to be followed in the late 40's and 50's by television.

Stimulated by space research programmes, enormous technical progress has been made in electronics. It was appropriate that people in many parts of the world could watch the first American moon landing on July 21st, 1969 on television, and in 1970 some could even watch the third landing in colour.

## LABOUR AND SOCIAL LEGISLATION

Trade unionism was not new in 1870, but until then it was weak and immensely handicapped. However, between 1870 and 1890, unions were granted legal recognition in most industrial countries, and they were allowed to exist in Russia after 1906. The first groups to organize themselves successfully were the skilled workers, but in the economic prosperity of the late 80's and early 90's a series of dramatic strikes, like the London dockers' strike and the Ruhr coal strike of 1889, marked the beginnings of organization among the unskilled or semi-skilled workers. All the early unions met with considerable opposition from employers, but in the relatively stable labour conditions of Europe this was gradually overcome, and the unions were generally recognized as the proper representatives of the employees. In the U.S.A., however, the vast influx of immigrants before 1921 severely weakened the bargaining position of the workers, particularly the unskilled, and the employers were able to delay the rise of unions to effective power until the early 1940's, nearly a generation after immigration had almost ceased.

The early trade unions were far from united amongst themselves, even in their general aims. Three main types can be distinguished. First, those which were solely concerned with the improvement of wages, hours, and conditions of work. The skilled unions generally conformed to this type, and deliberately avoided political affairs. Roman Catholic workers, too, who wished to dissociate themselves from Socialists, formed non-political unions which were moderately important in Germany and Italy. The second type, while sharing the economic aims of the non-political unions, also wanted to secure social reform—and ultimately a Socialist society—by political action, e.g. by getting representatives into parliament. This type became increasingly important after 1870 in Britain and Germany, and formed the basis of the organized support of the British Labour Party and the German Social Democratic Party. The third group was dominated by the Syndicalists, who played the leading part in French and Italian unionism in the first decades of this century, and who found adherents among the unskilled workers in the U.S.A. Syndicalists argued that workers could bring the life of a country to a standstill if they all joined in a general strike. They argued that this all-powerful weapon should be used to overthrow the existing political systems, which could then be replaced by a new form of government based on the workers' unions. The Syndicalists, unlike the Communists, who also wished to overthrow the existing state systems, would have nothing to do with political parties. Syndicalism was an important but limited phase in the history of trade unionism. In the First World War the majority of workers found that their patriotism urged them to support the systems they had wished to destroy, and the Syndicalists, like the Communists and extreme Socialists who opposed the war, lost most of their following.

Although the majority of trade unionists paid lip-service to international solidarity, in fact attempts at international organization have met with little success. In 1909 the International Federation of Trade Unions was formed, and by 1919 60 per cent of the world's trade unionists were affiliated to it, but it never attempted to exert political influence, and its membership fell in the 1930's when trade unionism was weakened in many countries by the depression, and in Germany by oppression. The Communist International, formed in 1921, became the largest international trade union body, but 97 per cent of its membership came from the U.S.S.R. After the Second World War a rigid division divided the Communist from the non-Communist unions of the world. Trade unions have always been more successful in securing benefits for their members within the existing framework of society than in securing changes in the framework itself.

Nevertheless, governments were not unmindful of the growing strength of organized labour and of their responsibilities towards its welfare. By 1914 every European country outside Russia and the Balkans had introduced laws governing hours and conditions of work, and safety regulations for factory workers. Germany led the way in social legislation with the introduction in the 1880's of accident and sickness insurance, and old age pensions. Britain did not introduce old age pensions until 1908, or sickness insurance until 1911. But part of the National Insurance Act of 1911 provided for unemployment pay for certain trades. This was the first national scheme for unemployment insurance, and it served as a model for other countries, though little was done until the 1920's. The important change that was taking place at the end of the 19th century in much of western Europe was the growing acceptance of the idea that governments were responsible for the social welfare of their peoples.

## THE END OF FREE TRADE

For most of the 19th century the dominant economic doctrine in Europe was that of Free Trade. The supporters of this doctrine argued that governments should not attempt to control trade artificially, by such means as subsidies to lower the price of exports, or tariffs to raise the price of imported foreign goods. To act thus, they argued, was not only bad for trade, but was in the long run a waste of time. Trade would always find its own level. There was a good deal of sense in this. For example, when Britain was almost the sole—and certainly the cheapest—manufacturer of railway engines, there was little point in another country's placing a tariff on imported railway engines. The chief effect of this would be to reduce the number of engines the country could afford. There was equally little point in the British government's putting tariffs on, say, French wines. If

Free Trade were universally practised, Britain would sell more manufactured goods, the French would sell more wines, and so forth.

The chief exponents of Free Trade were to be found in Britain, and this was scarcely surprising while Britain led the world in manufacturing activity. British manufacturers wanted cheap food to keep their wage bills low, cheap raw materials to keep the prices of their products low, and no tariffs, so that they could sell their goods at competitive prices in less industrialized countries. British industry stood to gain all by Free Trade, but its propaganda was so persuasive that other countries were partially converted to it, and between 1860 and 1880 made considerable tariff reductions.

The growth of industrialization in other countries, however, in the late 19th century led to the abandonment of Free Trade. While cheap British goods were allowed to flood into France and Germany, for example, the infant industries of those countries faced ruin. Foreign manufacturers demanded protection, and gradually their governments gave it them. Germany imposed tariffs in 1879 followed by France, Austria-Hungary, Italy and Russia in the early 1880's. The U.S.A. had always pursued a protectionist policy, and in the second half of the 19th century its tariffs were high, and rising. In 1913 this trend was temporarily reversed, but even then import duties averaged 27 per cent. In 1930 American tariffs hit an all-time high, and other countries retaliated by raising theirs. Even Britain acknowledged defeat, and in 1932 introduced a general tariff of 10 per cent, and protective duties of up to 33½ per cent on some manufactured goods. Free Trade was at an end, for the time being at least.

Free Trade had been part of a general doctrine known as *laissez-faire*. This idea, in its broadest interpretation, meant that governments should interfere with the economic and social lives of their peoples as little as possible—that governments governed best when they governed least. People who maintained this belief logically opposed factory legislation and social insurance as well as tariffs. As we have seen, most industrial countries accepted the need for the regulation of factory employment quite early in their industrial histories, though social insurance generally followed more slowly. In the U.S.A. the effective demand has usually been for *laissez-faire* at home, coupled with heavy protection from abroad. President Hoover, who signed the Hawley-Smoot tariff in 1930, declared himself opposed to any measures which would undermine the 'rugged individualism' of Americans.

## WAR—SLUMP—WAR

The First World War caused governments to exercise unprecedented control over industry, agriculture, and commerce. When the war was over, that control was largely abandoned, and a trade boom followed in the 1920's which concealed the structural cracks left by the war in the world economy. The victorious nations were heavily in debt to the U.S.A. and to Britain.

Germany was in economic disorder, and so was Russia. The redrawing of the map of Europe, by breaking up the Austro-Hungarian Empire and creating an independent Poland, had shattered the old economic divisions. The problems involved in this situation were serious, though they need not in themselves have led to disaster.

The really disastrous feature of the post-war economy was the dependence of the world on the financial stability of the U.S.A. Before the war Britain had been the largest international creditor. After the war, Britain's place was taken by the U.S.A., though both Britain and France built up their foreign investments to a considerable level again in the 1920's. But whereas before the war most of the money that was lent to foreign countries was used to promote production in undeveloped areas, and thus created wealth to repay loans, after the war much of the money went to European governments and public bodies who used the money to repay loans, to pay reparations (in the case of Germany) and to undertake public works. Thus the post-war loans were often not creating wealth, but were merely increasing the commitments of the borrowers to the creditor nations.

The disastrous consequences of this situation appeared in 1929. The U.S.A. had enjoyed a productive boom so spectacular that most Americans thought that life was going to go on getting better and better for ever. But by 1928 production of some goods had saturated the market, and prices began to fall. Unfortunately, speculators in shares paid little regard to production figures, and prices on the stock market soared to quite unrealistic heights. A great many businesses, as well as private individuals, had staked heavily on continued prosperity by borrowing considerable sums of money. When they began to have doubts about that prosperity, panic set in. The Wall Street[1] crash came in October 1929. Share prices tumbled down as people rushed to get rid of them while they could. Banks failed, businesses went bankrupt, production fell, and unemployment rose. Public confidence was shattered, and nothing short of sweeping government action could repair the damage.

European countries now found that American bankers wanted their money back, and at the same time the volume and the value of international trade fell. Unemployment rose nearly everywhere. The Nazi party in Germany had a magnificent situation to exploit. But governments elsewhere suffered crises, too, and one of the most important effects of the depression was that it caused countries to be acutely self-centred in their attitude to international problems. They were too busy saving themselves to worry about their neighbours.

Only the U.S.S.R., with its very limited foreign trade, remained almost untouched by the depression. Germany and Britain recovered most quickly, and after 1936 their production rose to new heights, though they still had a comparatively large number of unemployed. France and the U.S.A. recovered more slowly.

[1] The New York Stock Market.

The depression was finally lost in the turmoil of the Second World War, which in itself created new economic problems. Vast areas were devastated, and at the end of the war Germany and Japan were both at an industrial standstill. Furthermore, the economic pattern of Europe had undergone two changes: first, when Hitler had conquered much of the Continent and had subordinated the economic resources of those countries he controlled to the needs of Germany; second, when the iron curtain fell through the middle of Germany and divided western Europe from the East. The U.S.A. again emerged as the leading creditor nation, though now her position was one of absolute supremacy. Britain had had to part with the greater part of her foreign assets in the early years of the war.

But much had been learned from the lessons of the inter-war years. Financial help from the U.S.A. during the war in the form of lend-lease had done much to ease the problem of post-war debts. No attempt was made by the Western Powers to exact reparations, though the U.S.S.R. took goods and machinery from Eastern Germany.

The major post-war economic problem was the shortage of dollars to pay for imports from the U.S.A. But the U.S.A. rose to its responsibilities as the wealthiest and most powerful nation in the world. Through the agency of various United Nations bodies and by individual agreements with nations, the U.S.A. poured out money to aid recovery, though American tariffs made it difficult for European nations to earn as many dollars as they should have liked to by their exports.

The key-note of post-war economic policies has been international co-operation. In 1947 twenty-three countries joined in a General Agreement on Tariffs and Trade (G.A.T.T.) which provided for some substantial tariff reductions, and bound the signatories not to extend or increase existing tariffs. In the same year, the European Recovery Programme was approved by the U.S. Congress. This programme, known as the Marshall Plan, came into operation in 1948, and made available U.S. dollars for European recovery. A special body, called the Organization for European Economic Co-operation (O.E.E.C.) was formed out of the sixteen participating countries and the western zones of Germany. The members were required to increase their production and to adjust their trade so that they could balance their payments as nearly as possible. By 1951, when the scheme came to an end,[1] some $12 500 million had been provided under the Marshall Plan.

Economic recovery was rapid and genuine after the Second World War, though the dollar problem remained. Regrettably, one of the factors which eased the difficulties of the adverse trade balance between the U.S.A. and Europe was the enormous expenditure incurred by the U.S.A. on defence in Europe, both directly and through the agency of the North Atlantic Treaty Organization (N.A.T.O.) set up in 1949. In fighting what was termed the 'cold war' against the Communist countries, the U.S.A.

[1] O.E.E.C. continued to exist, and the U.S. continued to provide economic aid through new agencies.

dispensed dollars liberally to the undeveloped, the uncommitted, and the undefended countries. Politics and economics go hand in hand.

## THE EUROPEAN COMMUNITY

In some ways, one of the most interesting examples of international co-operation since the war is rooted in economics.

*E.C.S.C.* In 1950 M. Robert Schuman, then French Foreign Minister, proposed a community to control the coal and steel resources of France, Germany and any other interested European countries. From this proposal emerged the European Coal and Steel Community which was set up in 1952 by Belgium, France, Western Germany, Italy, Luxembourg and the Netherlands. E.C.S.C. is governed by a High Authority which is independent of the governments of the member states, and yet has absolute control over the production of these two vital commodities. The avowed object of this community was to remove rivalry among the countries of western Europe.

*E.E.C.* In 1957, the six member states of E.C.S.C. signed the Treaty of Rome, which established the European Economic Community (E.E.C.). The treaty provided for the extension of economic integration between the Six over a period of twelve years. By the end of that period, the members aimed to have

1. No customs duties or trade quotas between each other.
2. A common customs tariff with non-members.
3. Free movement of labour and capital between member countries and interchangeable professional qualifications.
4. Common policies for agriculture and transport.
5. Fair competition within the Community.
6. Integrated economic policies, supported by the necessary social and economic legislation.
7. A European Social Fund to aid employment and raise living standards.
8. A European Investment Bank.
9. Association with overseas countries and territories to improve trade and development.

This ambitious programme has run into some difficulties, notably in the attempts to formulate a common agricultural policy, but the foreign ministers of the member nations have pressed ahead with energy and achieved significant progress. By July 1st, 1968, the E.E.C. became a Common Market in fact with the abolition of internal customs duties and the adoption of a common external tariff.

*EURATOM* A separate Treaty of Rome in 1957 set up the European Atomic Energy Community. Its object was to pool the technical and industrial resources of the Six, for the production and development of nuclear energy.

THE GOVERNMENT OF THE EUROPEAN COMMUNITY

E.C.S.C., E.E.C., and EURATOM are all governed by a single authority which consists of a Commission, a Council of Ministers, the European Parliament, and the European Court of Justice.

The Commission, which controls policy, consists of nine (originally 14) members who are independent of the member governments. The Council of Ministers consists of ministers from each member country, and its composition varies according to the matters up for discussion. This is the main decision making body.

The European Parliament is formed by 142 members nominated by the parliaments of the member states. This body must be consulted on all major issues and it can, by a vote of no-confidence, dismiss the Commission.

The European Court of Justice, first set up in 1952 to serve the E.C.S.C., exists to settle disputes arising out of the Treaties. Cases may be brought by member governments, corporations, or individuals. The Court's verdicts are binding on all member states.

The European Community is concerned solely with a limited aspect of the life of a limited area of Europe, but in involves the sacrifice of some significant sovereign rights. Its evident success in promoting economic growth among its members has encouraged other countries, notably Britain, to try to join.

BRITAIN'S APPLICATION FOR MEMBERSHIP

Britain first sought admission to the Community in 1961, but her application was vetoed by France in January 1963. General de Gaulle, then President of France, was himself too much of a nationalist to be wholly attracted by the political aspirations of those working towards a united Europe. He wanted Europe to be strong so that its voice could be heard in world affairs alongside the voices of the U.S.A. and the U.S.S.R. But he wanted the voice of Europe to have a strong French accent. Britain, he feared, was too much distracted by Commonwealth interests and too subservient to the U.S.A. to be a good, committed, European.

In 1963, de Gaulle was probably right. Public opinion was, on the whole distrustful of signing away sovereign powers to a supra-national European authority. Fear that Britain would be left behind in a world economic race if it *failed* to join was the driving force behind Britain's application.

In January 1960, Britain, Sweden, Norway, Denmark, Austria, Switzerland, and Portugal (Finland became as associate member in 1961) set up the European Free Trade Association (E.F.T.A.). E.F.T.A. was set up under pressure from industrialists in the Seven to establish a free trade area as a platform from which to negotiate with E.E.C. for a single integrated market in Western Europe.

In 1967, Britain, by far the largest economically of the E.F.T.A. countries, Eire, Denmark, and Norway began the second attempt to join E.E.C.

By this time, Britain was less concerned with Commonwealth interests, but anti-Marketeers in Britain had marshalled their forces to point out that the price Britain might have to pay for entry could be too high. While General de Gaulle remained President of France, Britain's entry seemed likely to be indefinitely postponed. Neither his resignation in April 1969, nor his death in 1970, accelerated the pace of the negotiations. But, with the possible exception of France, the Six wanted a wider Western European community. The negotiations became a matter of bargaining for terms acceptable to all parties and interests. (See p. 203 for map of E.E.C. and E.F.T.A. countries.)

The British negotiations with E.E.C. have concentrated attention on the economic aspects of the European Community, but the Schuman Plan from which the movement began aimed to achieve political harmony through economic integration. If a strong Europe uses its power to flourish at the expense of others it will have betrayed the hopes of its founders. If it remains true to their ideals, it might show the way by which international rivalry may be removed.

# 2  France, 1870-1914
## *The Internal Affairs of the Third Republic*

### THE COLLAPSE OF THE SECOND EMPIRE

Few wars can have been as unnecessary or as far-reaching in their catastrophic results as the Franco-Prussian War of 1870–71. The quarrel between France and Prussia over the acceptance by a Hohenzollern prince of the vacant Spanish throne, which the French regarded as their preserve, had been settled when the King of Prussia, head of the Hohenzollerns, arranged for the withdrawal of the candidature. The French had scored a diplomatic triumph; a triumph which was sorely needed to bolster the crumbling prestige of Napoleon III's Empire. But the French Ministers were not content to let the matter rest there. Backed in their country by a wave of anti-Prussian hysteria they themselves had fomented, they demanded a formal guarantee that the candidature would never be renewed. This insolent demand was designed to show Europe, and the French people, who had every cause to think otherwise, that the Second Empire could play a part in foreign affairs worthy of the First. In the famous Ems telegram (see p. 26) the Prussian King politely declined to give such a guarantee. Bismarck, his chief Minister, edited this message before publication to make it sound like a rebuff to France.

The Ems telegram was, of course, the excuse for the war, not the cause of it. The cause lay in the belief, current in both countries, particularly since the Prussian defeat of Austria in 1866, that the movement for German unification must inevitably produce war between France and Prussia. Had the French wanted to preserve peace they would not have acted as swiftly as they did on receipt of the distorted telegram, but feeling ran high in Paris. Honour had to be satisfied. Bismarck had neatly turned the diplomatic tables. It was now France who faced war or humiliation, yet in the eyes of Europe she remained the aggressor. The consciences of the French Ministers were, however, clear, and on July 19th, 1870, Napoleon III, who did not share his Ministers', or his wife's, enthusiasm for war, nor their confidence in victory, declared war on Prussia. In the streets the mobs chanted 'À Berlin'. 'The Army', declared the Minister of War, 'is ready down to the last gaiter button.'

In fact France was woefully unprepared. Militarily her organization was chaotic, her reserves inadequate, her plans unrealistic. Diplomatically, she was isolated. Indeed, it is difficult in retrospect to see why most people

*Map 1. Europe 1870 before the Franco-Prussian War*

expected a French victory. Within a month of the declaration of war the main French Army was besieged in Metz. The force which went to relieve it was surrounded and hopelessly outnumbered at Sedan, and, on September 2nd, 84 000 men, 2700 officers, 39 generals, and the Emperor Napoleon III surrendered to the enemy. The Empire was at an end.

## THE GOVERNMENT OF NATIONAL DEFENCE

The fall of the Empire did not mean the end of the war. A provisional government, called the Government of National Defence, was formed, and the Third Republic was proclaimed. Leaders were found from the ranks of the Deputies who had been in opposition to Napoleon III. Gambetta, a thirty-two-year-old barrister, occupied the key position of Minister of the Interior and prepared to carry the struggle to victory. Jules Favre, the new Foreign Minister, summed up the spirit of the new ministry when he declared, 'We shall yield neither an inch of our territory, nor a stone of our fortresses.'

Paris was surrounded, but, with the exception of three aged Deputies who were sent to Tours to represent the Government, the Government of National Defence remained in the capital, and kept up a picturesque but erratic communication with the provinces by means of carrier pigeons and balloons. When help from outside failed to be forthcoming, Gambetta left Paris by balloon, assumed the post of Minister of War as well as of the Interior, and galvanized the wilting provinces into action. New armies, untrained and ill-equipped, were formed. Orleans was reoccupied. But the hope of victory was short-lived. Metz fell, and the German Army, which had been strained to its limits by the two great sieges of Metz and Paris, now had troops to deploy against the scratch armies of the Republic. Paris survived four bitter winter months, facing artillery bombardment and starvation, but on January 28th, 1871, the inevitable capitulation came, and the Government, from which Gambetta indignantly resigned, accepted Bismarck's armistice terms.

The terms provided for the election of a National Assembly with authority to conclude a peace treaty. The elections held in February reflected the general desire for peace. In the new Assembly which met at Bordeaux, the Republicans, associated with the war and defeat, had only 200 seats, while the Monarchists had 400, and the Bonapartists 30. Thiers, a veteran statesman of seventy-three, was called upon to head the new Government, and he was well-equipped to do so. Although an outspoken critic of Napoleon III's Empire, he had cautiously declined to join the new Government after Sedan. He had instead undertaken private missions to the Great Powers vainly seeking help or mediation. In this way he had served his country without being implicated in the war. He now had the unenviable tasks of concluding the peace and of beginning the reconstruction of France.

## THE TREATY OF FRANKFURT

The terms of the Treaty of Frankfurt, which ended the war, were considered at the time to be monstrously harsh. France was to pay 5000 million francs within three years, and to submit to an army of occupation, which was to be withdrawn gradually as the instalments of the indemnity were paid. Alsace and Lorraine, with their rich mineral deposits, and a population of some 1 600 000 were to be handed over to the recently-proclaimed German Empire. Germany, and indeed the whole world, was to pay dearly for this transfer of territory. There could be no rapid reconciliation between France and Germany, as there had been between Austria and Prussia after the War of 1866.

## THE COMMUNE

Before the peace was concluded civil war broke out in Paris. Although the city had been starved into submission, there were still many passionate Republicans who wanted the struggle to go on. They felt that they had been betrayed by the Government. Already Paris had suffered the humiliation of a German victory march (a concession granted by Thiers in return for retaining the fortress of Belfort). Once again in French history the cleavage between Paris and the rest of France was apparent. The Monarchist dominated Assembly represented conservative, Catholic, rural France, and had scant sympathy with the needs and desires of the Parisian working men. Three tactless moves by the Assembly produced a revolt. First, the Assembly left Bordeaux and moved not to Paris but to Versailles. Clearly, the Government knew that its policies were going to be unpopular in Paris. Then the Assembly passed resolutions ending the suspension of payment of commercial bills and household rents which had been in force since August 1870. The countless unemployed in Paris faced ruin and their one source of subsistence was removed by the third act of the Assembly which ordered the ending of National Guard pay and the disarmament of the force.

When the Government troops went to seize the artillery from the heights of Montmartre, the National Guard resisted. Thiers at once withdrew the regular soldiers and laid siege to the city. The revolutionaries set up a municipal council, called a Commune. This body, like the whole tragic episode to which it gave its name, was a throwback to the Jacobin days of the Great Revolution. Extreme, atheistic, disorganized, it was incapable of giving any coherent lead. Its chief successes were against its 'enemies' within the city, who were ruthlessly hunted by a Committee of Public Safety. The real power was in the hands of the National Guard, which was by no means unanimous in recognizing the authority of the civil power.

Thiers obtained permission from the Germans to increase the Government troops from 40 000 to 80 000 men. As these advanced against the well-armed but ill-disciplined Communard forces, the Terror in Paris mounted. Hostages, including the Archbishop of Paris, were shot. The Tuileries, the Palais de Justice, and the Hotel de Ville were burnt. More terrible was the retribution brought by the Government troops, anxious to prove themselves after the defeats of Metz and Sedan, as well as to restore order. They killed at least 20 000 in the terrible week in May.[1] In addition 13 450 were imprisoned and 7500 deported.

The Commune marked the end of the old revolutionary tradition which had been a recurrent feature of French political life since 1789. Its chief rallying point, the National Guard, was abolished in August. It also marked the end of the domination of Paris over the rest of the country. Communes had, it is true, been set up in other big cities in France in 1871, but these were poor imitations and were easily suppressed. The Commune was essentially a Parisian movement, and with its defeat Paris lost its special significance in French politics.

Once the Communard extremists had been banished, those conservative elements who had hitherto equated Republicanism with atheism and Socialism were ready to support the purged Republic. At a terrible price the way had been cleared for Thiers to begin his work of rebuilding the nation.

### THE ESTABLISHMENT OF THE THIRD REPUBLIC

The recovery which France made after the calamities of 1870–71 was remarkable. Communications were restored and the economic life of the country re-established with amazing energy and rapidity. To everyone's astonishment, and to Germany's consternation, the indemnity was paid well before it was due, and by September 1873 the last German troops were forced to leave. It was a measure of the confidence the middle classes had in the conservative nature of the new régime that they subscribed so readily to the public loans raised to meet this debt. Their confidence was not misplaced. The Republic was conservative. The only significantly new measure enacted by the Government was the introduction of conscription in 1872. Men were to serve five years and then go on the reserve. The system was not universal. The country could not afford a large army, so men were selected by ballot. Priests were exempted, and men who could provide their own equipment were required to serve only one year. The key-note of these years was the restoration of normal life and the strengthening of the nation's defences. As these aims were gradually fulfilled, the big question which faced the Assembly was the fundamental one of the constitution. What form of government should France now have?

### THE MONARCHISTS

The Monarchists, whose majority was overwhelming in the National Assembly, represented two distinct groups, the Legitimists, who supported

[1] The Terror of 1793–94 had taken 15 months to dispose of a mere 2596.

the Bourbon Comte de Chambord, and the Orleanists, who supported the Comte de Paris. The ancestors of both these men had occupied the throne of France.[1] The problem of division would eventually resolve itself. The Comte de Chambord was childless and on his death the succession would automatically pass to the Orleans branch. But time was not on the side of the Monarchists. They had been elected to power, not because the people wanted monarchy, but because they wanted peace. Already, in the by-elections of July 1871, the Republicans, purged of their extremists, had won 100 out of the 118 seats. If this trend continued the Monarchists would soon lose the opportunity to effect a restoration. Consequently, they were dumbfounded when the Comte de Chambord declared that he would return only on condition that the tricolour were replaced by the white flag of the Bourbons, for they knew that the French people would rather lose the monarchy than their flag.

Somehow the Monarchists had to keep the door to the throne open until the Comte de Chambord changed his mind or died, but it was no easy task. When Thiers violated the agreement he had made on taking office that he would remain impartial in party matters, and declared himself in favour of a Republican form of government, the Monarchists became alarmed that the door would be slammed in their faces. Accordingly, in March 1873, they passed a law which prevented the President from communicating with the Assembly except on special occasions. It was in this way that the French President came to occupy a position more like that of the British sovereign than that of a President of United States, who wields considerable executive power.

Shortly after this, Thiers resigned and the Assembly elected as President a thoroughly reliable Monarchist, the Duc de Magenta, Marshal Mac-Mahon. In the autumn, a further attempt was made, with the support of the Comte de Paris, to bring the Comte de Chambord to accept the throne, but he clung to the white flag. Still the Monarchists played for time. On November 1873 MacMahon's term of office was prolonged for seven years. But the Assembly could not prolong for ever its task of drafting a new constitution to replace the provisional government France had had since the fall of the Empire, and in 1875 the debates began.

## THE CONSTITUTION OF 1875

The Republican constitution, which was passed in 1875, reflected the hopes of the Monarchists, or, more precisely, those of the Orleanists, The new Republic was, in effect, a constitutional monarchy without a monarch. The word Republic was included in the constitution only after an amendment which was passed by 353 votes to 352. There was to be a President, a Senate, and a Chamber of Deputies. The President was to be elected by an absolute majority of the Senate and the Chamber meeting together as a

[1] The last Bourbon representative, Charles X, had been replaced after the 1830 revolution by Louis Philippe of the younger royal line, the house of Orleans.

National Assembly. He was to be elected for seven years and could then be re-elected. The Senate consisted of 300 members, each of whom had to be at least forty years of age. There were 75 life members nominated by the National Assembly, and 225 who were to serve for nine years. One-third of the elected members were to come up for re-election every three years. The Electoral Colleges in each Department which chose these Senators were constituted with a heavy rural, and thus conservative, bias. The Chamber of Deputies had 600 members, each at least twenty-five years old, elected for four years by popular suffrage. Although the constitution gave the President the authority to dissolve the Chamber before its term had expired, there was such a storm when MacMahon did so in 1877 that that power was never again used. As there was no possibility that they might suddenly have to face an election, Deputies tended to behave irresponsibly.

The Constitution lasted, with only minor amendments, until 1940. Because of its deliberate vagueness, it proved flexible enough to allow development. Because it represented a compromise, and was not the work of a single dominant group, it lasted longer than any other form of government in France since 1791.

### THE REPUBLICANS IN POWER

The elections of 1876 gave the conservative groups a majority in the Senate, and the Republicans a sweeping victory in the Chamber. Three years later the Republicans gained control of the Senate, and proceeded to fill the civil service and the judiciary with their loyal supporters. When they proposed to replace a number of generals, MacMahon resigned, and the Republicans gained control of the Presidency by the appointment of Jules Grévy.

The Republicans, who were now in complete power, were no longer revolutionaries. Even Gambetta had become respectable. He had left the Radicals and formed a group called the Opportunists, but both the Radicals and the Opportunists represented the petit bourgeoisie, or lower middle class. As yet the industrial labouring classes had no spokesmen. France was still predominantly a rural country, and Socialism found few adherents. Most of those Republicans who had Socialist leanings were still in exile. Indeed, had social reform loomed large in the Republicans' programme, they would not have won the success they had. As it was, they had been helped to power by some moderate Orleanists, who were frightened by the growth of Bonapartist support in the 70's. Accordingly, the Republicans concentrated on political matters.

First, they set about healing old wounds. In 1879 the Senate and the Chamber of Deputies returned to Paris. A partial amnesty was granted to Communards, followed two years later by a full amnesty. On July 14th, 1880, the anniversary of the Fall of the Bastille was made an occasion of national festivity. Next, measures were taken to democratize public institutions. The practice of having life Senators was abandoned in 1884; entry into the civil service was made dependent on a competitive examination; all Communes, except that of Paris, were allowed to elect their own mayors (though they were still subject to the control of the Prefect, a Government official); furthermore, workers were allowed to form unions. But to many Republicans, the chief obstacle in the way of complete political democracy was the Church, and in particular its control of education.

## THE EDUCATION LAWS

Two out of five million children in France were educated in Roman Catholic schools. Therefore, a considerable proportion of the people came under the influence of Right-wing opinion. On the Continent the political terms Right and Left are not used in the same way as they are in this country. The Right means Catholic and Authoritarian (anti-Republican). The Left means Republican and anti-Clerical. The Left is again split between Socialists and anti-Socialists. The Republicans determined to purge France of the political influence of the Church. Similar outbursts of anti-clericalism occurred in other European countries at this time, stimulated amongst other things by the growing agnosticism which had followed new scientific discoveries. The case for educational reform was reinforced by the widespread conviction that the Prussian educational system had contributed as much to the victories of 1870 as had the well-organized Army.

In 1882 State primary education was made free, compulsory, and free from all Church supervision. Already, in 1880, the Jesuits and all other unauthorized religious organizations (which had increased under the Second Empire) were disbanded. Catholic universities were deprived of the right to confer degrees. Military chaplaincies were abolished, clergy were removed from the administration of charities, Sisters of Mercy from hospitals, and divorce was instituted. The Roman Catholic Church lost a great deal when the State became responsible for primary education, since the change was effected with such bitterness on both sides that nearly all the new village schoolmasters were staunch Republicans and rabid anti-clerics.

## THE REPUBLIC IN DANGER

French domestic affairs in the 80's and 90's were dominated by three crises which threatened the very existence of the Republic.

1. *The Boulanger Crisis.* The elections of 1885 left the Opportunists without a clear majority and they were forced to rely on the Radicals for support. Clemenceau, the Radical leader, thus wielded considerable power although he was not in office, and he used this power to push one of his protégés, General Boulanger, into the post of Minister of War in Freycinet's Cabinet of 1886. Boulanger was impressive in appearance, rode a black circus horse called Tunis, and had a keen eye for publicity. He soon

became the idol of the people. Songs were written about him and he was hailed as 'Général Revanche', the man who would win back Alsace-Lorraine. The Opportunists and the Monarchists, alarmed by his dangerous popularity, combined to defeat Freycinet's Ministry and have the General posted to Clermont Ferrand. When Boulanger left Paris, hysterical crowds at the Gare de Lyon tried to prevent his departure by lying on the rails in front of his train.

Boulanger was popular because the Republic was unpopular. People were disillusioned by the way it was working and there was a growing demand for constitutional revision, which they hoped their hero would bring about. Matters were made worse by the Presidential crisis of 1887. Grévy was forced to resign after his son-in-law was found to be selling medals and decorations, Thiers was dead, Clemenceau hated Jules Ferry, the obvious candidate, and so the Assembly was reduced to voting for the worthy but insignificant Carnot.[1] Carnot could not compete in popular appeal with Boulanger, who soon attracted to his banner every discontented group in France, including the Monarchists and Bonapartists. Boulanger won six out of seven by-elections[2] in 1888, and when in January 1889 he won a traditionally Republican seat in Paris, it looked as if he could seize power overnight. He refused, however, to act unconstitutionally, and while he hesitated, the Government acted. Plans were made to try him for treason, and his disappointed followers heard of his flight to Brussels, where in 1891 he committed suicide. The panic passed the moment the General showed his political timidity. But the Republic had had an unpleasant shock, and the general effect of this crisis was to rally all parties to the defence of the Constitution of 1875.

2. *The Panama Scandal.* Ferdinand de Lesseps, engineer of the Suez Canal, together with Eiffel, who built the Tower, and other engineers, began the construction of a Panama Canal in 1881. The canal was to be at sea level, and the work ran into a number of serious technical difficulties. The project was also hampered by disease. Consequently, very much more money was needed than had at first been contemplated. There had been plenty of goodwill for the Company at the beginning of the enterprise and the public would have subscribed more than had been asked for, but as the work proceeded and disaster followed disaster and the Company had to raise successive loans, money became increasingly difficult and increasingly expensive to get. No Government help was given until 1888, when the Chamber authorized an issue of lottery bonds, but these failed to produce the amount required and the Company went bankrupt. Over 800 000 Frenchmen lost money. In 1892 accusations were made by an anti-Jewish paper that the Company had distributed bribes to members of parliament through a Jewish financier to enlist their support in raising money. When investigations began, this financier committed suicide, and another Jew

---

[1] Clemenceau was popularly quoted as saying, 'Let's vote for the stupidest.'

[2] It was possible for one man to be a candidate in several different constituencies though he could sit for only one of them.

named Herz, who had been blackmailing him, fled to England. Proceedings were taken against five Deputies and five Senators, though only one, a former Minister of Works, who rashly confessed, was condemned. However, the scandal eclipsed either permanently or temporarily the careers of a number of parliamentarians, including that of Clemenceau, whose newspaper was financed by Herz.

The scandal had important results. It poisoned the political air for a number of years to come. It increased anti-Jewish feeling in the country. It brought to the fore in place of the old leaders younger men like Poincaré and Delcassé. Socialism gained some ground, but the people did not desert the Opportunists, or Progressists, as they had come to be called. Instead they became more cynical about government, and there followed a period of confusion and disappointment in politics akin to that which had fostered Boulangism.

3. *The Dreyfus Case.* Soon after the Panama Scandal, the third, and most dramatic, crisis began to brew. In France, it is usually referred to simply as 'L'Affaire'. In 1894 a Jewish staff officer named Dreyfus was convicted of giving military secrets to Germany, and was deported to Devil's Island for life. Although some people thought that he should have been shot instead, the case aroused no particular interest at the time. The Jews, who had been discomforted by the Panama revelations and the anti-Jewish feeling which had followed them, wanted the matter forgotten as quickly as possible. However, the leakages of information continued and Colonel Picquart, the head of the Intelligence Service, began investigations, and discovered that the chief evidence in the case, the *borderau* (memorandum), was written not by Dreyfus, but by a disreputable officer named Esterhazy. When he reported his findings to his superiors, he was told that fresh evidence of Dreyfus's guilt had come to light, and he was promptly posted to North Africa. Picquart, however, made public his suspicions and, under pressure, the War Ministry allowed a charge to be brought against Esterhazy. In 1898 a secret court martial acquitted Esterhazy, and Colonel Picquart was dismissed the service.

The storm broke when Clemenceau's new paper *L'Aurore* published an 'Open Letter to the President of the Republic', written by Emile Zola, the eminent French novelist, which accused certain high-ranking officers by name of having rigged the Dreyfus trial. This letter, headed 'J'Accuse', made a public issue of the case. France divided into those for and those against Dreyfus, those who wished to bring the matter into the open to diminish the power of the Army and the Church, or even to uphold the principle of public justice in a democratic Republic, and those who wished to hush the matter up, 'for the honour of the State', or for the reputation of the Army, or to deal a blow at the Jews.

The Government now foolishly tried to produce the fresh evidence of Dreyfus's guilt which they had previously claimed to possess, but Colonel Henry, who had succeeded Picquart as Head of Intelligence, admitted that he had forged it and committed suicide. In 1899 Dreyfus was retried, found 'guilty with extenuating circumstances', and his sentence was reduced to ten years' imprisonment. This decision infuriated the anti-Drefusards and Dreyfusards alike, and so the President made an unhappy compromise by pardoning Dreyfus. The struggle went on until 1906 when a Court quashed the verdicts of both trials. Dreyfus was decorated with the Legion of Honour and both he and Picquart were promoted.

The result, politically, was a defeat for the militaristic and anti-semitic Right, and a victory for the anti-militarist and anti-Clerical Radicals, who were to dominate the politics of the Third Republic for the remainder of its existence.

### THE WALDECK-ROUSSEAU MINISTRY 1899–1902

The principal reason why the Dreyfus case dragged on so long was that no Ministry in the closing years of the 19th century was strong enough to be able to withstand the criticism that the reopening of the case was bound to cause. At last, however, in 1899 a leader was found in the person of Waldeck-Rousseau, a disciple of Gambetta, and a man of strong personality and independent views. He formed a distinguished Ministry, based on a Left-wing coalition, which included Millerand, the first Socialist in Europe to reach Cabinet rank, as Minister of Commerce. This Ministry lasted the unprecedented length of time of three years, during which time it was able to restore some stability to French government. The force which bound together the Republican bloc on which Waldeck-Rousseau based his power was the anti-militarism and the anti-clericalism of the Left. Under this régime a purge of the Army was carried through, changes were made in the High command, and the power of promotion was transferred from the army authorities to the Ministry of War, so that henceforth military advancement depended on political favour. But the burning issue of the time was the relationship between the Church and State.

### THE END OF THE CONCORDAT 1905

The attack on the Church was primarily directed against the religious orders, which Waldeck-Rousseau denounced as a dangerous rival power in the State. Some of these were dissolved and others had to apply for legal recognition. Waldeck-Rousseau retired through ill-health in 1902, and the work was carried on by Combes, who had been a professor of theology and was now a bitter anti-clerical. Applications for authorization were turned down en bloc. In 1903 a new Pope, Pius X, took office and he was as uncompromising as Combes. The result was the renunciation by the Republic of the Concordat of 1901, the agreement made between Napoleon and the Pope by which Roman Catholicism had been recognized as the State religion of France. The Republic ceased to recognize or subsidize any form or worship. Church revenues were to be handed over to lay organizations called *associations culturelles* who were to arrange the conduct of worship. The Pope refused to recognize these associations and so the Government, with their support confirmed by the election of 1906, handed over Church property to public relief organizations and to local municipalities. The clergy were left the use of the churches.

Henceforth, the clergy were dependent entirely on the contributions of their parishes, and many were desperately poor. The clergy declined in numbers, but improved in quality, since there were few attractions for the insincere. Furthermore, since some priests took jobs to earn a living, a new link was made with the people. Anti-clericalism did not die in 1907, but the ending of the Concordat removed its bite, and social reform moved to the political forefront.

SOCIAL UNREST

Waldeck-Rousseau's Ministry carried out a number of measures of social reform. A Labour Department had been set up by Millerand, trade unions had been encouraged, and a law passed providing for the gradual introduction of the ten-hour working day. But, except for the introduction of old age pensions in 1910, very little was done after his retirement. In 1906 the Syndicates, or trade unions, meeting at Amiens declared in favour of using the general strike weapon to destroy capitalism. A period of intense industrial unrest followed, which culminated in the post office workers' strike of 1909. Clemenceau, who had fought his way back into politics in the vanguard of the Dreyfusards, and who at last had reached the premiership, did not hesitate, Radical though he was, to use troops against the strikers. He won, but he destroyed the Republican bloc. In 1910 there were further strikes, and Briand, a former Socialist and the new Prime Minister, acted with equal resolution and broke the railway strike by calling up the strikers as army reservists to run the trains.

POLITICAL UNREST BEFORE 1914

Briand fell from office in 1911, and in the next three years there were seven cabinets. The Third Republic had faced and survived many disasters since 1870, but it had not emerged unscarred. The people had little respect for their political system. In fact, bitter experience, before and during the Third Republic, had caused the French to mistrust their leaders, and particularly strong leaders, as a matter of principle. Ministries which seemed likely to be strong enough to get things done were overthrown, often by their own parties, lest they abused their power. Weak and frequently changing governments were the price Frenchmen felt bound to pay in order to preserve their liberty. This attitude to government remained until the end of the Third Republic and was inhertired by the Fourth. The Deputies were much too greatly influenced by local interests or by the demands of powerful organizations, and eve-of-election vote-catching schemes too often replaced real government. While Germany was rearming, military service in France was, in 1905, reduced from three to two years, and military and naval expenditure cut. This was a particularly popular measure because it ended the exemption hitherto granted to priests. When the three-year term was restored in 1913, the Left-wing groups joined forces to oppose it and won the elections of 1914 on the strength of that opposition. It was somewhat ironic that these men were in power when the Third Republic came to face the greatest threat to its existence yet.

# Appendix to Chapter 2

### THE EMS TELEGRAM

1. The test of the message from Ems to Bismarck.

Ems, July 13, 1870.

His Majesty writes to me: 'Count Benedetti spoke to me on the promenade, in order to demand from me, finally in a very importunate manner, that I should authorize him to telegraph at once that I bound myself for all future time never again to give my consent if the Hohenzollerns should renew their candidature. I refused at last somewhat sternly, as it is neither right nor possible to undertake engagements of this kind *à tout jamais*. I told him that I had as yet received no news, and as he was earlier informed from Paris and Madrid than myself, he could see clearly that my government had no more interest in the matter.' His Majesty has since received a letter from Prince Charles Anthony. His Majesty, having told Count Benedetti that he was awaiting news from the Prince, has decided, with reference to the above demand, on the suggestion of Count Eulenberg and myself, not to receive Count Benedetti again, but only to let him be informed through an aide-de-camp: 'That his Majesty has now received from the Prince confirmation of the news which Benedetti had already received from Paris, and had nothing further to say to the ambassador.' His Majesty leaves it to your Excellency to decide whether Benedetti's fresh demand and its rejection should be at once communicated to both our ambassadors, to foreign nations, and to the press.'

2. The text prepared by Bismarck for publication.

'After the news of the renunciation of the Hereditary Prince of Hohenzollern had been officially communicated to the Imperial government of France by the Royal government of Spain, the French Ambassador further demanded of his Majesty, the King, at Ems, that he would authorize him to telegraph to Paris that his Majesty, the King, bound himself for all times never again to give his consent, should the Hohenzollerns renew their candidature. His Majesty, the King, thereupon decided not to receive the French Ambassador again, and sent the aide-de-camp on duty to tell

**Bismarck.** The Chancellor at his desk. He was extremely fond of his dogs, one of which can be seen in the foreground.

**The Third Republic.** *Top left* Gambetta. *Top right* Dreyfus. This photo is interesting as it is the official police one taken of all convicted criminals. Note the uniform stripped of its decoration. *Left* Boulanger.

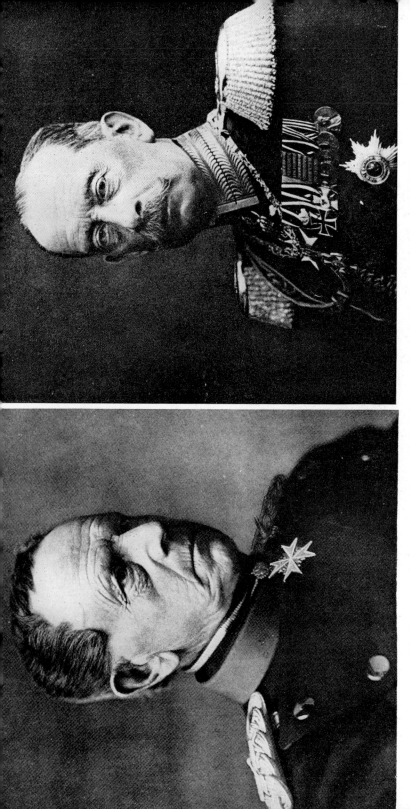

**The Creators of the German Army.** *Left* Moltke, the victor of the Franco-Prussian War, 1870 (p. 15). *Right* Schlieffen, whose plan for a knock-out blow on France failed in 1914 (p. 77).

**The Last Days of Imperial Russia.** *Above left* The evil monk Rasputin (p. 49). *Above right* Kerensky, the moderate leader overthrown by the Bolsheviks (p. 50). *Below* Nicholas II at army manoeuvres.

him that his Majesty had nothing further to communicate to the ambassador.'[1]

The important effect of this contraction is that the King's message through an aide-de-camp to the French Ambassador appears to be his immediate answer to the French demand for the perpetual renunciation of the Hohenzollern candidature. In fact, the message was sent because the King had at last received confirmation of the withdrawal of the candidature, and saw no point in further discussions.

# 3  Bismarck and the German Empire, 1871-1890

Otto von Bismarck was born on April Fool's Day, 1815. After a brief, and unsuccessful, career in the civil service, followed by a rather longer, and more notable, career as a diplomat, he was summoned in 1862 to Berlin to become Prime Minister and Foreign Minister of Prussia.

Bismarck came to power as the result of a constitutional struggle in Prussia between the King and his Parliament, in which the Liberals had a large majority. The precise issue, which concerned the composition of the Army, need not trouble us here. Bismarck, backed by the Army, reduced it to simple terms—either the King or Parliament was supreme. In Bismarck, the King found an ally—and a master. Though he had had no previous ministerial experience, Bismarck managed to dominate both Crown and Parliament. He was to continue to do so for over a quarter of a century.

Bismarck's dramatic elevation to supreme power was very unorthodox, and indeed there was little that was conventional about him. Even after he had become Chancellor of the German Empire in 1871 he never bothered to observe the social courtesies expected of a man in his position. He rarely troubled to see diplomats, or even visiting royalty. He never dined out. His favourite image of himself was a Junker, a Prussian country squire devoted to country pursuits. It is true that he acquired two large estates in return for his political services, one at Varzin after the Austro-Prussian War of 1866, and another (ten times larger) at Friedrichsruh, after the Franco-Prussian War of 1870. He certainly spent a great deal of his time on these estates—more and more as he grew older and more confident that, however inconvenient his absences from Berlin might be, he could not be dispensed with. He had an almost fanatical interest in planting trees, unlike his contemporary Gladstone (as Bismarck once noted), who found relaxation in chopping them down. But the life of a Junker was, for him, no substitute for the excitement of diplomacy. He was happy in the

[1] Both texts taken from Grant Robertson's *Bismarck*.

country only while he retained the reins of power. He never identified his interests with those of his fellow landowners.

Bismarck was an emotional man, easily moved to rages or tears, or both. He was also a big man, with gross appetites. He ate, smoked, and drank too much. At one time he smoked fourteen cigars a day, and once declared his intention of drinking 5000 bottles of champagne before he died—in addition, that is, to the other wines, brandy and beer he consumed. He ate vast meals, including a large supper immediately before going to bed. He suffered from a variety of ailments, the most persistent of which was indigestion. Between 1878 and 1883 he had such a severe twitch in his face that he grew a full beard to hide it. Only one medical adviser had much control over him. He took Bismarck in hand in 1883 and managed, oddly enough, by putting him on a diet which consisted (it is said) exclusively of herrings, to reduce his weight from eighteen to fourteen stone.

### THE CREATION OF THE EMPIRE

In his early years of power. Bismarck aimed to extend Prussian control over the German states. He had two opponents to reckon with, Austria and the German Liberals. When Bismarck took office, Austria's voice was predominant in the Diet of the German Confederation. She had to be silenced. The German Liberals, though anxious to remove Austria's influence over the states, did not wish to replace it with Prussia's. They wanted a united Germany into which Prussia, like the other German states, should be absorbed. Bismarck had to move carefully, but when opportunities for advance were presented, he moved quickly.

Prussia's victory over Austria in the Seven Weeks' War of 1866 deprived Austria of her voice in German affairs. All but the southern states joined with Prussia in the North German Confederation which was set up in the following year. Although the member-states retained their separate existences and continued to control their own local affairs, the power which really mattered was wielded by Prussia. The King of Prussia was President, Bismarck Chancellor, of the Confederation. They controlled the Army and the Navy, and foreign affairs.

The south German states, Bavaria, Wurtemberg, Baden, and Hesse-Darmstadt, were not so easy to absorb. For one thing, they were much bigger than the numerous states of the north. Two of them, Bavaria and Wurtemberg, were kingdoms. Furthermore, they valued their independence. But the creation of the North German Confederation made it increasingly difficult for them to maintain their independent position. They joined with the Confederation in a common tariff system, and they all had military treaties with Prussia. When the Franco-Prussian War broke out in 1870 Bismarck played upon the south German fears of French plans to acquire land east of the Rhine. Very reluctantly they were dragged into the war against Napoleon III.

While the siege of Paris was still proceeding, Bismarck concluded treaties with each of the south German states, by which they agreed to join with the northern states in an enlarged confederation to be called the German Reich, or Empire. Bismarck needed all his diplomatic skill to secure these agreements, but by negotiating with the states separately and by exploiting their mutual jealousies, he was able to attain his ends, at the cost of some concessions to their independence not enjoyed by the northern members. He rightly believed, however, that once the states had agreed to accept William I of Prussia as their Emperor, he would have little cause to regret the concessions made to them. William would have the power, and Bismarck knew well how to handle him.

Bismarck's diplomatic juggling was triumphantly successful. This was the sort of work he enjoyed and excelled at. On January 18th, 1871, the result of his labour was publicly displayed. In the Hall of Mirrors at the palace of Versailles, symbol of the French monarchy at the height of its power, William of Prussia was proclaimed the first Emperor of the German Reich.

## THE CONSTITUTION

The constitution of the Empire was similar to that of the North German Confederation. The Empire was a federal state with power divided between the Central Government and the twenty-five states from which it was formed. The states preserved their own constitutions, their rulers, and their parliamentary and administrative systems. They were responsible for their own internal affairs and they could raise their own taxes, though they also had to observe the federal laws and to collect federal taxes. The federal Government was responsible for relations with other countries and for inter-state matters. That is to say, it handled foreign affairs, concluded treaties, controlled trade, banking, coinage, railways, and postal services. Certain exceptions were made in the case of the southern states. Bavaria and Wurtemberg for instance, retained control over their own railways and postal services, and Bavaria was allowed to control her own army in peace time. Throughout the Empire there was universal male suffrage and universal military service.

The federal Government consisted of the Kaiser, the Chancellor (Bismarck), and two representative bodies, the Bundesrat, or Federal Council, and the Reichstag. The Bundesrat was made up of delegates from the states in proportion to their importance. Of the fifty-eight seats in the Council, Prussia had seventeen and Bavaria was next highest with six. Although Prussia did not have an overall majority, a coalition of many states would be required to oppose Prussia's wishes successfully. The Reichstag was elected by the people as a whole, but its powers were slight. Like the Bundesrat, it could introduce legislation, but it soon lost most of its control over taxation, and at no time could it force the resignation of ministers. Ministers were responsible to the Chancellor, and he was responsible to the Kaiser alone.

The German Empire was created in a hurry against some determined opposition and it is little wonder that it was a curious hotch-potch of different ideas. Although it was called the German Empire, and although it was hailed by many as the fulfilment of German nationalism, it neither included all Germans nor excluded all non-Germans. Many Germans remained in the Austro-Hungarian Empire, while the new German Reich included Frenchmen, Danes, and Poles. Again, although the ties which bound the Empire together appeared loose, and although there was a framework of democratic government, in fact the Prussian leaders were supreme. While William I lived, that meant that Bismarck was supreme.

## PROBLEMS FACING THE EMPIRE

1. *The Kulturkampf.* The formation of the German Empire immediately brought Bismarck into conflict with the Roman Catholic Church. The struggle between the two was known as the *Kulturkampf*—the struggle of civilizations. The issues involved were both religious and political, though for Bismarck the problem was essentially political.

Broadly speaking, Prussia and the northern states were Protestant, while the states in the south and along the Rhine were Catholic. The North German Confederation had, therefore, been predominantly Protestant, but the formation of the Empire had brought in a large number of Catholics. To protect their interests the Catholics formed a political party called the Centre, which attracted not only Catholics but also those who were opposed to Bismarck's Empire.

The Roman Catholic Church was facing great difficulties in 1870. The Italians had taken advantage of the removal of French troops from Rome, when war broke out with Prussia, to seize the Pope's remaining territories. Furthermore, the scientific discoveries of the 19th century seemed to many to make nonsense of religious beliefs. With his back to the wall, the Pope tried to increase his control of Catholics everywhere. This extension of papal control was known as ultramontanism.[1] Ultramontanism and Nationalism were regarded as being incompatible. Since both Church and State were staking claims for the final obedience of their peoples, Catholics might well be faced with an impossible choice. Matters were made worse by two papal pronouncements. The first was the Syllabus of 1864, which condemned many current ideas, including Nationalism and Liberalism, as mortal errors. The second was the doctrine of papal infallibility, which was declared an article of faith in 1870. This doctrine declared that when the Pope made an official pronouncement on matters of faith or morals, he could not be wrong. Henceforth, all Catholics were required to accept this dogma.

The German bishops at the Vatican Council which issued the decree of papal infallibility had protested strongly against it, but they were overwhelmed by the Italian bishops. Nevertheless, when the decree was

[1] Beyond the mountains (i.e. the Alps).

announced, some German Catholics refused to accept it and formed a group known as the Old Catholics. When Old Catholic professors and teachers were dismissed from posts under the control of Catholic bishops, Bismarck seized the chance to take up the cudgels against the Catholic Church.

The Kulturkampf was fought chiefly in Prussia,[1] though its repercussions were felt thoughout the Empire. In 1871 the Catholic section of the Prussian Ministry of Religion and Education was abolished, and in 1872 the Catholic rights of supervision of Catholic schools were withdrawn. In the same year, the Jesuits, leading exponents of ultramontane ideas, were expelled from the whole Empire. In the years 1873–75 the so-called 'May Laws' were passed in Prussia, under the direction of Falk, the Minister of Religion and Education. By these the State took over the control of education, and of the appointment and dismissal of clergy, Catholic and Protestant. Civil marriage was made compulsory in Prussia and later in the whole Empire. This meant that the legal basis of marriage was a ceremony conducted by State officials, though people could still have a separate religious ceremony as well if they wished to. All religious orders in Prussia, except nursing orders, were dissolved. State financial help for the Catholic Church was withdrawn, and the clause in the Prussian constitution which guaranteed Catholic rights was repealed. Many clergy and bishops were dismissed, imprisoned, and even deported.

Bismarck failed to break the Catholics. Indeed, they increased in strength. In the election of 1874 the Centre party gained over 90 seats out of the 382 in the Reichstag. In the next few years Bismarck was faced with grave problems in foreign affairs, while at home he was increasingly troubled by the Socialists. Clearly he should withdraw from the Kulturkampf, which he was losing anyway. Bismarck wanted reconciliation with the Catholics at the lowest possible price. Therefore his withdrawal was gradual. When Pius IX died in 1878, Bismarck looked forward to easier relations with the papacy, but Leo XIII, though more moderate than his predecessor, was just as insistent on the removal of the anti-Catholic laws. Bismarck blamed Falk for the May Laws and Falk resigned in 1879. In 1880 the repeal of the May Laws began and by 1887 the Kulturkampf was over. But the regulations relating to civil marriage and the State inspection of schools remained and the Jesuits were not readmitted.

The Old Catholics were too few in number to be of any use to Bismarck, and persecution had helped to strengthen the unity of the main body of German Catholics. Even Protestants had been alarmed by the increased State control over religion and education. Bismarck had underestimated his adversary, but he had retired with skill. The end of the Kulturkampf did not, however, bring about the collapse of the Centre Party. It remained with some one hundred members in the Reichstag, prepared now to support much of Bismarck's policy, but not unquestioningly.

[1] Prussia had quite a considerable Catholic population in the Rhine Provinces, which she had acquired in 1815.

2. *The Federal Budget.* The German Empire was insecurely based financially. The federal Government was allowed to levy only indirect taxes, i.e. customs and excise. Direct taxes, i.e. taxes on property and income, could be levied only by the states. The federal budget was balanced by what were called 'matricular' contributions from the separate states. These were sums calculated on the basis of the population of each state.

Nine-tenths of the federal budget was for the Army. In 1874 Bismarck quarrelled with his allies in the Reichstag, the National Liberals, and with the General Staff over the size of the Army. The General Staff wanted Germany's military establishment to be fixed permanently. This would have made a permanent mockery of any discussion of most of the budget. The National Liberals, though divided on the issue, were prepared to authorize the establishment for four years at a time. Bismarck, by threatening the Emperor and the Army with his resignation, and the National Liberals with the dissolution of the Reichstag, managed to force through a compromise measure by which authorization was given for seven years. The Army was effectively preserved from parliamentary control.

Bismarck, who belonged to no political party, became increasingly irritated by the failure of the National Liberals to obey him blindly. At the elections of 1877, the National Liberals, which had been by far the largest party in the Reichstag, suffered severe losses to the Conservatives and to the Centre. Bismarck saw his chance to kill a number of birds with one stone. Both the industrialists and the landowners were demanding the introduction of tariffs. The industrialists wanted protection chiefly from British manufactures and the landowners from Russian wheat. By the introduction of tariffs and by making peace with the Catholics, Bismarck perceived he could secure the support of the Conservatives and the Centre and command a majority over the National Liberals. He could also secure greater financial independence, since the tariffs, which were to replace the matricular contributions, were to be agreed to for years at a time.

After bitter opposition from most of the National Liberals, Bismarck announced in 1879 the end of Free Trade in the Empire and introduced protective tariffs. The National Liberals were thus dealt a blow from which they never really recovered, though the story of liberal parties in other countries suggests that their days were numbered anyway. The Reichstag became an even bigger mockery of parliamentary government than it had been, and men of ability employed their talents in business rather than in politics. It is little wonder that the German people found it impossible to work parliamentary institutions when they had them again after the First World War.

3. *The Socialists.* Even before the Empire was created, industry had begun to expand in Germany. In the last quarter of the century, this expansion became rapid and Socialist ideas spread with comparable speed. The workers saw the wealth of their country growing immensely, but their share in it was small. They therefore wanted political power in order to improve their economic position. Bismarck disliked the idea of anyone

other than himself having any real political power, and Socialism was wholly repugnant to him. Like many propertied and middle-class people, he regarded Socialists as thieves and murderers. He was determined to crush Socialism.

First he tried repression. In 1878 he introduced the anti-Socialist law which prohibited workers' organizations, publications, and meetings, and gave the Government powers to expel Socialists from where they lived. The law was renewed four times under Bismarck, but its effect on the workers was the same as that of the May Laws on the Catholics. Under persecution they became united and strengthened. The small number of Social Democrats in the Reichstag increased.

Since repression on its own was not wholly effective, Bismarck decided to supplement it with a little bribery. He proposed a series of laws which were to improve the conditions of the workers, and thus remove their desire for political power. The first laws which made up Bismarck's system of State Socialism were passed in 1884. These provided for accident and sickness insurance, and they were followed up in 1889 with the introduction of pensions for old people and for those permanently incapacitated. These measures were remarkable in that they were the first of their kind in the world, but they failed utterly in their object. The Socialists wanted a voice in the running of the country, not lollipops.

## THE FALL OF BISMARCK

In 1888 William I died. Bismarck had long feared that his successor, Frederick III, would introduce a liberal ministry when he became Emperor. But in 1888 Frederick was mortally ill with cancer of the throat, and three months after his accession he died. Bismarck's fears passed. Frederick's son, William II, was only twenty-nine years of age, and Bismarck regarded him as a silly, vain boy of no consequence. Bismarck was so used to controlling his sovereign, so sure that his services were indispensable, that he treated William with contempt and condescension. He entirely misjudged his new master. William was young, but he was also ambitious and anxious to direct the affairs of his country. He urged that the repressive policy against the Socialists should be abandoned. Tension between the two men grew, and Bismarck experienced the bitter disillusionment of seeing his former supporters seeking the favour of the Emperor.

The break came in 1890. William and Bismarck had a violent row, during which Bismarck flung his despatch case across the room. While gathering up the papers which had scattered out of it, Bismarck 'accidentally' allowed William to read some unflattering remarks Alexander III of Russia had written to Bismarck about him. But William had the last laugh. After Bismarck had spent three days composing his letter of resignation which he hoped would rouse nation-wide support for his recall, William would not allow him to publish it. He merely announced that the Chancellor had retired for health reasons. 'I am better than I have been for years past', commented Bismarck. But all that he could do now was to write his memoirs.

No one can deny that Bismarck was a great man in the sense in which historians use the term. He dominated the affairs of his country and of Europe for a quarter of a century. He was an inveterate juggler. Nothing pleased him more than to achieve a simple result by complex manoeuvres. That is why he preferred diplomacy to government. But in spite of his apparent success, the legacy of his work in Germany and in Europe proved disastrous. If he is to be given credit for controlling all the events he claimed to have controlled, he must equally take much of the blame for their consequences.

# 4  Bismarck's Foreign Policy, 1871-1890

The irony of Bismarck's life is that he had to spend the later part of his career struggling against the consequences of his earlier actions. The tragedy of it, for him and for the world, was that he struggled in vain. He was frightened of the German nationalism he had invoked to demand unification; he was frightened of the generals whose victories had achieved it; and he was frightened of France, whose defeat had finally brought it about. In 1871 he had got all that he wanted—a Prussian-dominated German Empire. He now had to defend it against France, who, he thought, wanted to destroy it, and against those of his own people and his own generals who, he knew, wanted to extend it.

The loss of Alsace-Lorraine was, in itself, no bar to a Franco-German reconciliation, after a decent lapse of time. Some reasonable claim could be made for their inclusion in the new German Empire—a very strong claim in the case of Alsace. Lorraine was certainly a mistake—it was too French. Bismarck never wanted to take it, but for once he bowed to the strategic demands of the generals. Nevertheless, the Germans had won a decisive victory, and a little land-grabbing was not an unforeseeable, nor unusual, consequence. Had the French won, the frontier would have been pushed a little the other way. Most people outside France accepted the annexation as natural, and most people inside France would have been prepared to forget it, but for the bitter memory of Sedan. Only the return of the provinces could expiate that shame. The French were not bent on a war of revenge. But if any opportunity to recover the provinces presented itself, such as a German defeat by a coalition of Powers, they would be ready to seize it. 'Till they have repaired their error,' wrote Gambetta, 'no one will lay down his arms. The peace of the world will remain at the mercy of an incident.' Whatever his private feelings, no Minister of the Third Republic ever dared admit publicly that he accepted the Treaty of Frankfurt as irrevocable. And no one in Germany would have believed him if he had. The idea of a Franco-German war dominated the policies of both France and Germany after 1871. France worked to get allies and so avoid a repetition of the isolation in which she had found herself in 1870, and Bismarck worked to keep her isolated.

As a first step, Bismarck sought to ensure the friendship of the two other great continental Powers, Austria-Hungary and Russia. In 1872, Francis Joseph, Alexander II, and William I met in Berlin and formed the *Dreikaiserbund* (League of Three Emperors). It was not an alliance of any sort, merely a general agreement on solidarity against social revolution. To get more agreement than this was almost impossible (though Bismarck spent nearly twenty years trying to do so), since Austria-Hungary and Russia were rivals in the Balkans, and Germany had no interest there at all, except in preventing their rivalry from providing an ally for France. Events in the Balkans[1] were, in fact, to keep Bismarck far busier than any events in the West, and he, by his actions before and during 1870, had more than a hand in their making. Austria, pushed out of Germany and out of Italy in 1866, had now only the Balkans in which to expand. Russia had taken advantage of France's distraction in 1870 to renounce the Black Sea clauses,[2] and she, too, was looking to the Balkans.

Although the Dreikaiserbund was directed against the 'revolution', Bismarck, in fact, feared the Monarchists in France very much more than he feared the Republicans. He could use the Republicans as a bogy to persuade his own people that France was threatening the Reich, and to persuade the despotic Governments of Austria-Hungary and Russia that the whole structure of their régimes was in danger. The Monarchists were too much influenced by the clericals for his liking, and he was fighting the clericals at home.

What has come to be called the 'War Scare' of 1875 may have been designed merely to distract attention from the Kulturkampf. But he found sufficient excuse for it in the rapid recovery that France had made under Thiers. News in 1875 that France had carried out organizational changes in her Army and had ordered a large number of cavalry horses from Germany raised fear of a rapid counter-attack. Bismarck forbade the export of horses and a vigorous press campaign, in which Bismarck claimed to have no hand, was carried on in Germany, claiming that French attack was imminent, and urging that attack was the best form of defence. When a German Foreign Office official uttered the same threat to the French Ambassador at a dinner at the British Embassy, Decazes, the French Foreign Minister, lost no time in communicating the conversation to the heads of governments and to *The Times*. The despatch in *The Times* caused

---

[1] For details see Chapter 6.
[2] Those clauses of the Treaty of Paris 1856 which forbade Russia to have warships or fortifications on the Black Sea.

widespread consternation. Both Britain and Russia made strong representations to Germany, and the alarm died down.

We cannot know what Bismarck intended by the scare. He may have used it to strengthen his position at home. He certainly wanted to discourage France from doing anything provocative. He may even have hoped to bully France into an alliance. Instead, France used the opportunity to alarm other Powers, and she succeeded. But the coalition which loomed against Germany was concerned only to preserve the *status quo*, not to support France in any territorial adjustments, and since Bismarck wanted no territorial adjustments he was well satisfied. Two months later, everyone's attention was occupied by the Balkan crisis.

The details of the Balkan crisis of 1875 to 1878 culminating in the Congress of Berlin do not concern us here,[1] but the effect of the events of those years was to shatter the Dreikaiserbund and to drive Germany into closer support of Austria-Hungary. Russia's attack on Turkey in 1877 was clearly against Austria-Hungary's interests in the Balkans. Bismarck was forced to choose between his neighbours. If he backed Russia against Austria-Hungary he would drive Austria-Hungary to seek support from Britain and France. Germany and Russia together were probably strong enough to defeat Austria-Hungary even with allies, but Bismarck did not want the Habsburg Empire to collapse, since his own policy at home, and the position of Prussia in the German Empire, depended on the continued existence of Austria-Hungary as a Power, albeit a weak one. If, on the other hand, Bismarck backed Austria-Hungary against Russia, his position was little better. Russia was useful to Germany by keeping the Poles down, and if Russia lost the support of Germany she might be driven into alliance with France, and Germany would be faced by a war on two fronts. It was on these lines that the pattern of European alliances was later to develop, but in the 1870's France was not ready to abandon her interest in maintaining Turkey in order to gain Russia's alliance, nor was Russia prepared to support a French war of revenge in the West.

Bismarck tried to avoid choosing between Russia and Austria-Hungary by acting as 'honest broker' at Berlin in 1878, but the Congress revised the Treaty of San Stefano by which Russia had made peace with Turkey, and accordingly inflicted a defeat on Russia. By his very neutrality, Bismarck had inevitably alienated Russia, and in consequence he had to rely more heavily on Austria-Hungary. In 1879 this fact was recognized by the Dual Alliance. The treaty pledged each country to support the other against a Russian attack. If either were attacked by another Power, the other would remain benevolently neutral. Bismarck did not fear a single-handed attack by France, and if Russia joined France, Austria-Hungary would join Germany. He saw this treaty as a means of fobbing off the demands of those Germans who wanted a 'Greater Germany', and also of keeping Austria-Hungary from alliance with Britain and France. If he could tie Austria-Hungary to Germany, he hoped he could keep her friendly with

[1] See Chapter 6.

Russia. In fact, Germany found herself tied to Austria-Hungary, and committed to supporting her in the Balkans.

The Dual Alliance was kept secret (until 1888, at least), and Bismarck was able to follow it up in 1881 with a renewal of the Dreikaiserbund, but this time the League was based on a firm treaty with military commitments. If one of the three Powers were involved in a war with a fourth the other two were pledged to observe a benevolent neutrality. Thus if Germany were involved in a war with France she would not have to fight Russia as well. A special clause in the treaty provided for joint consultation in the event of a dispute concerning Turkey. Thus neither Russia nor Austria-Hungary could pursue her ambitions in the Balkans, which would have forced Bismarck to make again the embarrassing and dangerous choice between his allies that he had had to make in 1878. This second agreement, though impressive on paper, and comforting to Bismarck, was of little value in itself. It was made possible only by the weak position of Russia after her diplomatic humiliation at Berlin in 1878. While Russia was weak and isolated, Bismarck was in no danger and in no need of paper guarantees; but Russian and Austrian ambitions in the Balkans could not be reconciled indefinitely by a treaty designed to protect Germany's interests.

Nevertheless, Bismarck continued to set great store by diplomatic juggling. He urged Great Britain to take over Egypt and France to take over Tunis.[1] In 1881 the French formally declared their protectorate over Tunis, and Italy, bitterly resentful of the French action, joined with Germany and Austria-Hungary to convert the Dual Alliance into a Triple Alliance in 1882.[2] Bismarck was now satisfied that France was isolated.

In 1884 and 1885 Germany acquired her first colonies. Bismarck had always opposed those who had demanded that Germany should join in the race for colonies in which the other Powers were participating. He saw clearly that Germany's destiny lay in Europe, and that any distraction overseas could only help her enemies, particularly France. If Germany had colonies, she would need a navy to protect them, and that would arouse British opposition. Why Bismarck acted against his well-reasoned convictions for two years, and for two years only, is rather obscure. It has been suggested that the pressure of public opinion was too much for him to withstand. But Bismarck was not given to allowing public opinion to guide his foreign policy. A. J. P. Taylor[3] suggests a more characteristic line of argument. In 1884 the Reichstag elections were approaching. In earlier elections Bismarck had always raised the cry, 'The Reich is in danger'

---

[1] The ruler of Egypt, Khedive Ismail, was saved temporarily in 1875 by Disraeli's purchase of his shares in the Suez Canal Company ($\frac{7}{16}$ of the total) but in 1876 he finally went bankrupt. In 1878 Britain and France joined together in a Dual Control to govern Egypt. Following a nationalist rising in 1881 and the bombardment of Alexandria in 1882 by the British Navy, the French declined to join Britain in the military occupation of Egypt, and Franco-British relations were strained for a long time to come.

[2] Although Italy retained the right not to go to war against Great Britain.

[3] *Struggle for Mastery*, pp. 292–303.

either from France or from Russia, in order to terrify the electorate into returning his supporters. In 1884, however, the Reich was clearly in danger from no one. Bismarck was busily fostering good relations with France, which, under the government of Jules Ferry, was anxious for peace and stability in Europe in order to pursue a vigorous colonial policy. The Dreikaiserbund and the Triple Alliance between them deprived Bismarck of any possible enemy—except Britain. The best way to bring about a dispute with Britain was to demand some colonies. In fact, Bismarck acquired the colonies (S.W. Africa, the Cameroons, Togoland, and Tanganyika) without managing to quarrel with Britain, who was much too concerned about her relations with France in Africa to worry about Germany. However, in 1885 the government of Jules Ferry fell, because of the unpopularity of his colonial schemes, and France resumed her hostility towards Germany. By now, the Reichstag elections were safely over, and Bismarck had no need of a dispute with Britain. What is more, the Eastern Question was flaring up again with the reunion of Bulgaria and Eastern Rumelia. He no longer had any interest in colonies, and Germany acquired no more while he was in power.

The Balkan crisis of 1885–87[1] forced Bismarck once more to oppose Russia in the Balkans. Russia, who had supported the Big Bulgaria in 1878, now opposed the joining of Bulgaria with Eastern Rumelia. Britain and Austria-Hungary, who had broken up the Big Bulgaria, now supported it. The bankrupt policy of supporting Turkey, which Britain and France had pursued throughout the century, was now abandoned. Bismarck was desperately anxious to maintain friendship with Russia. In 1887 he concluded the Reinsurance Treaty—which was to hold good for three years— by which each agreed to maintain benevolent neutrality in the event of war with a third Power,[2] but this treaty was negotiated under the threat of war between Russia and Germany. Russia again gave way in the Balkans, and Austria-Hungary emerged strengthened. Bismarck still had faith in a pro-Russian policy. Negotiations for the renewal of the Reinsurance Treaty were in progress when he was dismissed in 1890. The negotiations were abandoned, but it was already clear to the Russians that they must look elsewhere for useful allies.

# 5   Russia, 1855-1917

The Crimean War is chiefly remembered today for the incompetence displayed by both sides. Every schoolboy knows of the charge of the Light

---

[1] See Chapter 6.
[2] The terms would not apply if Russia attacked Austria-Hungary, or if Germany attacked France.

Brigade, of the terrible conditions endured by the sick and wounded until Miss Florence Nightingale swept into action, and of the endless struggle she had to get supplies, equipment and help. What alarmed the Russians so much was that, in spite of their superior numbers, in spite of their obvious advantages in lines of communication, and in spite of the stupidity of their opponents, they lost the war. Alexander II, who came to the throne in 1855 in the middle of the war, was not slow to see the need for reform after the Peace of Paris of 1856. One of the lessons of the war seemed to be that a freeman was a better soldier than a serf.

## THE REFORMS

1. *The Emancipation of the Serfs 1861.* Alexander actively encouraged the desire for liberal reform which had been created by the war. He allowed some important political magazines to be founded, and, in the relaxed atmosphere, the universities expanded and became centres of keen political interest. Nevertheless, there was as yet no organized public opinion, and everyone looked to the Czar, not only to carry out reforms but also to suggest what measures should be undertaken. The first, and the fundamental, reform announced by Alexander was the emancipation of the serfs.

By the edict of 1861 the peasantry were freed from their obligations of service, dues, and obedience to the gentry. The greatest problem in the emancipation of the serfs was the allocation of land. To have given the peasants freedom without land would have been to invite revolution. On the other hand not all landowners would agree to give up some of their property. The final settlement was not uniform over the whole country, but altogether the peasants received about half the cultivated land. Most peasants had a good deal less land to cultivate for themselves after their emancipation than they had had before. Even then, the land did not become their own property, but was vested in the village Commune, which henceforth exercised much of the authority formerly enjoyed by the gentry. For instance, no peasant could leave the village without the permission of the Commune. The landowners received from the Government immediate compensation for their lost lands and services, while the peasants purchased the land from the Government by the payment of redemption money to be spread over a period of forty-nine years. The Commune was responsible for collecting this money.

Although at first vigorously opposed by many landowners, the emancipation was in fact a great blessing to them. Most of the gentry were heavily in debt, and the compensation they received was generous and opportune. Freed from all responsibility over their serfs, many of them sold their remaining land, and left for the more congenial life of the cities. The peasants were not so favoured. They no longer had to seek permission before marrying. They could own property. They had legal rights. But they still were liable to corporal punishment. They had their movements restricted. No Commune would allow a peasant to escape his responsibilities before leaving the village before the redemption money had been paid. The system employed in granting emancipation had avoided, or at least postponed, a rush from the land to the towns, and the creation of a politically dangerous proletariat.

Nevertheless, the emancipation was generally well received. But it was only the beginning of reform. Such a fundamental change in the structure of the State could not fail to bring about many changes.

2. *The Zemstvos.* By a law of 1864, Alexander set up local elected councils (Zemstvos) to deal with roads, hospitals, food, education, and public welfare in general. This measure was second in importance only to the Emancipation itself. The Zemstvos had no police or military authority and were therefore popular. They came to be regarded as the voice of the people. The mere existence of these locally elected bodies emphasized the autocratic nature of the Czar's administration.

3. *The Law.* Later in 1864, the legal system was reformed. Courts were to be made free of all class distinctions and independent of government officials. Judges were to be adequately paid and to be irremovable. Trials were to be held in public and the jury system introduced. Local justice was to be administered by Justices of the Peace elected by the Zemstvos. Although much of the value of judicial freedom was destroyed in the years which followed by overriding repressive measures, nevertheless the law was never repealed and it remained the standard by which legal action was judged.

4. *Army Reform.* The inefficiency of the Army which had been so clearly demonstrated in the Crimean War led to the sweeping Army Reform of 1874. Conscription was extended from the peasants to cover all classes, training was reorganized, and education was provided for. Most Russian peasants who could read and write learned to do so in the Army.

## REACTION

In April 1866 a young student made an unsuccessful attempt on Alexander's life. From that time the Government lived in fear and suspicion of students. Count Dmitry Tolstoy, a stern reactionary, was appointed Minister of Education and tightened government control of schools and universities. By a law of 1871 he revised the curricula of the gymnasia (grammar schools) to include much more Latin and Greek, to the exclusion of science, geography, and history. This was designed to make the universities increasingly the preserve of the upper classes, since poor children were unable to reach the standard in classics to enter the gymnasia, and only pupils from the gymnasia could enter the universities.

The Zemstvos, too, felt the reaction. In 1868 their power to levy rates was restricted and from 1866 the publicity of their debates was put under the control of the local governors. Many able men, no longer finding service of the Zemstvos attractive, resigned.

Restrictions were also placed on the press and the legal reforms were curtailed. By a law of 1878 political cases were to be tried by court martial.

## BAKUNIN AND THE INSURRECTIONISTS

The Radical students were divided into two main groups, the propagandists and the insurrectionists. The propagandists believed that the world would be changed by education and persuasion, while the insurrectionists, who followed Michael Bakunin, called for armed rebellion. Bakunin, who had escaped from Siberia in 1862 and had gone into exile in Geneva, preached anarchism, that is to say, that the State should not be reformed but abolished. Bakunin differed sharply from Marx (see p. 44), who wanted to use the machinery of the State to bring about a better world. The insurrectionists congregated in the poorer parts of the big cities and waged determined war on the police. Violence was temporarily halted by patriotic feeling in the Bulgarian war of 1877, but after the humiliating Treaty of Berlin the outbreaks were renewed. One of the chief targets in the campaign was Alexander himself. More than one attempt was made to blow up the Imperial train. In 1880 a workman systematically carried small quantities of dynamite into the Winter Palace in St. Petersburg and blew up the Imperial dining-room. The Emperor's life was saved because his guest was half-an-hour late. The Government was so alarmed that it decided to moderate its policy. A Supreme Commission of Administration was appointed under General Loris-Melikov, who was given complete control even over his Ministers. By his generous and imaginative policy Melikov won the confidence of the liberals. In February 1881 he proposed a scheme for enabling elected representatives of the people to assist the government in legislative work. He also planned commissions to reform administration and finance. These reforms delighted the liberals and terrified the revolutionaries, who gained most popular support when repression was greatest. They redoubled their efforts to assassinate Alexander. Streets in St. Petersburg were undermined. Squads of assassins were trained. On March 13th, 1881, the very day on which he signed Melikov's scheme for legislative reform, a bomb was thrown at his carriage. The Emperor was unhurt, but he dismounted to speak to some of the Cossacks who had been wounded. As he was speaking, a second bomb was thrown and this tore the Emperor open. He died in the Palace an hour and a half later.

## ALEXANDER III: 1881–1894

The assassination of Alexander II shocked and horrified conservative and liberal opinion alike. The terrorist gangs lost most of the support they had and the police were able to wipe most of them out. Alexander III, a well-built, strong, courageous, but simple man, had never approved of the liberal policy his father had attempted to pursue just before his death.

Nevertheless, his instinct was strong to carry out his father's wishes and he might have put Melikov's proposals into practice had it not been for the advice of his former tutor, Constantine Pobedonostsev.

Pobedonostsev, who had been appointed procurator of the Holy Synod in 1880 (the office created by Peter the Great to control the Church), was highly intelligent, and thoroughly reactionary. He was devoted to Russian Czardom, summed up in the autocracy, the serfdom, and the Orthodox Church. Under his direction severe restrictions were placed on the universities, the press, the law courts, and religious groups other than the Orthodox Church. The reforming work of the Zemstvos was curtailed by a law of 1889 which gave the gentry predominance on the Councils. The most bitterly resented measure was the law of 1889 which established land captains. These were chosen from the poorer gentry and operated directly under the Minister of the Interior. Their duties were to supervise every detail of peasant life; their powers were similar to those of the pre-emancipation landowners. They also took over the work of the Justices of the Peace.

## ECONOMIC CHANGES

Although they could not own land individually, the peasants were leasing more and more land, and by 1917 something like three-quarters of the cultivated land was in peasant hands. In spite of the legal difficulties many peasants began to colonize Siberia. Others went to the cities, especially to St. Petersburg or Moscow. They would retain their claim to land in their village and send money back to the Commune. Later on they would return to the country and leave their place in the town to be taken by some relative. Some villages depended on this income from the towns for their prosperity. Where possible some worked in local factories and continued to cultivate their land, while others engaged in cottage industries, which were promoted energetically by the Zemstvos.

Russia was developing rapidly industrially. Mining, because it was easier to develop than some other forms of industry, became very important, but foreign enterprise and capital contributed to a considerable industrial growth in the Donets region. When Sergius Witte became Minister of Finance in 1892, the economic development of Russia increased apace. Witte had risen from station-master to the head of the South Western Railways and now, under his guidance, Russia added to her railway mileage more rapidly than any other country in Europe. Witte established Russia's finances firmly and was thus able to attract foreign capital.[1] One of his minor financial successes was the creation of a State monopoly of vodka.

Russia was now no longer isolated from industrial Europe, but industrialization brought with it the beginnings of a factory class which required

[1] Most of these investors lost their money, when the Bolsheviks repudiated the debts in 1917.

legislation. Factory laws limiting the hours of work for women and children were passed in 1882–86 with the important provision of factory inspectors with extensive powers. These measures, however, provoked the cry of 'Socialism' and, for a time after 1890, the employers were able to nullify this legislation.

## NICHOLAS II: 1894–1917

Alexander III died in 1894 and he was succeeded by his son Nicholas II. Nicholas had great personal charm, but neither the strength of will to be a successful autocrat, nor the intelligence to rule in accordance with Russia's needs. His stupidity was breathtaking. His obstinate adherence to the principle of autocracy was catastrophic. His wife Alexandra, formerly Princess Alix of Hesse-Darmstadt, whom he married shortly after his father's death, was a fitting companion for him. Deeply religious, she embraced the faith of the Orthodox Church on her marriage with all the fervour of the sincere convert. She was quite as stupid as Nicholas, and equally determined that the autocracy of the Czars should in no way be diminished, but her will was as strong as her husband's was weak. Only the thought that they were devoted to each other and were murdered together by the Bolsheviks produces any real sympathy for this wretched couple. Their reign began, as it was to end, in tragedy. It was the custom after the coronation for small presents to be distributed to the poor of Moscow by the new Czar and Czarina. While Nicholas and Alexandra were doing this, a rumour spread round the crowd of 300 000 that had gathered that there were not enough presents to go round. A wild scramble resulted, in which hundreds of people were crushed to death.

### REPRESSION

Nicholas determined to stamp out all ideas, beliefs, and customs that he disliked. Government spies were everywhere. Police permission was necessary before anything other than the smallest party could be held in St. Petersburg. Jews were particularly cruelly persecuted. Alexander III had introduced laws which placed severe restrictions on the movement, education, and employment of Jews. Nicholas added to these restrictions, and the police were employed to carry out or incite pogroms (armed attacks) on Jews. Nor was repression confined to Russia. Nicholas increased his powers over Finland in spite of the rights guaranteed to her when she was annexed in 1809, and which Alexander III had confirmed as recently as 1881. Only the Baltic provinces of Estonia and Livonia (Latvia) were granted any concessions. There, Nicholas reversed the Russianization policy of his father, and restored the German barons to their predominant position.

## MARX AND MARXISM

One of the results of the spectacular growth of industry which had begun in Alexander III's reign and which continued under Nicholas, was the spread from the west of the Socialist ideas of Karl Marx.

Marx was a German of Jewish extraction, although he was baptized and brought up a Lutheran. With Friedrich Engels, he wrote the famous *Communist Manifesto* in 1848, but his ideas were chiefly expounded in his great book *Das Kapital*, the first volume of which appeared in 1867. Marx asserted that all wealth came from man's labour, but that the poor sold their labour to the employer, or capitalist, at less than its full value. The development of capitalism, he maintained, depended upon the capitalist cheating the worker of this 'surplus value'. Class warfare between the proletariat, i.e. the workers, and the capitalists was therefore inevitable. Equally inevitable, in his view, was the collapse of capitalism owing to contradictions within the system as well as to the power of the proletariat. The victory of the proletariat would be followed by the establishment of a classless society.

Marx, who died in 1883, would have ridiculed the idea that the Communist Revolution should first succeed in Russia, which had neither a factory proletariat nor a capitalist bourgeoisie. He, and his followers—including Lenin—looked to Germany to lead the way.

## THE SOCIAL DEMOCRATS

In 1898 a number of small groups which had been organized by Gregory Plekhanov and his associates to study the writings of Marx joined together to form the Social Democratic Workmen's Party. Between 1900 and 1902, the rival Social Revolutionary Party was formed. Both these organizations, of course, were compelled to operate secretly in Russia, though they both existed openly in exile in western Europe. The S.R.'s represented the old Russian revolutionary tradition. Their appeal was to the peasant, their method terrorism. In contrast, the S.D.'s, preaching Marxism, directed their efforts towards the industrial worker.

The S.D.'s were themselves divided right from the start between those who wished to bring about an improvement in the economic conditions of the workers within the existing framework of the State, and those who wished to overthrow the political system and seize control of the State. The party actually split over a point of organization. At the Second Congress of the Party in 1903,[1] the question of whether the party should be a mass organization of sympathizers or whether it should be a restricted, tightly controlled group of active organizers, was put to the vote. Lenin, who supported the latter alternative, secured a majority of two. Hence-

[1] Which opened in Brussels and moved across to London while in session, the delegates arguing all the way over.

forth, he called his followers the Bolsheviks (the majority men) and his opponents the Mensheviks (the minority men).

Lenin, who was born Vladimir Ulyanov, was the son of an inspector of schools who had worked his way up to a position of minor nobility. Lenin's elder brother, Alexander, an S.R., was executed in 1887 for his slender share in a plot to assassinate Alexander III. Highly intelligent, Lenin had thrown himself whole-heartedly into the revolutionary movement, but he had no faith in the bomb-throwing methods. In 1897 he was arrested, imprisoned, and sent to Siberia.[1] When his term was up in 1900, he left Russia for Switzerland, where he joined other exiled revolutionaries to form the party newspaper *Iskra* (the Spark), which was smuggled into Russia. His emergence in 1903 as the leader of the Bolsheviks accelerated the pace of revolutionary activity, but the position of the revolutionaries was strengthened by the Czar's unpopular and disastrous foreign policy.

## THE RUSSO-JAPANESE WAR: 1904–5

After the setback she received in 1878 at the Congress of Berlin, Russia turned her attention to Asia. Nicholas inherited the policy of expansion in the Far East from his father, though after his tour of 1890–91, during which he had laid the foundation-stone of the terminus of the Trans-Siberian railway at Vladivostok, he himself became immensely attracted by the opportunities for autocratic grandeur which the East seemed to offer. A clash with Japan, which also had ambitions in the crumbling Chinese Empire, thus became probable. Nicholas personally directed affairs with Japan and friction increased as Russia poured troops into Manchuria and levered her way into Korea. Assured by the treaty of 1902 of Britain's neutrality if she had to fight Russia alone, and of Britain's help if Russia were joined by another Power, Japan delivered a surprise attack on Port Arthur in February 1904. The war was utterly disastrous for the Russian forces. Port Arthur fell, the Russian naval forces were destroyed, and the great land battle of Mukden, which lasted for fourteen days, ended in a Russian retreat. Any lingering hopes the Russians may have entertained disappeared with the tragi-comic episode of the Baltic Fleet. In October 1904 the Russian Baltic Fleet set out on its journey half-way round the world to restore the naval balance in Chinese waters. Early in their voyage, the trigger-happy Russians fired on some English trawlers off Dogger Bank which they took for Japanese warships. Only the prompt offer of satisfaction by Russia averted a major crisis. When the fleet eventually came within range of Admiral Togo's guns off Korea in May 1905, most of it was put out of action in three-quarters of an hour. Only two cruisers and

---

[1] Being sent to Siberia under the Czars was not so terrifying as many people imagine. The political offenders were exiled rather than imprisoned. They lived in wood cabins in remote and desolate settlements and were able to receive letters, newspapers, and books. Lenin wrote several books during his enforced leisure. The life was undoubtedly bleak and dull, but not physically exhausting or cruel.

two destroyers escaped to Vladivostok. Thanks to the skilled negotiating of Witte, Russia escaped lightly by the Treaty of Portsmouth (New Hampshire) 1905. She lost Port Arthur and the Liaotung peninsula, southern Manchuria, and the southern half of the island of Sakhalin, to Japan. Korea was recognized as a Japanese sphere of influence. Long before the treaty was signed Russia was in the grip of revolution.

## THE REVOLUTION OF 1905

The war was a private adventure of the Czar and was unpopular with most Russians even before the news of the calamities reached home. Discontent soon showed itself. In July 1904, Plehve, the Minister of the Interior and chief architect of internal repression, was assassinated. The Zemstvos took heart at the appointment of Sviatopolk-Mirsky, known for his liberal views, as Plehve's successor. At the Zemstvo Conference of November 1904, the representatives called unanimously for freedom of person, conscience, speech, meeting, the press, association, and education; for equal civil rights for all irrespective of class, nationality, or religion; for a wider system of voting for the Zemstvos; and for reforms to meet the needs of the peasants and factory workers. The only point on which they disagreed was whether the elective national assembly which they demanded should have legislative authority or be merely consultative. The majority favoured legislative authority. The Czar characteristically told the conference that it had no business discussing political matters. He promised reforms of his own, but there was to be no national assembly. At once professional men (authors, lawyers, professors, journalists, doctors) organized meetings which adopted the Zemstvo programme in its entirety and each group formed itself into a union—the first trade unions in Russia —to bring this programme into effect.

One of the persistent beliefs among the poor and downtrodden was that the Czar was misled by his advisers, and that if only he were aware of their sufferings he would meet their needs. On Sunday January 22nd, 1905, Father Gapon, an eccentric but persuasive priest who had established a representative organization among factory workers, decided to lead his followers to the Winter Palace to petition the Czar personally. The authorities took fright and the procession, carrying icons and portraits of the Czar, and singing religious and national songs, was brutally mown down by fire from troops stationed at strategic points. Perhaps as many as a thousand were killed.

Bloody Sunday aroused far more feeling than could have been produced by any number of Zemstvo resolutions. A wave of strikes spread throughout the country. The Governor-General of Moscow was killed by a bomb in the Kremlin in broad daylight. The S.R.'s abandoned all talk of forms of government and adopted the rallying cry 'All land for the peasants' which was instantly successful. Riots broke out all over the countryside, estates were ransacked, and the landlords driven out (usually unharmed).

At Odessa, on the Black Sea, the crew of the Battleship *Potemkin* mutinied and seized their ship. In October a general strike spread throughout the country. In St. Petersburg a Soviet, a workers' council, was formed, with Trotsky as its Vice-President, to assume control of the revolution. On the advice of Witte, the Czar issued a manifesto announcing that a legislative Duma, or parliament, elected by popular franchise would be summoned in the near future. The general strike was called off in November, but disorders and mutinies remained widespread. Order was restored only by the wholesale execution of peasants, and the burning of villages.

The revolution had failed, but it had not been wholly ineffective. Russia was never again to be ruled without any semblance of a representative institution. The revolution had divided the liberals from the revolutionaries and it had shown that, amongst the revolutionaries, it was the peasants and the S.R. party, rather than the factory workers, the soviets, and the S.D.'s that had the power.

*Map 2. Russo-Japanese War, 1904–5*

## THE DUMAS

The first Duma met in May 1906. The S.D.'s at first boycotted the elections and only joined in half-heartedly when it was too late. An overwhelming majority of the seats went to groups opposing the Government, and the Cadets, the Liberals, were the largest single party. The parties were almost unanimous in approving the moderate programme of reform that was submitted, and when most of it was rejected by the Government, their unanimity in support of a vote of censure was complete. But the

Duma was powerless to make the Government resign. Indeed, the Government, assured of financial independence by the French loan of 2000 million francs negotiated by Witte in April, felt strong enough to dissolve the Duma, and the attempt by some of the Cadets to organize civil disobedience (by such acts as the refusal to pay taxes) until the Duma was restored, was a complete failure.

Witte had been dismissed shortly after he had concluded the French loan, and the dominant Minister was now Stolypin. As a provincial governor in 1905, Stolypin had shown great courage and determination, as well as great brutality, in restoring order in his province. When he dissolved the First Duma, he called another to meet in March 1907, but in the intervening time he introduced a revolutionary change in peasant society by diminishing the power of the village Commune. The responsibility of the Commune for the collection of the redemption money ended with the cancellation of those payments in November 1905. Peasants were now allowed to leave their villages without permission, and they were also allowed to consolidate their scattered strips into single holdings, which they could henceforth hold as their personal property. They could also be elected to the Zemstvo and were eligible for any rank in government service.

Stolypin did everything in his power to ensure that the composition of the Second Duma was favourable to him. The electoral law was changed, large numbers of people disfranchised, candidates excluded from the lists, voting papers delayed, and in fact there was general gerrymandering. The effect of all this was the reverse of what Stolypin wanted. The places of those Cadets who had protested against the dissolution of the First Duma and who accordingly were excluded from standing for the Second, were taken by more Left-wing groups, including the S.R.'s and the S.D.'s. Every move made by the Second Duma was obstructed by the Government and after three months it was dissolved.

With the dissolution came the announcement of a carefully prepared electoral law, though such a move was illegal since by the Government's own ruling no such changes could take place without the Duma's consent. The new law left little to chance. Non-Russian parts of the Empire had their representation reduced or abolished altogether. Towns lost their separate representation and were merged into that of the provinces, where the gentry were placed in a controlling position.

The Third Duma, elected under the new law, met in November 1907. It was dominated by the Octobrists (the moderate Liberals who took as their programme the Czar's manifesto of October 1905), who gained a great deal of valuable insight into the workings of government. Their criticisms were restrained but sound, and, although the assembly was far from representative of the true wishes of the people, the conduct of the Octobrists earned respect both from below and from above. The Third Duma lasted its full term of five years. Stolypin, however, had acquired many enemies, and in 1911 he was assassinated while attending a theatre performance with the Czar in Kiev. His death, though at the hands of a revolutionary, was applauded, and probably arranged, by the reactionaries.

The Fourth Duma was elected in 1912, and its composition was very similar to that of its predecessor. Conditions were by this time improving in both town and country. The peasant reforms were taking effect, wages in industry were rising, and in 1912 health and accident insurance was introduced. Illiteracy was rapidly being conquered and by 1914 half the children of school age were attending school. The vision of Czarist Russia's undergoing a steady transformation into a constitutional democracy was shattered by the war, which brought out the extremes both of autocracy and of revolution.

## THE WAR: 1914-17

The outbreak of war swept the whole country up in a wave of patriotic feeling, but in spite of the military reorganization which had taken place, Russia was ill-prepared for the fight. Leadership was poor, munitions short, and medical services totally insufficient. The Russian soldier fought with pathetic gallantry but the corruption and inefficiency of the régime he was fighting for made his task hopeless. The losses were appalling. Manpower by itself was not enough.

Perhaps one of the greatest disasters to overtake the Russian armies was the decision of the Czar in August 1914 to appoint himself Commander-in-Chief. This step, urged on by the Czarina and greeted with consternation by nearly everyone else, was fatal for two reasons. First, the Czar was militarily incompetent and therefore a menace. Secondly, his absence at Headquarters increased the influence Alexandra had on affairs, and she was under the spell of the infamous Rasputin.

## RASPUTIN

Rasputin was a coarse, unkempt, foul-minded, Siberian peasant who, although never in religious orders, had acquired a reputation as a holy man. His connection with the Royal Family arose out of his apparently miraculous powers. The Czar's only son Alexis suffered from haemophilia and was liable to bleed to death following the slightest injury. He was naturally the object of Alexandra's constant concern. Twice when the doctors had despaired of the boy's life, Rasputin had prophesied his recovery and at once it had begun to take place. On one of these occasions Rasputin had been far away from the Czarevitch and he had sent his prophecy by telegram. The Czarnina, who was much given to mystical and spiritualist experiences, was convinced he was a 'Man of God', and refused to listen to the vile, but usually accurate, stories that were told about him. In July 1914 he warned the Czar that if he went to war he would be defeated. His prestige mounted as the defeats followed. From September 1915, he was the effective ruler of Russia. The Czarina wrote of him as 'our Friend', and

Ministers rose or fell in accordance with their expressed opinion of him. He scribbled instructions to every department of government and even issued orders and prophecies for the operations at the front. He was opposed to the war and equally opposed to anything which sought to diminish the Czar's absolutism.

The military disasters, the breakdown of the transport system which produced a major food crisis at home and at the front, and the scandalous domination of Rasputin over affairs, led to growing discontent. In October 1916 soldiers joined a group of strikers in Petrograd[1] they had been sent to disperse. There was urgent need for decisive, intelligent, and courageous action if Russia was to avoid terrible defeat and suffering. While Rasputin remained in favour, the Ministries were likely to continue to be filled by incompetents. Since Alexandra would not listen to reason, the only alternative was to assassinate 'the Man of God'.

On December 30th 1916, Rasputin was invited to the house of a relative of the Czar and there plied with cakes and wine which had been liberally laced with potassium cyanide. He remained unmoved. Accordingly, his would-be assassins shot him. Their nerves now thoroughly on edge, they were discussing what to do with the corpse when to their horror it rose and began to chase them. Several more revolver bullets were poured into Rasputin before he finally collapsed. His body was dumped in the Neva. Affairs had reached a sad state when respectable members of the Russian nobility felt compelled to participate in such a macabre episode.

Nicholas and Alexandra alone grieved his death, but they no longer counted for very much.

REVOLUTION

In March 1917 hungry crowds and strikers in the capital became involved in clashes with the police. On March 12th, two regiments of Guards joined the demonstrators, who then seized and distributed arms and ammunition, opened prisons, and set fire to the political police headquarters. All this happened spontaneously without any leadership. Two groups hastened to provide a lead. Representatives of factory workers and soldiers formed a Soviet, while the Duma set about forming a provisional government. Members of the Soviet had sworn not to participate in the provisional government, but when it was formed on March 14th under Prince Lvov, Alexander Kerensky, a Social Revolutionary who was both a member of the Duma and Vice-President of the Soviet, obtained permission to become Minister of Justice. The following day, Nicholas abdicated in favour of his brother Michael and was shortly afterwards placed under arrest. The refusal of the Grand Duke Michael to accept the throne left Russia with a provisional government but without a legal sovereign. The Government of Prince Lvov had less claim to any authority than the Petrograd Soviet, or

[1] The German-sounding name St. Petersburg had been changed at the beginning of the war.

indeed than any of the numerous soviets which had sprung up everywhere. The possibilities of the situation were suddenly realized by Lenin, who was champing at the bit in Switzerland.

## THE BOLSHEVIK REVOLUTION

By agreement with the German General Staff, Lenin and other Bolshevik leaders were allowed to travel through Germany to Russia in a sealed train. The provisional government was determined to continue the war, but already soldiers were running their units by committees on which officers had equal voting rights with other ranks, and military discipline was fast disintegrating. The Germans were not unnaturally anxious to unleash what further chaos they could. The Bolsheviks well repaid their train ride.

Yet despite their best effort, the Bolsheviks remained, ironically in view of their name, in the minority. At the all-Russian Congress of Soviets held in June there were 285 S.R.'s, 248 Mensheviks, and only 105 Bolsheviks. Lenin had to play his game carefully. Bringing about the fall of the provisional government was not enough; he had also to ensure that it was not replaced by the more popular Socialist groups. After an unsuccessful attempt to unseat the Government in July, Lenin was forced into hiding in Finland, but the position of Lvov became increasingly difficult and in August he was replaced by Kerensky, who formed another coalition Government of Liberals and moderate Socialists.

The last move was sudden and dramatic. In the early hours of November 7th (October 25),[1] the Bolsheviks seized the principal buildings of Petrograd. The Winter Palace, Kerensky's headquarters, was besieged, and Ministers were arrested. Similar coups took place in other large cities. On the following day the new Soviet Government came into existence with Lenin as its chairman.

The Bolsheviks succeeded in their daring seizure of power for three reasons. First, although greatly outnumbered, they were a well-disciplined and highly selected group, and as such presented a formidable striking force. Secondly, Lenin was an outstanding leader and he knew just when to strike hard most effectively. Finally, the Bolsheviks promised peace and food. The people were tired of the efforts to continue the war and they were hungry. The actual area under Bolshevik control though vital, was as yet very limited. The tasks facing the new Government were innumerable. None was more important than the establishment of peace and the provision of bread.

---

[1] The Gregorian Calendar, which was first introduced by Pope Gregory XIII in 1582 and which Britain adopted in 1752, was not used in Russia until 1918. Before 1918 dates were reckoned according to the Julian Calendar, which by then was thirteen days behind the Gregorian. The two revolutions of 1917 are therefore known as the February and October revolutions although they took place in March and November.

# 6   The Balkans

By 1870, the Turkish Empire, which at one time had stretched from the Indian Ocean to the Straits of Gibraltar and from the Persian Gulf to the gates of Vienna, was fast crumbling. The Turks had always been better fighters than administrators, better conquerors than rulers. Their policy of relying on periodic bouts of terrorism to keep their subject peoples in check had been moderately effective when their army had been efficient and when the Great Powers had been preoccupied elsewhere, but in the 19th century neither of these conditions remained. Without drastic internal reform Turkey could not hope to hold her own in a modern world, but misrule and corruption had eaten so deeply into her that only violent and sweeping changes could bring about reform, and such changes would give the restless subject peoples the chance they were waiting for to throw off Turkish overlordship. It had become impossible to reform the Turkish Empire and at the same time to maintain it. Consequently the Empire crumbled. In 1870, the Turkish Empire in Europe included four Christian national groups: Greeks, Slavs (Serbs and Croats), Rumanians and Bulgars, and two Moslem national groups: Turks and Albanians. Already the process of disintegration had begun. Since 1815 nationalist movements in the outlying parts of the Empire, combined with pressure from the Great Powers, had achieved Turkish recognition of the independence of a small Greek Kingdom, and a large measure of independence for the principalities of Serbia and Rumania. Montenegro remained, as it always had, secure behind its mountain barriers and independent of the Turk. But many Greeks, Serbs, Croats and Rumanians, and all the Bulgars,[1] remained wholly under Turkish rule.

Throughout the 19th century, Turkey was finding it increasingly difficult to deal with her problems of government, and at the same time the Christian peoples in her Empire were becoming increasignly determined to win national independence. The problems created by this process of disintegration were known as the Eastern Question, which was a constant and dominating factor in European policies from 1815 to 1914. The Eastern Question broke up such harmony as existed between the Great Powers after their defeat of Napoleon, it was in some degree responsible for the Crimean War, it determined Bismarck's alliances, and it set the scene for the outbreak of the First World War.

Broadly speaking, there were three possible solutions to the problem: (1) Turkey could reform herself internally; (2) Turkey-in-Europe could be absorbed by Russia and Austria, her two great neighbours, while Britain, France and Italy helped themselves to Turkey's African and

[1] Though in 1870 they were allowed to have their own religious head, instead of being under the Patriarch at Constantinople. This move increased their sense of nationality.

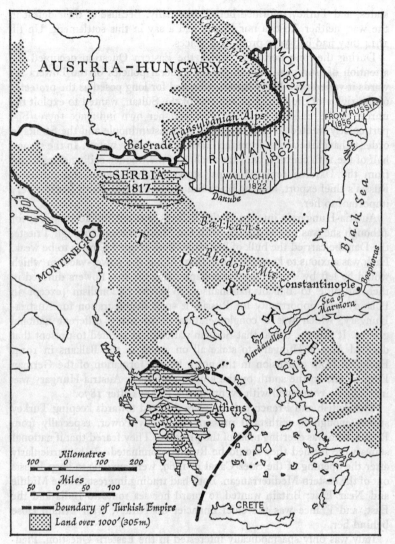

*Map 3. The Balkans, 1870*

Middle Eastern possessions; (3) the national groups in the Empire could be given national independence.

The final solution—if the problem can be said to have been solved finally—was a combination of all three possibilities. After the First World War the African and Middle Eastern parts of the Empire were in the hands of Britain, France and Italy, Turkey-in-Europe was divided into nation states, and Turkey reformed herself internally. Because of their defeat in the war, neither Austria nor Russia had a say in this settlement. Up till 1914 they had had very prominent voices.

During the long period in which the Eastern Question occupied the attention of European statesmen, the general policies of the Powers towards it varied very little. Russia, who had for long posed as the protector of the rights of the Christian subjects of the Sultan, wanted to exploit the unrest in the Balkans in order to extend her own influence there. She particularly wanted to gain control over Constantinople and the Straits in order to have free access from the Black Sea to 'warm water'. In the second half of the 19th century, with the decline of the wooden sailing ship, wheat from the Ukraine replaced ships' stores (timber, hemp and pitch) as Russia's chief export, and the Black Sea rather than the Baltic became very important to her.

Austria-Hungary's interest in the Balkans was not unlike Russia's, for although she was linked directly with the Mediterranean through Trieste, the Danube carried the bulk of her trade. Both wanted Turkey to be weak. Each was anxious to keep the other from filling the power-vacuum which would be left by Turkey's utter collapse. But the two Powers differed in their attitude to Balkan nationalism. Whereas nationalism (except in Poland) spelt opportunity for Russia, it spelt disintegration for Austria-Hungary, which was a conglomeration of so many different national groups. It was the threat that Serbian nationalism seemed to present that decided Austria-Hungary to stake all on a war in the Balkans in 1914. Excluded from expansion in the north by the formation of the German Empire, and in the south by the kingdom of Italy, Austria-Hungary was increasingly concerned with events in the Balkans after 1870.

The British and French policies were directed towards keeping Turkey strong enough to withstand pressure from any Power, especially from Russia, who was exerting most of the pressure. They feared that if national states were formed they would be Russian-dominated. Both, particularly after the opening of the Suez Canal in 1869, were anxious to keep Russia out of the eastern Mediterranean. Both had trading interests in the Middle and Near East; Britain wanted to guard her sea route to India and the East, and France was the chief financier of Turkey, with Britain close behind her.

Italy was only spasmodically interested in the Eastern Question. Piedmont had used the Crimean War and its peace conference as a means of enlisting help in the unification of Italy. After 1870, her interest lay chiefly in her desire for colonies in North Africa, and in the effect of Balkan crises on her neighbour, Austria-Hungary, against whom she had territorial claims.

Until Bismarck's fall in 1890, Germany had no interest in the Balkans, except in securing peace. While the Eastern Question remained unsolved, each crisis would force Bismarck to choose between supporting Austria-Hungary and supporting Russia, and he was anxious to remain friendly with both. After Bismarck's fall, however, when Germany became increasingly involved economically in Turkish affairs, and even more obviously committed to the maintenance of the Habsburg Empire, Germany's policy became closely aligned with that of Austria-Hungary.

## THE NEAR-EASTERN CRISIS: 1875–78

In 1875 the oppressed Serbs of Bosnia and Herzegovina rose in rebellion against the Turk. The immediate concern of all the Great Powers was to end the fighting. In December 1875, Andrássy, the Austro-Hungarian Foreign Minister, sent a Note to the Sultan on behalf of all the Powers, which demanded that he should carry out reforms to remove the grievances of the rebels. The Sultan, Abdul Aziz, agreed to the reforms, but had no intention of carrying them out. The rebels, for their part, continued to rebel, and the situation continued to deteriorate. In May 1876 the Eastern Powers drew up a second note to the Sultan, known as the Berlin Memorandum, which proposed an armistice with the rebels so that the reforms outlined in the Andrássy Note could be carried out. All the Powers adhered to this except Britain. Disraeli, the British Prime Minister, reversed his policy between the Andrássy Note and the Berlin Memorandum, partly because of his own pro-Turk sympathies, which were greatly reinforced by the despatches of Elliott, his Ambassador at Constantinople, and partly because of a feeling that the members of the Dreikaiserbund (see p. 35) were secretly planning to dismember Turkey. Following an entirely independent policy, Disraeli ordered the British fleet to Besika Bay, close to the Dardanelles.

By now the fears of the Powers were realized. The revolt spread to the Bulgarians, and soon Serbia and Montenegro joined them against the Turks. The Balkans were in ferment, and the Turks, roused to activity by the rebellions and by the interference of the Great Powers, experienced an upsurge of intense nationalist feeling on their own account. At Salonika a mob murdered the German and French consuls. At Constantinople the Sultan Abdul Aziz was deposed and, after making three attempts to throw himself out of the window, he finally committed suicide by slitting the veins of his arms open with a pair of scissors which he had been given to trim his beard with.[1] His successor, Murad V, went mad and was deposed three months later.[2] Against the Bulgarians the Turks loosed an army of irregular soldiers, known as Bashi-Bazouks, who terrorized the population by their atrocities, and slaughtered men, women and children in their thousands.

---

[1] Why he was given the scissors and then left alone remains a mystery. He was clearly in a suicidal mood, and suspicion should have been roused by his request to trim his own beard. As Sultan, his beard had been trimmed by the Imperial Barber as part of an elaborate ritual in which every hair was preserved.

[2] He lingered on as a dangerous prisoner of the Sultan until 1904.

Disraeli, acting in good faith on Elliott's despatches, declared the reports of the atrocities to be greatly exaggerated, but it soon became common knowledge that they were not. Gladstone, whose pamphlet *The Bulgarian Horrors and the Question of the East* sold 40 000 copies within a few days of issue, led a growing and influential body of public opinion to demand that Britain should intervene to check the Turk. The Bulgarian Atrocities made it impossible for Disraeli to go to war against Russia on the side of Turkey, and Russia knew this.

In the autumn of 1876, Czar Alexander II decided to adopt a stronger line. Turkey was winning its fight against the rebels, and the Serbian armies had been defeated. Accordingly, a Conference of the Powers met at Constantinople. Disraeli (he became the Earl of Beaconsfield in August 1876), who still clung to his pro-Turk and anti-Russian views, was represented by Lord Salisbury, who did not. The Conference proposed sweeping reforms, including self-government for Bulgaria. The new Sultan, the crafty Abdul Hamid II, spiked the guns of the Conference by proclaiming a liberal constitution, and rejected its demands. The Conference broke up in confusion and the Sultan was free to abolish the constitution, as he did in May 1877. The Sultan was firmly convinced that, as in the past, whatever the merits of the case, Britain would not stand by and watch Turkey be dismembered by Russia.

Russia, however, was now bent on war, and if all the Powers were not with her, at least none would stand against her. Austria-Hungary was bought off with the promise of Bosnia and Herzegovina. Britain was assured of the security of Egypt and the Suez Canal, and the freedom of Constantinople and the Straits. In April 1877 the Russo-Turkish War began. For nearly five months the Turks held up the Russian advance at Plevna. The effect of this resistance was far-reaching. The British public, ever on the side of the under-dog, forgot the Bulgarian Horrors, and was lost in admiration for the heroic Osman Pasha, the defender of Plevna. Weight of numbers told in the end, Osman Pasha capitulated, and an armistice was concluded at Adrianople in January 1878. By then the British people were clamouring for war against Russia, a sentiment shared by Queen Victoria.[1]

Peace was made by the Treaty of San Stefano 1878. Serbia and Montenegro were to gain territory and, together with Rumania, were to be recognized by Turkey as fully independent. A new, big, Bulgaria, with access to the Aegean Sea, was to be created. Southern Dobruja was to go to Rumania. Russia was to recover Bessarabia (which had gone to Rumania in 1856) and some other conquests in the Caucasus. Turkey undertook to carry out the promised reforms.

This Treaty was quite unacceptable to either Austria-Hungary or Britain, and both demanded that Russia submit it to a congress of the

---

[1] She even thought of abdicating. When told that the Russians were encamped on the shores of the Sea of Marmora, she is reported to have replied, 'Then they must get out!'

Powers. Beaconsfield backed his demand by calling up the reserves and by sending 7000 Indian troops to Malta. The British Fleet was already in the Sea of Marmora, and the British public pledged its support in a famous music-hall song introduced by the Great Macdermott, a music-hall star believed to be in Tory pay. The top-hatted audience at the London Pavilion went wild when they heard the chorus:

> We don't want to fight, but by Jingo, if we do,
> We've got the ships, we've got the men, and got the money too.
> We've fought the Bear before, and while we're Britons true,
> The Russians shall not have Constantinople.

Later, Gladstone's windows were smashed.

Russia submitted, and in June 1878 all the Powers met at Berlin to revise the terms of the Treaty of San Stefano.

## THE CONGRESS OF BERLIN 1878

The Congress of Berlin was a personal triumph for Beaconsfield. Largely by bluff he had forced the Russians to agree to it; he dominated its proceedings and ensured its success by arranging its conclusions before it met. By the time the Ministers gathered in Berlin, Beaconsfield had concluded secret agreements with Russia, Austria-Hungary, and Turkey. The principle point agreed to was that the 'Big Bulgaria' should be broken up, and that only the most northerly part should be entirely independent of Turkey. Even so, at Berlin, the Russians tried to evade the consequences of this agreement by insisting that Turkish troops should not be allowed to garrison Eastern Rumelia. The Russian motive in this was to deny the Turks the use of the Balkan mountains as a defensible frontier. However, Beaconsfield was a match for Prince Gortchakov, the Russian Chancellor. He ordered his special train to be ready to leave Berlin—'the first time that this weapon was added to the technique of diplomacy' (A. J. P. Taylor). Bismarck, the unhappy chairman of the Congress, who was trying to clear up the whole business without losing the friendship of either Austria, Hungary or Russia, persuaded the Russians to give way, and the crisis passed.

Bulgaria was trisected as planned. The new Bulgaria was declared a self-governing principality, Eastern Rumelia became a special province of the Turkish Empire under a Christian Governor, and Macedonia was entirely restored to Turkey. Austria-Hungary was given the right to occupy, though not to annex, Bosnia and Herzegovina, and Novibazar, between Serbia and Montenegro. For the rest the Treaty of San Stefano was confirmed. Russia took Bessarabia from Rumania, and Batum and Kars from Turkey. Rumania was given in return Southern Dobruja and the recognition of her independence. The independence of the enlarged Serbia and Montenegro was confirmed. To counteract Russia's gains from

*Map 4. The Congress of Berlin, 1878*

Turkey, Britain, by direct agreement with the Sultan, acquired Cyprus[1]
as a base in the eastern Mediterranean, though in fact she developed

[1] Public opinion was not altogether happy about the acquisition of Cyprus,
particularly after reports of ill-health among the first occupying troops. A music-
hall song of the time ran:

> Here's another little baby Queen Victoria has got,
> Another little colony, although she has a lot,
> Another little island, very wet and very hot,
> Whatever will she do with little Cyprus?

**British Statesmen.** *Above left* Disraeli (this photo was taken by the Queen's command in 1878). *Above right* Salisbury, the Conservative champion of 'Splendid Isolation' (see p. 66) speaking in the House of Lords. *Right* Edward VII, the personification of the Anglo-French entente (see p. 69). Behind is his brother, the Duke of Connaught.

**Bismarck's Successors.** *Left* Tirpitz, the creator of the Imperial German Navy (see p. 70). *Below* Bülow (in soft hat) confers with his successor, Bethman-Hollweg, at the railway station in Berlin (see p. 73).

**The Kaiser in Good Humour.** The Kaiser (with arm raised) has just said something which a general and an Austrian officer find very amusing. It was no doubt wise to find the Kaiser's jokes funny.

The Outbreak of the First World War. *Left* Grey, the Foreign Secretary in Asquith's Liberal Government in 1914. *Below* The famous Kitchener recruiting poster of 1914.

YOUR COUNTRY NEEDS "YOU"

**Military Leaders of the First World War.** *Above* Foch (see p. 86) arrives to inspect a British army detachment. *Below* Hindenburg (second from right) and German officers in June 1918.

**Wilson in Europe.** Wilson (in light macintosh) accompanied by King Albert of the Belgians receives one of the popular welcomes that had such an unfortunate effect upon him (see p. 90).

**Politicians at the Front.** *Above* Lloyd George (with bow tie) on a visit to the western front in 1916. *Below* Clemenceau acknowledges the cheers of British troops in the spring of 1918.

**Leaders of New Countries.**
*Left* Pilsudski, the leader of the recreated Poland (see p. 111). *Below* Masaryk (in peaked cap) whose dream of a Czechoslovak state came true at Versailles (see p. 112).

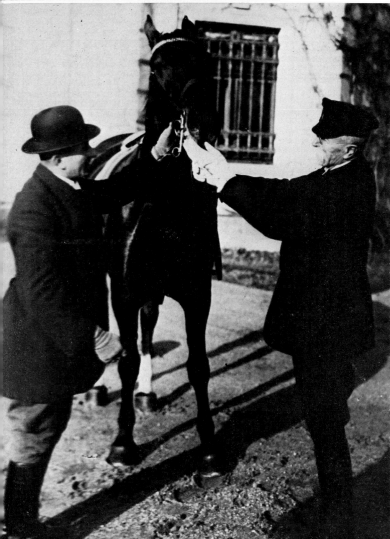

Egypt, which she occupied in varying degrees from 1882 to 1956, as her base in this area. The French were compensated by British and German consent to their seizure of Tunis in 1881. Italy acquired nothing except recognition as a Power by her mere presence at the Congress. In 1878 that was something. Germany alone gained nothing. Indeed, she lost a great deal, for Bismarck had been forced to side with Austria-Hungary and to allow Russia to be humiliated, and he needed the friendship of both (see pp. 36–7).

Beaconsfield returned from Berlin in triumph, bringing with him 'peace with honour'. But the Congress of Berlin was no great triumph. It is true that the Great Powers did not fight each other until 1914, but those intervening years were crowded with crises in which the Berlin settlement was amended. The Eastern Question had not been solved. No one was satisfied, except Beaconsfield, and his victory had been too easy. Britain had won 'a bloodless victory with a music-hall song, a navy of museum pieces, and no land forces, except the 7000 Indian troops' (A. J. P. Taylor). Her foreign policy for the next twenty years was based on the assumption that she could do so again. Britain was encouraged to maintain her bankrupt policy of extracting vain promises of reform from the Sultan and supporting him against Russia. Austria-Hungary had a foothold in the Serb provinces, and her relations with Russia, not to mention with Serbia, were bound to deteriorate. The Congress of Berlin had been a diplomatic exercise by the Great Powers. The Balkan peoples counted for nothing. But now there existed small national states representing the three Christian races, the Greeks, the Serbs, and the Bulgars. Balkan nationalism was henceforth increasingly difficult to ignore.

## THE BALKAN CRISIS 1885

That the new small Bulgaria would become a Russian satellite had been taken for granted by everyone: everyone that is, except the Bulgarians. When they discovered what Russian protection involved, a strong anti-Russian movement arose amongst the Bulgarians, and was supported by their sovereign, Prince Alexander of Battenberg. A further shock to the Berlin arrangements came in September 1885 when Eastern Rumelia proclaimed its union with Bulgaria. Russia opposed this enlargement of Bulgaria, and Britain supported it. This was in some ways a complete reversal of the positions taken up by both countries in 1878, but Britain's policy was more consistent than Russia's. Britain still opposed Russia in the Balkans, and she was very glad to be able to support Balkan nationalism at the same time, a policy which Salisbury, now Prime Minister as well as Foreign Secretary, had always favoured.

While the Great Powers hesitated to take action, Serbia launched an attack against Bulgaria. The Serbs had been bitterly hostile to the Bulgars ever since 1870, when the Turks gave the Bulgars a separate religious leader. Now the Serbs demanded territorial compensation for this expansion of their enemy. The Serbs were defeated in a fortnight, and would have been completely overrun had not Austria-Hungary ordered the Bulgarian Army to halt. Peace was signed in 1886, and the united Bulgaria was recognized internationally.

The Russians had again been forced to climb down for want of an ally, but they had not quite finished with Bulgaria. In August 1886 Prince Alexander was kidnapped by Russian agents and forced to abdicate. The Bulgarians rejected the Russian general sent to replace their Prince, and in November relations between the two countries were broken off. War seemed likely but Russia would not act until she knew what course the other Powers would follow. All the Powers had good reason for wishing to delay the declaring of their hands.

In June 1887 the Reinsurance Treaty was concluded between Russia and Germany. By this Russia promised to remain neutral unless Germany attacked France, and Germany promised to remain neutral unless Russia attacked Austria-Hungary. Germany also promised diplomatic support for Russia in Bulgaria and at the Straits. In July the Bulgarians elected a German prince, Ferdinand of Saxe-Coburg, as their sovereign. Russia opposed him. Britain, Austria-Hungary and Italy joined together in an agreement to maintain the *status quo* in the Near East. France was too occupied with Boulangism to be of any use or any danger to anybody, except inasmuch as Bismarck was given an excuse to increase the German Army.

The crisis ended very quietly. In February 1888 Bismarck published the terms of the Dual Alliance of 1879[1] between Austria-Hungary and Germany to show Russia that it was purely defensive, and joined with France and Russia in asking the Turks to declare illegal the election of Ferdinand to the throne of Bulgaria. Austria-Hungary, Britain, and Italy opposed them. Abdul Hamid was delighted to act on Russia's advice. Nothing, however, was done to remove Ferdinand, and he remained. Against Bismarck's wishes, William II, the young German Emperor, paid a state visit to Constantinople in 1889. The visit was a great success. The Sultan was delighted to find a new friend, and William saw a great future for German enterprise in Turkey. However, it put another nail in the coffin of Russo-German relations. The Russians were now convinced that once Bismarck fell they would have to look elsewhere for an ally.

Austria-Hungary was now the dominant Power in the Balkans. Russia was more concerned with her prestige than with anything else in the crisis. In the 1880's and 1890's Russia was far more interested in Persia and Afghanistan and the far East as spheres for expansion than in the Balkans. The warm waters of the Persian Gulf and the Yellow Sea seemed less troubled than those of the Mediterranean. It was only after being blocked by Britain on the Persian Gulf and by Japan in the Yellow Sea that Russia renewed her active interest in the Balkans. Her re-entry was marked by the crisis of 1908.

[1] Although not those of the Triple Alliance (see p. 37).

THE ARMENIAN MASSACRES

The absence of Russian interest in Turkey during this period is well illustrated by the Armenian Massacres. There were some two million Christian Armenians living under Turkish oppression in Asia Minor. In 1894 the Turks launched a series of murderous attacks against them, similar in barbarity to the Bulgarian atrocities, though on a larger scale. Public opinion in Britain forced the Government to demand yet again that the Sultan carry out reforms. Russia and France supported Britain in this, but neither would agree to the use of force. The German Kaiser made the most of the situation to further his policy of friendship with the Sultan in order to replace British influence in Turkey by German economic domination. Austria-Hungary regarded the massacre as a happy diversion which carried the issue of the Christian nationalism in Turkey out of the Balkans. Only Britain was prepared to move, and she would not move alone.

In August 1896 twenty Armenians attempted to force the hands of the Great Powers by staging an incident in Constantinople itself. Armed with bombs, they made a daylight attack on the Ottoman Bank and seized the buildings. Abdul Hamid, confident that the Powers would not intervene, ordered the wholesale slaughter of Armenians in the city. The English Director of the Bank, anxious to preserve the buildings, arranged for the twenty bomb-throwers, besieged in the bank, to be given a safe-conduct to his yacht, on which they left the country. But some six or seven thousand of their innocent compatriots perished in the three days and nights of the massacre. No Power moved.

CRETE

In 1896 a rebellion broke out in the island of Crete, which was inhabited mainly by Greek subjects of the Sultan. Greece sent troops to the island, Turkey declared war on her, and heavily defeated a Greek army on the mainland. The Powers intervened, but the divisions between them delayed a settlement. Finally, Britain, France, Italy and Russia forced the Sultan to withdraw all his troops and officials from Crete, and to grant it self-government within the Empire, but with Prince George of Greece as the governor. Germany, followed by Austria-Hungary, had already abandoned the other Powers to curry favour with Turkey. Neither Armenia nor Crete could provoke a great European crisis like that of 1878.

In 1898, William II, while on a tour to the Holy Land organized by Thos. Cook's, paid a second visit to Constantinople. The following year Abdul Hamid granted a concession to a German company to build a railway from the Sea of Marmora to Baghdad and the Persian Gulf.

THE YOUNG TURKS

By 1908 the Balkan situation was back to normal. Russia had returned from her Far East adventures, badly wounded, it is true, but none the less back. In 1908 a revolution broke out in Turkey led by a group of ardent Turkish nationalists known as the Young Turks. They succeeded in securing the support of part of the Army, and, faced with such a challenge, Abdul Hamid agreed to all their demands. He proclaimed himself a constitutional monarch, called a parliament based on universal manhood suffrage, abolished press censorship, and stopped all racial persecution. The Sultan felt strong enough in 1909 to attempt to overthrow the Young Turks, but he failed, and he was deposed in favour of his brother Mohammed V.

Meanwhile, the revolution had put the Eastern Question in an entirely new light. All the settlements which had been made so far, had been made on the assumption that Turkey was weak. Were Turkey to become strong again—and liberal—new problems would arise.

Austria-Hungary and Russia decided to secure their own position whatever happened. They concluded an agreement by which Austria-Hungary was to annex Bosnia and Herzegovina (which she had occupied since 1878) and Russia was to secure the opening of the Dardanelles.[1] Accordingly the two provinces were annexed, and, in keeping with the spirit of the times, Ferdinand of Bulgaria declared his country's independence and took the title of Czar, and Crete demanded incorporation into Greece.

Russia demanded a Conference of the Powers to discuss these breaches of the Berlin Settlement, so that she could bargain for the free passage of her warships through the Straits. Britain, in spite of her *entente* with Russia, had no intention of agreeing to the opening of the Straits. France was non-committal. Austria-Hungary and Germany opposed any conference. Germany was annoyed with Austria-Hungary, since her action was contrary to Germany's policy of friendship with Turkey, but she nevertheless supported Austria-Hungary to show Russia how annoyed she was by the Anglo-Russian *entente* of 1907.

No conference was held. Turkey received financial compensation,[2] and the crisis, which had threatened war for five months, passed.

The crisis left Serbia bitterly hostile to Austria-Hungary and ready to look to Russia for support. Bulgaria, too, drew closer to Russia. Germany had again been obliged to choose clearly between Russia and Austria-Hungary.

THE BALKAN WARS 1912–13

The Young Turks soon abandoned their liberal ideas and resorted to the same policy of racial persecution which their predecessors had pursued. The Italians took advantage of the swing of sympathy in Britain against Turkey to seize Tripoli, on the North Coast of Africa. The Turks resisted stubbornly, but they were forced to make peace when they found themselves faced with a war in Europe.

[1] By the Straits Convention of 1841, the Straits were closed to all foreign warships while Turkey was at peace.
[2] And the Sanjak of Novibazar (see map, p. 58).

Map 5. The Balkan Wars, 1912-13

Greece, Serbia, Montenegro and Bulgaria joined in alliance in 1912 to form the Balkan League. The reconciliation of Bulgaria and Serbia was brought about by Russia, who hoped that the alliance would form a defensive barrier against Austria-Hungary. But the League was intent on the dismemberment of Turkey.

Before the fighting began, Bulgaria and Serbia divided the spoils they expected to acquire. Serbia was to have Northern Macedonia and Albania. Bulgaria was to expand roughly to her San Stefano boundaries, with the addition, she privately hoped, of Salonika. Greece and Montenegro were to extend their frontiers to complete the expulsion of the Turk from Europe.

Montenegro first declared war on Turkey, and she was rapidly joined by Bulgaria, Greece and Serbia. Within a few weeks, the armies of the League were completely victorious. This time, however, the Powers insisted on a conference. Austria-Hungary insisted that an independent Albania be created, and Russia forbade Bulgaria to occupy Constantinople. The Conference met in London and drew up the peace treaty in May 1913.

Serbia and Montenegro were compelled to evacuate the Albanian territory they had occupied, which was now declared independent. Serbia, however, received Northern and Central Macedonia. Greece received Southern Macedonia, including Salonika. Bulgaria was to have Thrace and a stretch of the Aegean coast without a proper port. Turkey lost all her European possessions except for Constantinople and the Straits littoral.

Austria's insistence on the creation of Albania had prevented Serbia from obtaining an Adriatic coastline. It had also disrupted the short-lived harmony of the Balkan League. Serbia, thwarted in Albania, had compensated herself with Bulgarian-populated Central Macedonia. Bulgaria had done most of the fighting and had been robbed of her rewards.

In June 1913 Bulgaria attacked Serbia and Greece. Rumania and Turkey seized the chance to attack Bulgaria. In August the defeated Bulgarians agreed to the Treaty of Bucharest. Greece and Serbia kept their recent acquisitions in Macedonia. Rumania took Southern Dobruja from Bulgaria, and Turkey recovered Adrianople. Bulgaria was beaten for the moment, but she was bent on revenge on Serbia, and was prepared to ally with Austria-Hungary and Turkey to get it.

Serbia was now the leading Balkan state, and although she was content to count Bulgarians and Albanians among her subjects, she was becoming increasingly eager not to exclude any Serbs. Bosnia and Herzegovina were a thorn in the flesh of the militant Serbia. Serb propaganda convinced Austria-Hungary, if she needed convincing, that Serbia must be silenced or Bosnia must be abandoned. If Bosnia went, what part of Austria-Hungary would go next? The opportunity to silence Serbia came in June 1914 when a Serb murdered the heir-apparent to the crowns of Austria and Hungary, in a street in Sarajevo, the capital of Bosnia.

# 7 William II and European Diplomacy, 1890-1914

German affairs underwent great changes after Bismarck was dismissed in 1890. Policies were different, but even more striking were the changes in the methods by which policies were decided and carried out. Henceforth the Emperor played a leading part in foreign affairs and in the development of the Army and the Navy. Never again was a Chancellor to wield supreme power in the Empire. Never again was a Chancellor to hold office for the length of time that Bismarck had. There were no fewer than seven Chancellors in the remaining twenty-eight years of the Empire, and the most able of them, Bülow, held the post for only nine years. None came near the stature of Bismarck. In any case, there was no room for a Bismarck in the new system. William wanted to take over the work which had formerly been done by his Chancellor, but he conspicuously lacked the ability to do so. The result was that after 1890 Germany no longer had a strong government dominated by one man. Government became unco-ordinated and consequently policies were inconsistent and wavering. Various people who managed to win the Emperor's confidence were able to pursue conflicting policies side by side with each other. Bismarck had driven his team of horses single-handed, with the Emperors sitting in the coach. William climbed up beside the driver and invited his friends to take a horse each. No wonder the coach overturned.

William II, for all his outward bluster, was weak and unsure of himself. He was very theatrical in his behaviour, and frequently made dramatic utterances which embarrassed his friends and enemies alike. He was a showman, and he wanted the German Empire to be the greatest show on earth. He wished to delight his own people, while shocking foreign statesmen. He pictured himself both as a mighty autocrat and as a popular politician. He also fancied himself as a great soldier, the hero of his troops, or again, as the head of a great and glorious navy, the ruler of a splendid colonial Empire. He supported men who favoured expansion, but he never controlled their irreconcilable ambitions.

At home, his attempt to kill Socialism by kindness was a failure. When he refused to renew the anti-Socialist law in 1890, the Socialist organizations were free to come into the open again. As a result, the Social Democrats increased their vote, until in 1912 it stood at over four million, and made them the largest single party in the Reichstag. Not that that counted for anything in the German Empire. They still had no political power. The Government was independent of parliament. Bismarck had seen to that, and, by keeping so much power to himself, he had also ensured that there were no men of political ability and experience to succeed him. Nevertheless, the existence of a large and growing Social Democratic party did cause the Government to pay some attention to its public relations.

Abroad, William's policy led directly to catastrophe. He aimed to make Germany the mightiest country in the world, and although he hoped that it might become so before the other powers had woken up to the fact, he had an uncanny knack of making enemies faster than he need have done by saying the wrong thing at the wrong time. His actions brought him the enmity of Britain, France and Russia, and he became increasingly dependent on the friendship of Austria-Hungary. His other friends, Italy and Turkey, were of little value to him. Yet Britain, France and Russia did not wish for war with Germany. German policy forced them into an opposition camp.

### THE FRANCO-RUSSIAN ALLIANCE 1893

As we have seen in Chapter 4, Bismarck's policy of maintaining friendship with both Russia and Austria-Hungary was doomed to failure from the beginning. Bismarck alone had any faith in it, and even he was forced to side with Austria-Hungary when his two allies were in conflict. By 1890 The Russians were already convinced that Bismarck's policy would not survive his fall from power. They mistrusted William II, and rightly so.

In 1891 the first cautious steps were taken towards a Franco-Russian alliance. The French Fleet paid a courtesy visit to Kronstadt, and an *entente cordiale* was signed between the two countries. This friendly understanding was not turned into a military alliance until December 1893. The Czar was still anxious to keep good relations with Germany, and, as an absolute monarch, he was suspicious of French republicanism. The Panama Scandal of 1892 seemed to justify his suspicions. Had William II made serious efforts to destroy the Franco-Russian alliance he could have done so. However, the French backed up their friendship with Russia with considerable loans of money which enabled work on the Trans-Siberian Railway to begin in 1892.

Russia regarded this alliance merely as an additional safeguard to her position in Europe. She had no quarrel with Germany as such, and she wished to remain on good terms with her. France, too, now that she had an ally, felt less insecure, and her relations with Germany improved considerably. The power which was affected by the alliance was not Germany, but Great Britain.

### SPLENDID ISOLATION

In the last quarter of the 19th century British foreign policy was dominated by Lord Salisbury, who pursued a policy known as 'Splendid Isolation'. Nowadays we should probably call such a policy one of 'going it alone'. Britain kept herself free from alliances and commitments to other Powers. Salisbury argued that as Britain's Navy was strong enough to defend her shores and overseas possessions against all comers, alliances were of no value to her. They could serve only to entangle Britain in continental quarrels.

In the 1890's the two countries Britain disliked most were France and Russia. Relations were embittered with France over Egypt, and with Russia over the Balkans, Afghanistan and China. The French had never forgiven Britain for occupying Egypt in 1882 (see p. 37 n. 1). In 1898, when France tried to restore her prestige in that area, an ugly situation arose between the two countries. Kitchener had led a British expedition up the Nile from Egypt, and had defeated the Sudanese forces at Omdurman. He then learned that Captain Marchand, with a French detachment (complete with a collapsible steamboat), had entered the Sudan from the west, and had occupied Fashoda, higher up the Nile. Kitchener therefore went on to Fashoda with five gunboats and two thousand men. There was no bloodshed, but neither side would give way, and the politicians were left to fight it out at home. Both Governments claimed the Sudan, and there was deadlock. Britain was in by far the stronger position in that she had more troops than the French on the spot and could quickly get reinforcements from Egypt. The French were not really interested in the Sudan. All they wanted was to recover their prestige. The facts of the situation caused them to lose both the Sudan and further prestige. Neither Russia nor Germany responded to French requests for help, and Marchand withdrew unconditionally in March 1899, though an agreement was reached between the two countries about their respective spheres of influence. France was left free to develop French West Africa. Britain had withstood a war scare without having to seek help from anyone. The Fashoda Incident seemed to show the success of Splendid Isolation. So, too, did the Boer War (1899–1902).

In 1899 Britain went to war against the two Boer republics of Transvaal and the Orange Free State. Pro-Boer feeling ran high in France, Russia and Germany—as, indeed, it did in many quarters in Britain itself. William II had already shown sympathy with the Boers in 1895 when Dr Jameson (with the connivance of Cecil Rhodes, the Prime Minister of Cape Colony) had made his famous and stupid raid into the Transvaal in the hope of raising a rebellion there. The Kaiser had sent a telegram to Kruger, the President of the Transvaal, congratulating him on preserving his country's independence.

The outbreak of the Boer War put Splendid Isolation to the test, and it emerged triumphant. Although Russia proposed intervention, and the French agreed to join with Germany in any action she might take, Britain was allowed to defeat the Boers, after three years of bitter fighting, unmolested by any Power. The British navy was strong enough to prevent any interference. In any case, no power was ready for war, and no power would go to war over a colonial issue, as Fashoda and the later Moroccan crises showed.

Nor, for all their pro-Boer talk, were the Powers united in 1899. Germany had no wish to side with Russia and France against Britain. The Kaiser and Bülow, his Chancellor, paid a visit to England in November, and Joseph Chamberlain, the Colonial Secretary, who had already in 1898 tried to secure an Anglo-German alliance, made further proposals to William. Chamberlain approached the Germans again in 1901, but nothing came of his efforts. The alliance to many seemed a natural one—the greatest sea power with the greatest land power. But the Germans would not consider a straight alliance with Britain, which would not include Austria-Hungary and Italy. They played a complicated game of 'hard to get', trying to keep Britain as a friend, but not as an ally. What Germany really wanted was for Britain to get into more and more trouble with France and Russia. Germany particularly looked forward to an Anglo-Russian war in which both sides would weaken themselves while Germany took the pickings.

## THE ANGLO-JAPANESE ALLIANCE 1902

In 1900 all the European Great Powers joined in co-operation to put down the Boxer rising in China, when the foreign legations were besieged and the German minister at Peking was killed. William II insisted that Germany must lead the international force, and this was agreed to, though the two Powers most interested in China were Britain and Russia. Britain wanted to prevent Russian penetration into North China and she hoped to secure the assistance of Germany in achieving this by a convention signed in October 1900. Britain and Germany agreed to uphold the 'open door' principle in China (see p. 195). Germany however, never intended that this agreement should be used against Russia, for she had no wish to weaken her position in Europe for the sake of British policy in China. Japan, with a foothold in Korea, was as anxious as Britain to check the Russians in North China. Accordingly, in 1902 an Anglo-Japanese alliance was signed, by which both countries agreed to maintain the *status quo* in East Asia. Each country agreed to assist the other if it were attacked by more than one power. Japan was given security for her coming clash with Russia in 1904.

The Anglo-Japanese alliance, though marking the end of the period in which Britain was without allies, did not mark the end of 'Splendid Isolation'. Britain still played an independent role in the European balance of power. The Germans were pleased with the alliance in that it opened the way for a worsening in Anglo-Russian relationships.

## ANGLO-FRENCH ENTENTE 1904

Once the Anglo-Japanese treaty had been signed, negotiations began between France and Britain to resolve their colonial differences. The French were seriously worried by the challenge to Russia which the Anglo-Japanese alliance, in effect, offered. They dared not lose the friendship of Russia, but on the other hand they did not want war with Britain. Britain, for her part, was glad to remove the tension with France over Egypt.

The Anglo-French agreement of 1904 dealt chiefly with Egypt and Morocco. Britain was already established in Egypt, although, as we have seen, her presence there was resented by France. Morocco was as yet independent, but both countries were interested in its future. France was already in control of the adjacent territories of Algeria and West Africa. Britain had close trade links with Morocco but her concern was primarily caused by its strategic position. If Morocco fell into the hands of a strong naval Power, British strength in the Mediterranean and in the Atlantic would be threatened.

Public opinion in France was prepared for the new policy by the visit of King Edward VII to Paris in 1903. The King was greeted in the capital with pro-Boer slogans, but left to the accompaniment of wild cheering. By the terms of the agreement, France renounced her claims in Egypt and Britain gave France a free hand to develop Morocco. The *entente* dealt solely with colonial matters, and it was in no sense an alliance, though it did clear the ground for future co-operation.

### FIRST MOROCCAN CRISIS 1905

Before they had settled their differences, both Britain and France had sought German co-operation against the other in Morocco. Germany had refused to become involved. She had no interest in Morocco herself, and and she was happy for it to remain a cause of tension between Britain and France. The German Government now sought an early opportunity to restore the tension which had been eased by the *entente*.

In March 1905 William II visited Tangier and declared that Germany recognized the independence of the Sultan of Morocco. This was a direct and deliberate challenge to the Anglo-French agreement. It was designed to revive Anglo-French differences and to test the strength of the British assurances of diplomatic support for France over Morocco. The Germans pressed their challenge by demanding firstly, the dismissal of Delcassé, the French Foreign Minister who had negotiated the *entente*, and secondly, an international conference to discuss Morocco.

The French Prime Minister, Rouvier, anxious for good relations with Germany, forced the resignation of Delcassé, and agreed to the demand for a conference.

German power appeared triumphant, but it was a short-lived success. When the conference met at Algeçiras in 1906 only Austria-Hungary and Morocco supported Germany. Britain, Russia, Spain, the U.S.A. and even Italy—a member of the Triple Alliance—supported France. The conference affirmed the independence of Morocco, but France, with the help of Spain, was given the responsibility for policing the Sultan's territory.

The Kaiser's action had a boomerang effect. The crisis showed the weakness of the Triple Alliance and Germany's dependence on Austria-Hungary's support. It showed clearly that Germany was out to make trouble, and as a result Britain and France drew closer together. Highly secret military conversations, about which Grey omitted (purposely) to tell even the British Cabinet, began between the British and French general staffs. Outwardly nothing had changed. Britain still held herself free from

European alliances. Russia was still anxious for friendship with Germany. Nevertheless the crisis of 1905–6 gave some indication of the shape of things to come.

### ANGLO-RUSSIAN ENTENTE 1907

In 1907 Britain and Russia settled their differences in Persia. The two countries concluded an *entente* by which they tri-sected Persia. The northern area, including Teheran, the capital, was to be a Russian sphere of influence, the south-eastern area, bordering on Afghanistan, was to be a British sphere of influence. The remaining area was to be neutral.

After her defeat by Japan in 1905, Russia was no longer a rival of Britain in the Far East, and it suited both Britain and Russia to compromise over Persia. The *entente* had no wider implications; indeed, even in Persia, relations between the two Powers continued to be strained.

Britain now had *ententes* with France and with Russia, each of whom was in alliance with the other. This arrangement was termed the Triple Entente, which contrasted with the Triple Alliance of Germany, Austria-Hungary and Italy. There was nothing, however, in either the French or the Russian *ententes* which threatened the Triple Alliance or any of its members. The *ententes* dealt with the settlement of specific issues. Neither represented or even considered military alliances for future joint action. It was the crises which developed after the *ententes* were concluded which divided Europe into opposing camps.

### NAVAL RIVALRY

In 1897 Tirpitz became Minister of Marine, and plans were laid for a large German navy. The Naval Law of 1898 provided for a tremendous expansion of the small German fleet over the next six years. In 1900 these plans were doubled. This programme did not immediately alarm Britain, since she had a very large fleet and she was building rapidly herself.

The great problem of naval building at this time was the rapidity with which navies became obsolete. The introduction in the 1870's and 1880's of torpedoes, breech-loading guns, and steel armour, rendered earlier fleets useless. Britain was in a particularly vulnerable position, since she was utterly dependent for her security on a strong navy. A new invention, even one first introduced into the British Navy, meant that Britain then had more obsolete ships than any other Power. At any time another Power could begin to rival British sea-power on equal terms. It was the realization of this fact which caused alarm in British hearts in 1908–9

In 1906 H.M.S. *Dreadnought* was launched. Her distinctive feature was that she was the first all-big-gun ship. Earlier ships had carried four big guns and a number of smaller guns. The *Dreadnought* abandoned the secondary armament in favour of more 12-inch guns, which were mounted in revolving turrets to give maximum fire power. She was also the first battleship in the world to be driven by steam turbines. The Admiralty planned to lay down four Dreadnoughts a year.

The cost of rebuilding the British Navy from scratch with Dreadnoughts was immense, and in 1907 Britain tried to slacken the race with Germany by reducing her own building programme, but this merely tempted Tirpitz to accelerate, so that in 1908 Germany laid down four Dreadnoughts to Britain's two. In 1909 the British Admiralty asked for six, but the Liberal Cabinet, anxious to carry through a programme of social reform, agreed only to four. But public opinion, expressed in the music-hall refrain, 'We want Eight, And we won't wait', settled the issue, and eight were laid down at once. Lloyd George's 1909 budget had to find the unprecedented sum of over £15 million in new taxation.

German naval expansion struck at the basis of Splendid Isolation. It forced Britain to reassess her position in relation to other European powers. Neither Russia nor France was pleased with the estrangement of Britain and Germany. Germany's naval policy was chiefly designed for prestige. It produced unnecessary and unwanted rivalries between the European powers.

## BOSNIA AND CASABLANCA

1908 was a critical year. In the Balkans, the Young Turk revolution produced a war crisis which lasted well into 1909 (see pp. 61-62). The Kaiser provoked a private crisis of his own in October by giving an interview to the *Daily Telegraph* in which he declared himself one of England's few friends in Germany. He claimed to have prevented a coalition against Britain in the Boer War, and he also claimed that he had provided Queen Victoria with the plan of campaign for that war which her generals had successfully employed. This absurd piece of sensationalism produced an uproar in Germany, and led firstly to the dismissal of Bülow, the Chancellor, and secondly to the loss by the Kaiser of what control he had over German policy.

Another crisis of 1908 occurred over Morocco. At Casablanca the French arrested three German deserters from the Foreign Legion while they were in the charge of German consular officials. Austria-Hungary wanted Germany to reserve her energies for the Balkans, and France was not anxious for war, and so the matter was submitted to the International Court at the Hague. In February 1909 an agreement was signed by which Germany recognized French political interests in Morocco, while France recognized German economic interests there.

## AGADIR 1911

In April 1911, French troops, claiming that they were protecting the Europeans there, occupied Fez, the capital of Morocco. It seemed clear that the French intended to establish a protectorate over Morocco. In return for abandoning her interest in Morocco Germany demanded compensation from France in the Congo, and reinforced this demand by sending the gunboat *Panther* to Agadir. Britain became alarmed at the prospect of a German naval base on the Atlantic coast of Morocco.

The diplomatic manoeuvres of France and Germany were sharply halted by Lloyd George. In a speech at the Mansion House on July 21st, 1911, he publicly declared that Britain was ready to go to war if the price of peace was to allow herself to be treated 'where her interests were vitally affected, as if she were of no account in the Cabinet of Nations'. Deadlock was reached from which it was impossible for any country to withdraw without loss or prestige, yet no one wanted war. However, perhaps encouraged by a financial crisis which struck Berlin, Germany scaled down her demands, and in November an agreement was signed by which Germany recognized a French protectorate over Morocco in return for two strips of territory in the French Congo.

The Agadir crisis was more serious than either the Tangier crisis of 1905 or the Bosnian crisis of 1908-9. For the first time, German public opinion was whole-heartedly behind a warlike policy. Germany climbed down because of lack of unity in her ruling classes. Like Russia in 1909 she had accepted defeat without going to war. Neither Russia nor Germany was likely to do so again.

### THE BALKANS AND THE OUTBREAK OF WAR

The Balkan Wars of 1912-13 set the stage for the outbreak of war in 1914 (see pp. 62-64). Austria-Hungary was determined to crush Serbia at the first opportunity. She would have gone to war in 1913 had she had support. A year later she got the support she wanted.

On June 28th, 1914, Archduke Franz Ferdinand, heir-apparent of Austria-Hungary, was murdered with his wife while on a State visit to Sarajevo, the capital of Bosnia. The date of the visit was the Serbian national day, and this public display of Habsburg power over the annexed Serbian province could reasonably have been expected to provoke an 'incident' of some sort, though few precautions were taken to safeguard the royal visitor. The details of the planning of the assassination have never come to light. Franz Princip, who fired the fatal shot, was merely one of several students whom the organizers were prepared to sacrifice in order to make trouble. Almost certainly the head of Serbian Military Intelligence was intimately concerned in the plot.

Austria-Hungary, however, was not interested in investigations. The assassination was enough. Here was the chance to annihilate Serbia, if German support was forthcoming. William II gave his blessing. On July 23rd Austria-Hungary delivered an ultimatum to Serbia. The ultimatum accused the Serbian Government of complicity in the crime, and demanded, in addition to full compensation, what would amount to the military occupation of Serbia by Austrian forces. Serbia was called upon to agree to these demands within forty-eight hours. Serbia capitulated utterly, save on two points, which she asked to be referred to a decision of the Hague Tribunal or the Great Powers. Austria-Hungary rejected the Serbian request and began partial mobilization. The Kaiser and Bethmann-Hollweg, the German Chancellor, began to have second thoughts in the light of Serbia's submissive attitude. They urged Austria-Hungary to consult with Russia. But by the end of July Austria-Hungary had gone far enough to drag Germany with her, and it was the counsels of the military chiefs, not the politicians, which prevailed in Berlin. Sir Edward Grey tried to find a solution, as he had in 1913, by suggesting a Conference in London, but neither Austria-Hungary nor the German Army was interested in diplomatic solutions.

On July 30th Russia began mobilization, and Germany demanded that it should be cancelled. On August 2nd Germany declared war on Russia, and in the following day on France. With her war strategy based on the Schlieffen Plan (see pp. 77–79), Germany could not fight Russia without fighting France first—whether France supported Russia or not. On August 4th German troops invaded Belgium. At midnight Britain declared war. Ostensibly Britain's reason for going to war against Germany was to uphold the Treaty of London 1839, by which both Britain and Prussia had guaranteed Belgian independence and neutrality. Until Belgium was invaded, the British Cabinet had refused to give France any assurances of help against Germany.

Bethmann-Hollweg declared that Britain was waging war 'just for a scrap of paper'. But there was more in it than that. Britain could not have stood by and watched Germany, her naval rival, occupy and control the Belgian and French coastlines. Indeed Britain was already more closely committed than she realized to supporting France. By the Anglo-French Naval Convention of 1912, Britain had assumed responsibility for the defence of the North Sea and the Channel, while France concentrated her fleet in the Mediterranean. The French were able, on the strength of this, to extract from Grey, subject to Parliament's approval, a promise that if the German Fleet attacked French shipping and ports in the North Sea and the Channel, the British Navy would go to their defence. Morally, Britain could scarcely do less. She had taken advantage of the concentration of French ships in the Mediterranean to deplete her own forces there. It is difficult to see how Britain could have kept out of the war for long, even if Belgium had not been involved. The violation of Belgian neutrality enabled her to enter quickly and with unity. Cabinet, Parliament and people could join together in support of a simple, if somewhat misleading, war aim—the defence of the sanctity of treaties.

# 8   The Causes of the First World War

The published literature on the causes of the First World War is immense, and between them writers have managed to fix the blame for starting the war squarely on the shoulders, respectively, of Germany, Austria-Hungary, Russia, Serbia, France, Great Britain, colonial rivalry, capitalism, economic rivalry, naval rivalry, the arms race, and the system of alliances—to name merely the outstanding scapegoats.

There are several reasons why writers have been so anxious to establish the causes of this war above all others. Article 231 of the Versailles Treaty, which demanded Germany's admission of war-guilt, immediately provoked writers, not from Germany alone, to point out other guilty parties. The horrors of the war convinced many people that such a catastrophe must not occur again, and that if only the causes of the conflict could be discovered they could be removed. President Wilson based his peace plan on this reasoning. Furthermore, there was the unexpectedness of the First World War, which came as a shock to most people. There had been no major war, involving all the Great Powers in Europe, for a hundred years. Great changes had occurred in that time. Germany and Italy had emerged as nations. The Turkish Empire had been largely dismembered, and Africa had been opened up. All this had been brought about either by diplomacy or by localized and brief wars. The twenty years before 1914 were spattered with international crises, but however threatening they had seemed, a major war had been avoided. The last thing that most people expected to emerge from the Sarajevo crisis was a long, bitterly fought, world-wide conflict.

Let us look briefly at the chief problems which are alleged to have caused the war. First, Nationalism. Nationalism, the drive from peoples of the same language-group to form self-governing states, had been the dominant feature of European history in the 19th century. The completion of the process of creating nation-states in Europe was the guiding principle of the Versailles settlement. In 1914 there were various national groups which had not gained full unity and independence. Poland did not exist. Some Serbs, Bulgarians, Danes, Frenchmen, and Germans were living under foreign rule. Austria-Hungary was a hotch-potch of different nationalities. Nationalism was a very important problem. The quarrel between Austria-Hungary and Serbia was entirely one of nationalism. Austria-Hungary wanted to suppress Serbian demands for the completion of a great Slav state by the incorporation of Bosnia and Herzegovina. The success of nationalism meant the disintegration of the Austro-Hungarian Empire. This issue will explain the Austro-Serbian war, but it cannot alone explain the outbreak of a world war.

Second, Economic rivalry. This charge may be dealt with briefly. Both Germany and Britain were expanding industrial nations, but there is no evidence to suggest that the business men of either country brought pressure to bear on their governments to turn trade rivalry into armed warfare. Businesses flourish best in peace and there was a widespread fear that war would inevitably bring Socialism. In any case the men who took the operative decisions in government policies were aristocrats or professional diplomats who saw matters in a purely political, rather than an economic, light.

Third, Colonial rivalry. Germany was a late starter in the race for colonies. Britain and France had acquired much greater empires than Germany, and even small countries like Belgium and Holland had considerable colonial territory. There was a commonly-held belief at the time that big industrial nations must have colonies to provide them with cheap raw materials and to give them new, expanding markets, and opportunities for investing surplus capital, from which they could exclude their competitors. Colonies were valuable to maritime nations because they could provide naval bases and coaling stations. Perhaps most important of all in the eyes of people at that time, colonies gave a nation prestige. Powerful nations had colonies. Therefore, to prove herself great, Germany wanted 'a place in the sun'. Whatever may be the strength of these arguments, and whatever the ordinary German thought, German policy, from Bismarck onwards, had been primarily to exploit colonial issues such as the Moroccan crisis in order to gain diplomatic advantage in Europe, and only secondarily to acquire land. Germany's colonies were, in fact, run at a loss.

It is very tempting to fix the blame for the widespread nature of the war on the system of alliances. What began as a war between Austria and Serbia spread because Germany supported Austria, with whom she was allied, and opposed to Russia, who mobilized in support of the Serbs. France was allied with Russia, and Britain had *ententes* with them both. In fact, however, the two 'armed camps' of the Triple Alliance and the Triple Entente were not united amongst themselves. Italy was a very doubtful member of the Triple Alliance, and not only failed to support Austria-Hungary and Germany in 1914, but actually joined the fighting against them in 1915. Britain, right up to the outbreak of war, refused to be committed to any particular course of action by her *ententes* with France and Russia. Admittedly, both sides drew closer together in the years immediately before the war. Germany feared encirclement as much as Britain, France and Russia feared isolation. But the alliances themselves did not produce tension. They merely recorded the fact that tension existed. No country began fighting in 1914 to fulfil the terms of an alliance.

The arms race, another sympton of the tension between the nations, was of more fundamental importance. While the arms race could not create a crisis, once a crisis had occurred the military preparedness of the nations could affect its course. In preparing for a modern war, nations must aim for a peak of efficiency. Before that peak is reached they are unprepared; after that peak has passed, their weapons become increasingly obsolete and they must aim at a new peak. German plans were geared for the summer of 1914, the French for 1915, and Russia's for 1917.

No Government wants war for its own sake. What is important is how far a Government is prepared to risk war in pursuing its policies. By this test German policy cannot alone be condemned. France feared German expansion and feared being left without friends in the face of that expansion. She was prepared to go to war rather than lose Russian support. Britain pursued a selfish policy, willing to use the friendship of others, while being unwilling to give firm support in return. She weakened the Triple Entente by this attitude and, some have claimed, could have averted war had she made it clear to Germany that she would fight if France were attacked. Neville Chamberlain in 1938 was determined that this charge should not be repeated (see p. 152). In fact, Germany was quite prepared to fight France, Russia and Britain in 1914, just as Hitler was prepared to fight Poland, France, and Britain in 1939.

Russia's policy before the war was expansionist; she had been aggressive throughout the 19th century. After the Russo-Japanese war she was militarily weak, and she feared to move without the support of France and Great Britain. The Japanese had stopped her expansion in the Far East. Her friendship with Britain prevented her expansion towards the Persian Gulf, though there was considerable friction there. Only by extending her control over the Balkans and gaining the Dardanelles could she secure ice-free access to the seas. Her Balkan policy cut right across that of Germany and Austria-Hungary. Her support of the Serbs encouraged them to be bolder than they might otherwise have been. Russia was the first country to mobilize fully in 1914, and Germany's ultimatums to Russia and France were delivered in reply to that mobilization. The case against Russia is strong, but not conclusive. She was not prepared on her own to take the initiative in bringing about a war. She was weak and she knew it. Neither Britain nor France would support her aggressive plans. Full, rather than partial, mobilization was ordered very reluctantly by the Czar, because the Army had no plan for partial mobilization. War was likely to increase Russia's internal difficulties. On the other hand, there was a faint chance that a short victorious war might solve them.

Austria-Hungary's position was similar to Russia's. She was expansionist. In addition, she was reckless. Internally, the Empire was crumbling. A victorious war might provide some much-needed buttresses. She wanted, as her ultimatum clearly showed, to crush Serbia, but she dared not act alone. She had to have German support. Eleven months earlier she had been in the same position and Germany had not supported her. It was the change in German policy between 1913 and 1914 that produced a European war.

Germany did not consciously plan to provoke the war in 1914. Her leadership was too divided and wavering for such a programme to be possible. German interest in the Balkans was based on her desire to dominate it economically and to maintain the existence of Austria-Hungary. Given the German position in Europe, these were very reasonable policies. Germany's responsibility for the war lay in her inability to control her

General Staff. Early in 1913 the General Staff had decided that war between the Triple Alliance and the other powers was inevitable, and they had made preparations, including the widening of the Kiel Canal, to be ready by the summer of 1914, ahead of the plans of the other Powers. The Army had always played an important and independent part in Prussian politics. In July 1914 it was supreme. Neither the Kaiser, nor Bethmann-Hollweg, the Chancellor, controlled the last moves. The Chief of the General Staff, Moltke, had the last word. When Bethmann-Hollweg urged moderation on Vienna after the Serbs had all but capitulated to the Austrian demands, Moltke sent a private message to his opposite number in Austria urging him on. Moltke's message was obeyed. Austria had the support she needed and from then on military considerations dictated the moves. Fear of being caught unprepared led Germany to mobilize when Russia did so. The Army's Strategy, the Schlieffen Plan, required that a campaign against Russia should be preceded by an attack on France (see pp. 77-79). This was a military, not a political, plan, and when the German Army put it into operation by invading Luxembourg and Belgium, Britain was given just the excuse she wanted for entering the war. Here was a moral issue behind which the people could be united. Grey had been able to settle the Balkan crisis of 1913 diplomatically because the diplomats were still in charge. In 1914, in Germany, the Army was in charge, and the issue was settled militarily.

# 9   The First World War

No one expected the war which began in August 1914 to be a long one. The experience of the Austro-Prussian War of 1866, of the Franco-Prussian War of 1870, and of the Balkan Wars, indicated that modern wars were brief, and that the first campaigns were decisive. Accordingly, the key to success was preparedness. All the Powers had this thought in mind when they embarked upon the arms race in the years before the war.

Germany's war strategy, the Schlieffen Plan, was based on the assumption of a knock-out blow in the West being delivered in the first round. That is one reason why Germany acted so promptly after learning of Russian mobilization. In a short race, the one who beats the gun may well be the winner.

After the first few months had passed, and with them the hopes and fears of a lightning victory, the two sides were remarkably evenly balanced. In spite of the expensive tactics of some commanders, neither side was likely to lose the war for want of men. Want of munitions was another matter. Russia exhausted her meagre supply of arms before 1914 was out, and this

industrial failure was decisive in the East. But in the West the mighty resources of German and Britiish industry were ranged against each other
and both were capable of sustaining a long war.

The Central Powers had a considerable geographical advantage in
Europe. All their lines of communication were internal, and the well-
planned railways could be used to switch troops from one front to another
swiftly. The Allies, on the other hand, although severely handicapped in

*Map 6. Europe in 1914*

their communications between the Eastern and Western Fronts, were able
to blockade the Central Powers in Europe, and make them dependent on
the territories they occupied or raw materials.

However, these factors became important only as the war went on. In
August 1914 it was the actual, not the potential, power of the two sides
which was important. The Central Powers then had a clear advantage.
Germany was the only Power at the peak of her war-preparedness. In the

West she was able to field 2 million men against 1 million Frenchmen and the 160 000 men of the British Expeditionary Force. Austria-Hungary mobilized 2 million as against Russia's 1½ million. The fate of Europe hinged on the success or failure of the Schlieffen Plan.

The plan which Schlieffen had originally drawn up was never in fact put into operation. The Chief of the German General Staff in 1914, Moltke,[1] introduced a number of modifications. The original plan provided for a weak left wing to stand on the defensive around Metz, while a massive right hook went through Luxembourg and Belgium, down the Channel ports, and encircled Paris. The main French armies could then be trapped and forced to surrender. Moltke modified this plan by strengthening the left wing in order to prevent a possible French advance into Lorraine. To do this he had to weaken the right hook.

When the Germans crossed the frontier on August 4th, the Belgians fought a stout delaying action. Brussels fell on August 20th, and Namur on the 25th. The main Belgian army fell back on Antwerp, and Moltke detached two corps from the advancing right wing to deal with it. Two more corps were withdrawn to deal with the Russian threat in East Prussia. The German momentum was slowing down as that of the Allies was building up. On August 22nd the British Expeditionary Force reached Mons, though it was soon forced to fall back with the French.

At the end of August, the German commanders in the field, frightened by the widening gaps between them, took a decision on their own initiative which effectively destroyed what was left of the Schlieffen Plan. The First Army on the right wing, which should have swung round Paris to the north, west and south, was diverted to meet the Second Army, which was making straight for Paris, somewhere east of the city. What had been planned as a swinging right hook had emerged as a jab from the elbow. And it fell short of the target.

French armies which had been held back to defend Paris were now freed, and early in September the British and French launched a counter-attack in the Battle of the Marne. The German armies, out of touch with the High Command, which was still in Luxembourg, fell back to the Marne and then to the Aisne. In October Antwerp fell to the Germans, but the Channel ports were kept open by the successful defence of Ypres.

The modified Schlieffen Plan broke down finally because of bad leadership, but there is no reason to believe that well-conducted and unmodified it would have worked much better. The plan gave the defenders a great advantage in communication over the attackers. The railways, centred in Paris, could be used to transport troops quickly to any point of the circumference of the German march.

Before the end of 1914 both sides had dug themselves in. Miles and miles of trenches stretched from the Vosges to the sea. For nearly four years the war on the Western Front was a hopeless and demoralizing struggle be-

---

[1] He was the nephew of the great Moltke, the victor of 1870. His indecisive character was in part concealed from his countrymen by his famous name.

tween two seemingly impregnable forces. Terrible casualties were suffered by both sides as the armies advanced or retreated a few hundred yards, or perhaps a mile or two, from one line of muddy trenches to another. In the stark, shell-shattered fighting area of northern France, men had time to reflect on the horror and waste of war. A strange comradeship linked the men in the trenches—even enemies—and separated them from those who had not shared in their experiences of mud, water, lice, rats, dysentery, poison-gas, shelling, and death. Out of all the misery came many good intentions, including the resolution that this war should end all wars.

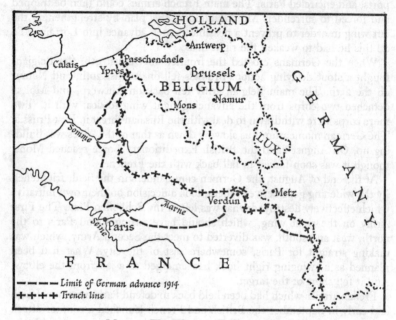

*Map 7. The Western Front, 1914–18*

Sudden victory came nowhere in 1914. In the East, the Russians, who had mobilized their forces much more quickly than anyone had imagined possible, invaded East Prussia and Galicia. The Germans, with the bulk of the forces engaged in the West, were temporarily panic-stricken by the rapid advance of a numerically stronger Russian force.

The two corps were switched from Belgium, fresh commanders (Generals Hindenburg and Ludendorff) were sent to take over operations, and at the end of August and in early September the Russians were overwhelmingly defeated at the battles of Tannenberg and the Masurian Lakes. The Russians lost some quarter of a million men. These could readily be replaced; but the arms and equipment they lost represented the accumulation of years of production. The Russian forces remained numerous, but they became increasingly inefficient.

Against the Austro-Hungarians in Galicia the Russians had more success, but by December 1914 Hindenburg was able to halt the Russian advance. Both sides were exhausted, and the Russians had little hope of refreshment. On the Balkan front, the Serbs had repelled the invading Austro-Hungarians and had retaken Belgrade.

*Map 8. The Eastern and Balkan Fronts, 1914–18*

1914 closed with deadlock on all fronts. Only in Germany's marooned colonies was anything decisive achieved. Most of these were in allied control by 1915. German East Africa (Tanganyika) held out until 1916, and even then isolated pockets of resistance remained.

Turkey's entry into the war on the side of the Central Powers in November 1914 had effectively cut off Russia and Serbia from help from the west. Britain and France, therefore, decided to send an expedition to force open the Dardanelles. There was considerable opposition to the plan in both countries. At best it would be a difficult operation and, by diverting men and supplies from the Western Front, it might fatally weaken the defence of France. On the other hand, if it succeeded, Serbia and Russia could be kept in the war, and the Central Powers would be forced to fight well-equipped soldiers on two fronts. Had it succeeded, the war might have been won more quickly. Furthermore, since the Allies promised Russia the Straits and Constantinople, the Czarist régime might have survived the war and the Bolsheviks might never have seized power. Greater issues than were dreamed of hung on the success or failure of the Dardanelles Campaign.

An unsuccessful attempt in March 1915 to force the Straits by naval forces alone was followed up in April by landings of British, Australian and New Zealand troops on the Gallipoli peninsula. The troops hung on to their positions throughout the summer, but their position became increasingly difficult, and they were withdrawn.

The plan as carried out had little chance of success. The Turks were prepared for it, it was planned much too hurriedly, and it never enjoyed the whole-hearted support of the British and French Governments.

In October 1915 Bulgaria joined the Central Powers and, together with an Austro-German army, overran Serbia. Franco-British troops landed at Salonika, though Greece was neutral, but they were unable to do more than hold a bridgehead there.

New hopes of opening up a more mobile front against the Central Powers arose with Italy's declaration of war against Austria-Hungary in May 1915. Italy was anxious to get what she could out of the war, and was open to bids from both sides. Since most of her territorial claims were against Austria-Hungary, the Allies were in a position to make the higher bid. By the secret Treaty of London (April 1915) Italy agreed to enter the war within a month, in return for the promise of Trentino and the South Tyrol, Istria (including the port of Trieste), half Dalmatia, Adalia (in Asia Minor), and a protectorate over Albania. She hoped by these gains to strengthen her mountain defences in the north and to secure full control over the Adriatic. To her later regret, she did not demand, nor was she granted, the promise of the port of Fiume, nor was she promised any specific colonial territories, though Britain and France did agree to 'compensation in principle' if they acquired the German colonies.

Italy proved, as it happened, a very doubtful asset to the Allies in 1915, and later became a liability. She certainly engaged the major part of the

Austrian forces, but her entry came too late to prevent a renewed Austro-German offensive against the Russians. In August 1915 Warsaw fell, and the Russians were driven from Poland altogether.

In an oblique way, the only crumb of comfort the Allies could gather from 1915 was the sinking of the British liner *Lusitania* with the loss of 1200 lives. Britain and France had imposed a complete naval blockade in Europe. No ships were allowed to go to German ports, and even the imports of neutral countries were severely restricted so that no goods should reach enemy hands. The United States strongly objected, as it always had, to having its ships searched and goods confiscated while it was at peace. However, Germany helped to solve the crisis by declaring the western approaches of Britain a zone of war, which neutrals would enter at their own risk. The sinking of the *Lusitania* in April 1915 swung American opinion against Germany, since 118 American citizens perished in the disaster. President Wilson warned Germany against a repetition, and for the next two years Germany abandoned unrestricted submarine warfare.

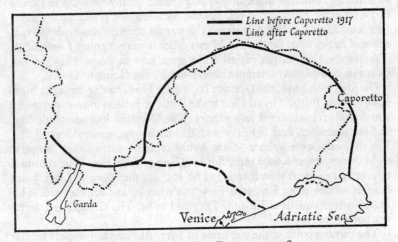

Map 9. *The Italian Front, 1914–18*

In 1916 Falkenhayn, Moltke's successor, decided to concentrate his attack on the West. His plan was to mass enormous forces in an onslaught against the vital and heavily defended fortress of Verdun and to continue his attack until the French had exhausted their reserves. Under the leadership of General Pétain, and inspired by the slogan 'Ils ne passeront pas!' the French held on to Verdun for nearly five months. When Falkenhayn called off the attack in July, the French had lost 350 000 men, the Germans 330 000.

One of Falkenhayn's mistakes was to underestimate the importance of the British Army. It had grown immensely since the early days of the war, first with volunteers, and then, after January 1916, with conscripted men.

On July 1st the British and French launched an attack on the Somme. The tank, a new British invention, was employed for the first time, though its uses were imperfectly realized. The Battle of the Somme, which marked the emergence of Britain as a military power, dealt a shattering blow to the morale of the Germans. When the raw conscripts became fully effective the British Army would be formidable indeed. After the Somme Falkenhayn was replaced by Hindenburg. Nevertheless, the British lost 400 000 men and the French 200 000, against the German 500 000. Still no decisive victory had been won.

The Russians, contrary to Falkenhayn's calculations, had been able to launch an offensive in June, and had won some considerable successes against the Austro-Hungarians. Rumania felt sufficiently encouraged to declare war on Austria-Hungary in August. But the Germans quickly overran Rumania and seized her wheat and oil supplies.

The only major naval engagement of the war took place in 1916. British naval policy was to contain the German surface ships within the North Sea so that they could not block British and French supply routes. The Straits of Dover were easily sealed off, but the northern exit presented a greater problem. After the U.S.A. entered the war an attempt was made to lay a chain of mines from Scotland to Norway, but it was not entirely successful. Therefore almost all the capital ships were kept at Scapa Flow, in the Orkneys, to await any attempted break-out by the German Navy.

On May 31st, 1916, the German High Seas Fleet, having emerged from Kiel, met the British Grand Fleet at the Battle of Jutland in an engagement which both sides claimed as a victory. The Germans lost one battleship, one battle cruiser, four light cruisers, five destroyers, and 2500 men. The British losses were greater—three battle cruisers, three heavy cruisers, eight destroyers, and 6000 men. But the German High Seas Fleet returned to port and the next time it emerged far out into the North Sea, two years later, it was en route for Scapa Flow to surrender and scuttle itself. The British were cautious at Jutland. They had to be. The Grand Fleet dared not be destroyed.

The turning point of the war came in 1917. At first the prospect for the Allies was bleak. In March Czar Nicholas of Russia abdicated in face of wholesale strikes and mutinies. The provisional governments which followed tried to carry on the war, but their task was hopeless. Russia was militarily paralysed, and all the people wanted was food and peace. In December, the Bolshevik Government, which had seized power the previous month, began negotiations with Germany.

The collapse of Russia was, however, more than outweighed by the U.S.A.'s declaration of war against Germany in April 1917. At the beginning of the war isolationist feeling in the United States had been strong. Americans saw no need to concern themselves in European squabbles. Furthermore, a number of American citizens were immigrants from Central Europe, and had national sympathies with the Central Powers. British interference with American shipping antagonized many others. But as the war went on the United States drew closer to the Allies. She did a great deal of trade with the Allies, particularly in war materials, and German handling of American opinion was unskilful and sometimes inept.

What placed the United States firmly on the road to war was the German resumption of unrestricted submarine warfare in January 1917. In the same month, the British intercepted a message from the German Foreign Secretary to his Minister in Mexico, offering the Mexican Government Texas, New Mexico, and Arizona in return for Mexican help if the U.S. entered the war. The British lost no time in communicating the message to Washington.

Even so, President Wilson hesitated, but the terrible shipping losses of February and March appalled the Americans. With the collapse of the Czarist régime in Russia, Americans felt they could rightly enter the war —for democracy.

The resources of the U.S. in men and materials were immense. The Allies now had a tremendous potential superiority over the Central Powers. The big question was—could the help come in time? Germany staked all on starving Britain and France into submission before U.S. aid could become effective. Her submarines very nearly succeeded in severing the connection between the Allies and their newly-acquired 'Associated Power'.

Britain and France desperately tried to take the offensive on land while they had supplies, but their losses were terrible, and they were unable to break through. The French were at the end of their tether, and serious mutinies broke out in their ranks. Much of the British Army lay dead in the mud of Passchendaele. The Italians were disastrously defeated by an Austro-German army at Caporetto. Only the speed of their retreat saved the front, which henceforth had to be buttressed by French and British troops. However, with the development of anti-submarine devices and with the organization of the convoy system, the worst of the submarine menace was over by the end of the year. The U.S. Navy quickly proved its usefulness.

On the forgotten fronts of Egypt and Mesopotamia 1917 brought victories. In Mesopotamia, the British, advancing from the Persian Gulf, recaptured Kut, which they had lost in 1916, and drove the Turks from Baghdad. Allenby, advancing from Egypt, entered Palestine and took Jerusalem on Christmas Day.

Perhaps, however, next to the entry of the U.S.A. into the war, the best thing that happened to the Allies in 1917 was the appointment of Clemenceau as Prime Minister of France. He took office in November, and rallied the wilting French with his ringing assertion, 'Je fais la guerre!' Like Lloyd George, who had replaced Asquith as Prime Minister of Britain in December 1916, Clemenceau proved a great war leader, determined on nothing short of total victory.

With the failure of her submarine campaign, Germany staked all on a successful offensive in the West in the spring of 1918. She now had no worries in the East. The cripplingly severe treaties of Brest-Litovsk and

Bucharest were signed with Russia and Rumania in March and May respectively. All the German forces could be concentrated against France. On March 21st Ludendorff launched his attack.

All the Allied forces in France were placed under the unified command of the French Marshal Foch. His strategy was to allow the Germans to exhaust themselves while he built up reserves to strike a punishing counter-blow when they were exhausted. His plan was wildly successful. The Germans swept through to the Marne, but by the end of July the force of their offensive was spent.

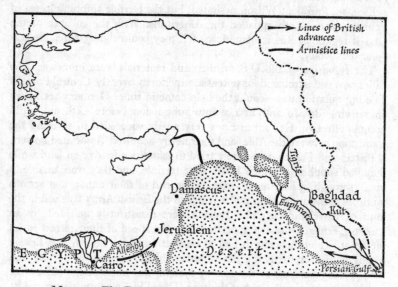

*Map 10. The Egyptian and Mesopotamian Front, 1914–18*

Nothing could stop the Allied offensive when it began in earnest in September. By then the American forces, which had been pouring into France at the rate of more than 250 000 a month, were playing a full part in the fighting.

The Central Powers collapsed. In 1917 the Greek King, who had opposed the Allies' forces at Salonika, was overthrown, and Greece entered the war. In mid-September 1918 the Allies launched from Salonika an attack against Bulgaria, which surrendered within a fortnight. Allenby entered Damascus in October, and the Turks signed an armistice. In the same month at Vittoria Veneto the Italians routed the Austro-Hungarians, who sued for peace. The German people were starving, and strikes and mutinies were breaking out. The German generals had no alternative but to insist on their Government's making peace.

The first request for peace was made to President Wilson on October 3rd (see p. 89). On November 9th the German Emperor abdicated. The guns ceased firing at 11.0 a.m. on November 11th.

So ended the first total war. It was distinguished from previous wars not only because it was widespread, but because it was a battle between nations rather than between professional armies and navies. Millions of civilians were conscripted into the armed forces. Others experienced a foretaste of bombing from the air which was to become a gruesome feature of the Second World War. All, on both sides, suffered the privation caused by blockade. Furthermore, it was the first technological war, a war of new destructive weapons and counter-devices which could be produced only by great industrial nations. Numbers of fighting men were no longer important in themselves, as the collapse of Russia showed. The small industrialized countries which joined in the fighting were a hindrance rather than a help to their allies. In terms of industrial output, Britain and Germany were head and shoulders above all other countries in Europe. The United States had a much greater output than either of them. The winning of the battle for the Atlantic supply-line ensured the final victory of the Allies.

# 10 The Versailles Settlement

In January 1918 President Wilson announced in a speech to Congress the terms on which a peace settlement should be based. They may briefly be stated as follows:

1. Open covenants of peace, openly arrived at.
2. Freedom of navigation of the seas, in peace and war.
3. The removal of all economic barriers to international trade.
4. The reduction of armaments to the lowest point consistent with domestic safety.
5. The adjustment of colonial claims, bearing in mind the interests of the colonial peoples.
6. The evacuation of all Russian territory. Russia to be free to develop her own institutions and to be given every assistance she needed or desired and to be welcomed into the League of Nations.
7. Belgium to be evacuated and restored.
8. France to be evacuated, the invaded portions restored, and Alsace-Lorraine to be returned to her.
9. The Italian frontiers to be readjusted along clearly recognizable lines of nationality.
10. The peoples of Austria-Hungary to be accorded the freest opportunity of autonomous development (later altered to independence).

11. Rumania, Serbia and Montenegro to be evacuated; the occupied territories restored; Serbia given access to the sea.
12. Turkish portions of the Ottoman Empire to be assured a secure sovereignty, but the other nationalities under Turkish rule to be allowed to develop independence. The Dardanelles to be permanently opened to ships and commerce of all nations.
13. An independent Polish state to be created and given access to the sea.
14. A general association of nations to be formed.

*Map 11. Treaty of Versailles: Germany*

There was nothing particularly original in the ideas contained in these Fourteen Points. Lloyd George had made a similar speech a few days earlier. They expressed at that stage of the war the desires of many of the Allied statesmen and people. Furthermore, these utterances had considerable propaganda value. In speeches in February, July and September, Wilson added to his Fourteen Points, what were called the Four Principles, the Four Ends, and the Five Particulars, but apart from the important statement that the Peace should contain 'no annexations, no contributions, no punitive damages', these contained little that was not inherent in his original proposals.

Germany did not become interested in peace proposals until the autumn, when her allies deserted her, and it became abundantly clear that nothing could save her from military defeat. During the ten months which passed between the framing of the Fourteen Points and the conclusion of the armistice, incidents occurred which greatly affected the temper of the

Allies. In March 1918 Germany concluded peace with Russia by the Treaty of Brest-Litovsk. Signed with a struggling Bolshevik Government, this treaty stripped Russia of land, peoples, goods, and minerals. In May Rumania was forced to sign a similarly crushing treaty with Germany. These two treaties left little doubt about Germany's attitude, as a victor, to peace-making. In defeat she was no less vindictive. Her retreating armies wantonly destroyed mines and buildings in France and Belgium. Perhaps what raised the greatest horror was the sinking of the S.S. *Leinster*. On October 16th (eleven days *after* the German request for the mediation of President Wilson) the Irish Mail Steamer *Leinster* was torpedoed off Kingstown, with the loss of 450 men, women, and children. This act alone could account for much of the bitterness which hung over the Paris Peace Conference.

On October 5th, Prince Max of Baden, the German Chancellor, asked President Wilson to negotiate a peace on the basis of his Fourteen Points and his subsequent pronouncements. After seeking certain assurances from Germany, Wilson conferred with his allies who made two qualifications, one relating to the question of Freedom of the Seas, and the other to reparations. The Allied Prime Ministers met the President's special envoy, Colonel House, who reassured them on their problems. Wilson's Second Point, he said, was not intended to stop blockading, and, as far as reparations were concerned, Germany must pay 'for damages done to the civilian population of the Allies and their property by the aggression of Germany by land, by sea, and from the air'. Colonel House was anxious to obtain the rapid approval of the Premiers and to do so he pointed out the wide interpretations which could be put upon Wilson's statements. The Allies, too, for all their doubts, were anxious to be convinced, for they feared that their rejection of Wilson's plans would lead to the loss of American support, and possibly even to a separate peace. Accordingly, the terms of the armistice were agreed and signed on November 11th.

Whatever they had been in January, the Fourteen Points were no longer in November 1918 regarded by anyone, Allied or enemy, as a bribe to induce Germany to surrender. The complete collapse and surrender of Germany and the other Central Powers was a matter of a few weeks at the most. The German Government sued for peace at the urgent request of its own High Command. The Allies agreed to use the Fourteen Points as the basis for settlement because Germany's request indicated that such a settlement would be acceptable to her. The Fourteen Points, therefore, seemed most likely to secure a lasting peace. Although the Allies were in a position to insist on an unconditional surrender, this, they argued, would be humiliating to Germany and would produce resentment and a desire to repudiate the terms when an opportunity arose. As we shall see, the Germans did resent the Versailles settlement and did repudiate it as soon as they could. Wherever in the peace treaties the Allies departed from the German interpretation of the Fourteen Points they were accused of violating the armistice terms and of having caused the Germans to lay down their arms on false pretences. Because the Germans were not allowed to negotiate the peace treaty these charges were soon widely believed to be true not only in the defeated, but in the victorious countries as well.

By the terms of the armistice, Germany was required to evacuate all occupied territory and to withdraw beyond the right bank of the Rhine, to surrender large quantities of guns, aeroplanes, her fleet, locomotives, wagons, and motor-lorries. The Treaties of Brest-Litovsk and Bucharest were to be cancelled. The blockade was to continue until the conclusion of the peace.

The continuation of the blockade led to much ill-founded abuse even at the time. It was only natural, however, that Germany should be deprived of the means of making war until she had signed the peace. The Allies at no time denied Germany such food as was available, but the demands on the limited food supplies immediately available were great and the need for help was greatest in other parts of ravaged Europe. The main reason why there was a delay in food going into Germany was the refusal of the German Government to allow its merchant ships to be used for this purpose and also its refusal to release gold to pay for the food. Only in March 1919 did the Germans give way and then only under the extreme pressure Lloyd George exerted on them when he learnt that British occupation troops were giving part of their own rations to the hungry civilians. Far from neglecting the work of relief, the Allies immediately organized under Herbert Hoover, a future president of the United States, a gigantic scheme for food distribution, in which Germany shared. Even Keynes, a severe critic of the Allies' treatment of Germany, recognized the worth of Hoover's work. 'The only man', he wrote, 'who emerged from the ordeal of Paris with an enhanced reputation.'

### THE 'BIG THREE'

The first session of the peace conference met in Paris on January 18th, 1919. Thirty-two states sent delegates, many of whom were accompanied by large technical staffs. If it was nothing else, this was the largest peace conference of all time. Germany was not allowed to send representatives. The full conference however, met very rarely. From the beginning the real control was assumed by a Council of Ten which consisted of two representatives from the United States, Britain, France, Italy, and Japan. Japan was interested only in what directly concerned her, and took little part in the general settlement. Orlando, the Italian Prime Minister, withdrew from the Conference in protest against Wilson's refusal to meet Italy's claims. Decisions were then taken openly, as they had always been taken effectively, by the representatives of the U.S., France, and Britain, Wilson, Clemenceau, and Lloyd George, the 'Big Three'.

Of these three, Wilson was the only head of state. He was also the representative of the most powerful state. He was a solitary, sombre, humourless man with an air of deep religious feeling. Presbyterian is the adjective

**The Russian Revolution.** *Above* Lenin addressing a crowd. *Below* Trotsky (right) as a leader of the Red Army. Note the form of Tartar cap worn by the Red Army in its early days.

**Hoover, Poincaré and Stresemann.** *Above left* Poincaré, the incarnation of French anti-German policy (see p. 110). *Above right* Stresemann, the liberal German Chancellor (see Chapter 15). *Below* The American, Hoover, responsible for much U.S. relief work in Europe after the First World War (see p. 103).

**Mussolini.** Attempting to symbolize the martial vigour of Fascism, Mussolini leads the famous 'at the double' march of the Italian Bersaglieri regiment.

**Atatürk and Franco.** *Above* Atatürk (in cloth cap) in a group of modern, western-dressed Turks (see p. 114). *Below* Franco greets senior officers at a reception in Madrid (see p. 115).

frequently affixed to him. He was highly sensitive to criticism and when the Paris press began to make fun of him he was both annoyed and shaken. He had high ideals, and in certain directions, great vision. He hoped for a peace founded on principle, not on the selfish national interests of the victors. But he also had considerable shortcomings, which were, in part at least, to cancel out his great qualities. He was a poor negotiator, clinging stubbornly and self-righteously to his own ideas and paying little regard to other views. When he did give way, he often did so unwisely. He took little trouble over public and press relations. He did nothing to hide his conviction that God and the people were on his side. As far as the people were concerned, he was probably too greatly influenced by the tumultuous reception he received in Paris and London. The picture which has emerged of Wilson as the righteous idealist outwitted by the clever and unscrupulous Clemenceau and Lloyd George is inaccurate. Wilson knew a trick or two. He once got his own way by ordering his ship to be made ready to sail. He was not at first fully aware of the complexity of the problems in Europe, though he was remarkably quick to readjust many of the ideas he had formed across the Atlantic. His greatest weakness, was, however, his personal position as the representative of the United States. In the Congressional elections of November 1918, Wilson's party, the Democrats, lost its majority in both the Senate and the House of Representatives. From the outset, there was the threat that the treaty the President was negotiating would be rejected by the Senate and thus invalidated. As his own position became more and more isolated, he put increasing faith in the Covenant of the League of Nations, trusting in that to solve the problems he found it either impossible or inconvenient to solve. The Covenant rather than the Fourteen Points became his instrument for achieving a just settlement.

In contrast to Wilson, Lloyd George and Clemenceau had clear support from their electorates. Lloyd George had won a resounding victory in the 'Coupon' Election of December 1918, which was marked by a wild display of hatred against Germany. Lord Northcliffe, then controlling *The Times* as well as the *Daily Mail*, contributed considerably towards creating and maintaining this hysterical outburst. The twin pillars of his campaign were the election slogans 'Hang the Kaiser' and 'Make Germany Pay'. No politician, not even Lloyd George, could resist the demand for revenge. 'We shall get out of her all you can squeeze out of a lemon and a bit more', shouted one oft-quoted politician, Sir Eric Geddes, 'I will squeeze her until you can hear the pips squeak'. Throughout the Conference, the *Daily Mail* kept up its clamour. In April 1919 the slogan 'The Junkers will cheat you yet' appeared daily on its front page. When the Germans reached Versailles for the signing, the slogan 'Lest we forget: Killed 670 986, Wounded 1 041 000, Missing 350 243', was added. Lloyd George did well, against this background, to be as moderate as he was.

A few days after the British General Election, Clemenceau received a resounding vote of confidence in the French Chamber of Deputies. Since the Conference was in Paris, Clemenceau was, out of courtesy, made Chairman. He dominated the proceedings. 'The Tiger', now an old man, sat for much of the time, his eyes closed, 'with an impassive face of parchment his grey-gloved hands clasped in front of him' (Keynes), occasionally opening his eyes and rapping out a short, uncompromising sentence. In February, an attempt was made on his life. He was hit in the shoulder blade and a bullet lodged near one of his lungs. Though he was seventy-eight years of age, he was back at work in a fortnight. He was tough, and he had one aim —to give France security, by making it impossible for Germany ever again to commit aggression. He had little interest in schemes which failed to provide effectively for this. He disliked the League because it did not guarantee military action. In Britain and the United States it became customary to attack Clemenceau for insisting on a vindictive peace. In France he was attacked by people of many shades of opinion for giving in to Wilson and Lloyd George.

## THE TERMS

The peace settlement consisted of five separate treaties signed with each of the enemy powers. The Treaty of Versailles made peace with Germany, the Treaty of St. Germain (1919) with Austria, the Treaty of Trianon (1920) with Hungary, the Treaty of Neuilly (1919) with Bulgaria, and the Treaty of Sèvres (1920) with Turkey. The treaty with Hungary was de-

*Map 12.  Treaties of St. Germain (Austria)
and Trianon (Hungary)*

layed because of the establishment of Bela Kun's short-lived Communist Government. The Treaty of Sèvres was rejected by the Government of Kemal after the revolution in Turkey and was replaced by the Treaty of Lausanne (1923). These treaties are dealt with separately here, except with regard to colonies, where it is convenient to examine the distribution of the lands formerly belonging to Germany and Turkey together.

## GERMANY'S FRONTIERS

Alsace-Lorraine was restored to France. Belgium received Moresnet outright, and Eupen-Malmédy after a plebiscite. Denmark was given North Slesvig after a plebiscite. The Saar territory was to be administered by the League of Nations for fifteen years, after which a plebiscite was to be held to decide its future. The coal-mines in the area were to be the property of France, and if, as a result of the plebiscite, the Saar returned to Germany, France was to receive compensation for the loss of the mines. (This actually happened in 1935.)

A new state of Poland was to be created out of the provinces of Posen, West Prussia, and the lands made available by the Treaty of Brest-Litovsk. Part of Upper Silesia went to Poland after a plebiscite. The frontiers were drawn so that Poland had a corridor through German territory to the sea. The port of Danzig was declared a Free City, under the protection of the League, but in customs union with Poland, who also controlled the city's foreign affairs.

Memel was to be administered by the League pending a decision about its future. The League acquiesced in its seizure by Lithuania in 1923.

The union of Germany and Austria was forbidden without the unanimous consent of the Council of the League. France had a permanent seat on the Council and would always veto such a move.

In Europe, Germany lost 28 000 square miles of territory, and some 7 million inhabitants or just over 10 per cent of her population, though in terms of actual German-speaking people permanently lost (i.e. excluding the Saar) the figure was less than 3 per cent.

## COLONIES

Germany's colonies and the conquered Turkish provinces were ceded to the Allies and distributed to the various Powers as mandates under the League. Each Power undertook to maintain certain principles in its mandated territories. They were to be governed in the interests of the colonial peoples. There was to be no exploitation, no slavery, and complete freedom of religion was to be observed. The territories were to be developed so that the peoples could eventually be given self-government, though it was recognized that this could be achieved earlier in some colonies than in others. Each Power was required to submit an annual report on its mandated territories to the League of Nations. The mandates system was an ingenious scheme devised to enable the Allies to seize Germany's colonies without seeming to contradict Wilson's pledge that there should be no annexations. However, it also set an admirable pattern for colonial government.

Britain received Palestine, Iraq and Transjordan from Turkey, and German East Africa (Tanganyika), and parts of Togoland and the Cameroons.

France received Syria and the Lebanon from Turkey and most of Togoland and the Cameroons.

Belgium received a strip of German East Africa, and the Union of South Africa was given German South West Africa.

In the Pacific, Britain, Australia and New Zealand shared the islands south of the Equator while Japan took those to the north. Japan was also granted, much to China's annoyance, since she too was on the Allied side, all German rights in Kiaochow on the Chinese mainland.

## REPARATIONS

Germany, as agreed in the armistice terms, was to pay compensation for the damage done to the Allied civilian populations. This principle was extended during the discussions to include the pensions to widows and orphans, and also separation allowances paid by the Allied governments. This extension was demanded by Lloyd George, under pressure from his Parliament, and agreed to by Wilson, though it was, and has remained, a highly debatable point.

The sum of reparations was not fixed in the treaty. It was to be determined by an Inter-Allied Commission before May 1st, 1921. By that date, Germany was to have paid 20 000 million gold marks (£1 000 million) to meet the immediate costs of the armies of occupation and of urgent imports into Germany. Any money remaining would be credited to the reparations account.

Germany was to surrender all merchant ships over 1600 tons, and a number of her smaller ships. In addition, for five years, Germany was to build ships to the annual tonnage of 200 000 to replace Allied shipping. France and Belgium were to receive large quantities of coal and large numbers of horses, cattle and sheep to compensate for their wartime losses.

All German property, including private property, in former German colonies and in Allied countries was confiscated.

The rivers Elbe, Oder, Niemen, and Danube (from Ulm) were to be internationalized and the Rhine was to be placed under a joint Commission. The Kiel Canal was to be open to all ships of all nations.

## DISARMAMENT

Conscription was to be abolished and the Army reduced to 100 000 men each serving for twelve years. Limitations were placed on German military equipment, and tanks, armoured cars, and military aircraft were prohibited.

The German Navy was limited in size and numbers and no submarines were permitted. (The German Fleet had surrendered at the armistice and had sailed to Scapa Flow where it scuttled itself.)

The right bank of the Rhine was to be permanently demilitarized to a depth of 50 kilometeres (32 miles).

## THE 'WAR-GUILT' CLAUSE

Article 231 of the Treaty stated: 'The Allies and Associated Governments affirm and Germany accepts the responsibility of Germany and her allies for causing all the loss and damage to which the Allies and Associated Governments have been subjected as a consequence of the war imposed upon them by the aggression of Germany and her allies.'

This was inserted to give a legal basis for the reparations claims, and it caused much bitterness in Germany.

## THE KAISER AND THE 'WAR CRIMINALS'

The Treaty further demanded that the Kaiser be handed over to the Allies for trial. This was included purely to satisfy the 'Hang the Kaiser' movement in Britain. Fortunately for everyone, the Kaiser was in Holland and the Dutch refused to hand him over. An attempt to bring 'war criminals' to trial was abandoned after a few test cases.

## OCCUPATION

The Allies were to occupy the left bank and bridgeheads of the Rhine for fifteen years. In fact, the first zone was evacuated in 1926, the second in 1929, and the third in 1930.

## AUSTRIA, HUNGARY AND BULGARIA

The Austro-Hungarian Empire was broken up and distributed to the various national groups. A new state of Czechoslovakia was formed. Serbia was greatly expanded to form Yugoslavia. Poland received Galicia and Italy received the South Tyrol, Trentino, Istria, and Trieste. The economic distress caused by this loss of land and people was considerable. The great city of Vienna was left like a head without a body.

Hungary lost Transylvania, rich in forests and ores, to Rumania, which also gained Bessarabia from the Russian land taken by Germany. Hungary also lost land to Yugoslavia and Czechoslovakia. Bulgaria gave up land to Yugoslavia and also lost her Aegean coastline to Greece.

## TURKEY

By the Treaty of Sèvres, Greece received Adrianople and Eastern Thrace in Europe, and the area round Smyrna in Asia Minor. The Straits from the

Dardanelles to the Sea of Marmora were to be demilitarized and put under the League of Nations. This treaty was signed by the Sultan, but the Turkish Nationalists under Kemal rejected the terms and retired to Angora (Ankara) out of reach of the Greek troops sent against them. In 1922 Kemal took the offensive and expelled the Greeks from the mainland. A new treaty was drawn up at Lausanne in 1923. Turkish sovereignty was recognized over Eastern Thrace and Adrianople and over the whole of Asia Minor. Turkey was the first ex-enemy to defy the peacemakers successfully.

The remaining Turkish provinces were either mandated or else given complete independence.

*Map 13. Treaties of Neuilly, Sèvres and Lausanne*

## THE BALTIC PROVINCES

The land taken from Russia by Germany by the Treaty of Brest-Litovsk was at the disposal of the Conference. Three new states were created on the Baltic, Latvia, Lithuania, and Estonia. The independence of Finland which had been won in 1917 as a result of the Russian revolution was recognized. The remaining land went to Poland and Rumania.

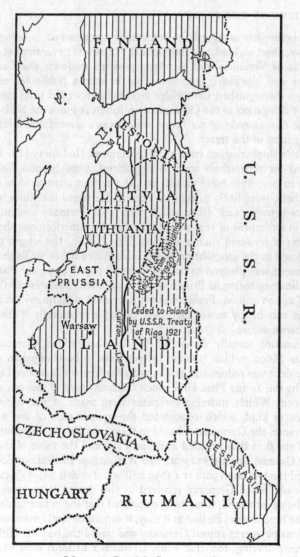

*Map 14. Russia's Losses, 1918–21*

THE LEAGUE OF NATIONS

Each treaty began with the clauses providing for the establishment of the League of Nations. Wilson insisted on this method of ensuring that his great dream should not be allowed to fade away. These clauses, the nature of the League, and its history, are examined separately in Chapter 11.

CRITICISMS OF THE PEACE

Even before it was signed the settlement was attacked as being cruelly vindictive, short-sighted, and impractical. Hitler was never tired of abusing the *diktat* of Versailles, but the pattern of his criticism was familiar in Germany and elsewhere long before he became a public figure. J. M. Keynes, a distinguished Cambridge economist, resigned from the British Treasury delegation to the Conference in June 1919 to write his book *The Economic Consequences of the Peace*, which was a powerful and influential condemnation of the treaty.

Keynes's chief criticism concerned reparations. He believed the amounts envisaged for reparations were totally unreal, were beyond Germany's capacity to pay, were quite unjust, and, if a serious attempt were made to collect them, were likely to ruin all Europe. He urged the Allies to cancel the debts between each other and to take from Germany a round £2000 million in settlement of reparations. Neither the American nor the British Government favoured such a solution. The U.S.A., the largest creditor, was opposed to the cancellation of the Inter-Allied debts, while the British Government was pledged to make Germany pay. The figure that caught the public imagination in Britain was the so-called 'business-man's estimate' of £24 000 million. France was not interested in Germany's capacity to pay. She was happy to see Germany ruined economically if that would make France secure.

The amount actually demanded by the Reparations Commission in 1921 was £6600 million (though interest was to be charged in addition until the debt was redeemed), and in 1929 the figure was reduced to £2000 million by the Young Plan. How much Germany paid of this can never be determined. Widely differing estimates were made of the value of the deliveries in kind, which constituted the greater part of the payment. Furthermore, the Germans included in their calculations such items as the value of the fleet they scuttled at Scapa Flow and the value of the labour done by German prisoners of war. The Washington Institute of Economics estimated the total sum paid at £1850 million, of which about £250 million was in cash. Since Germany received in this period large foreign loans which she never repaid, it has been calculated that she in fact made a profit out of the reparations! Be that as it may, it cannot be justly maintained that reparations payments ruined Germany and paved the way for Hitler. It is worth remembering, too, that while Germany's national debt was effectively wiped out by the wild inflation which her Government brought about in 1924, the Allied national debts remained burdened with the expenses of the war.

Nevertheless, the Allies would have done well to follow Keynes's advice in 1919. When the slump hit Europe in 1932, Germany defaulted on her payments, and the Allies in their turn defaulted on their payments to each other. The reparations scheme prolonged the bitterness of the war and benefited no one. Even had the Allies forced Germany to produce the goods and gold they demanded, they would only have succeeded in bringing unemployment and inflation on themselves, by flooding their own markets with goods their countrymen had not produced, and money they had not earned. Economically the plan was unsound; politically it was disastrous. There were better ways to express the Allies' disapproval of Germany.

The other chief criticism Keynes levelled against the treaty was that it took little account of the economic structure of Europe. Wilson, in his own words, was 'not much interested in the economic subjects'. His guiding principle was self-determination. His aim was to redraw the map of Europe so that all people speaking the same language should be together in independent states. He hoped to complete the movement towards this end which had caused so much fighting and unrest in the previous century. Not until he arrived in Paris did he realize fully the complexity of his task. The intermingling peoples of different languages, particularly in Eastern Europe, made it impossible to draw frontiers which would leave no alien minorities anywhere, unless people were forcibly uprooted from their homes. Even where reasonable lines of separation might be drawn, they were not always economically sound. Upper Silesia, for instance represented an economic unit and many Germans with financial interests there were said to hope it would go as a unit to Poland rather than be split up. Railways which had been planned to serve the large units of the German and Austro-Hungarian Empires were obviously unsuited to the needs of the new, smaller states. Where Wilson did depart from his principle of self-determination, it was for political, rather than for economic, reasons. For example, three million Germans in the Sudetenland were included in Czechoslovakia so that the new state could have the Bohemian mountains as a defensible frontier. Nevertheless, most of the economic adjustments of a technical nature, such as the rearrangement of railway systems and of sources of power supply, could be and were made. Clearly, great economic problems were involved in such a drastic rearrangement of European boundaries. Nevertheless, the will to self-determination was deeply rooted, and in retrospect Wilson's flexible adherence to this principle does not seem so very misguided.

## THE FAILURE OF VERSAILLES

The Treaty of Versailles, which President Wilson had personally negotiated at every stage, was rejected by the Senate of the United States. There were many reasons for this—personal dislike of Wilson, fear of entanglement in European affairs by membership of the League of Nations, and a general feeling of disgust at what appeared the petty squabbles of European statesmen. The result was to sabotage the treaty right from the beginning. France felt particularly aggrieved. She had sacrificed her more extreme demands for the annexation of German territory west of the Rhine

New States formed by the Peace Treaties

Note: Yugoslavia, which was formed by the expansion of Serbia to include Austro-Hungarian provinces and Montenegro was, in effect, a new state too.

*Map 15. Europe in 1923*

in return for a treaty by which the United States and Britain guaranteed her frontiers against attack. This treaty was to become operative only if ratified by all parties. The Senate rejected this agreement, too. France was thus left, as it seemed to her, without any security. The consequences of the failure of the United States to join the League are discussed in Chapter

11. The general effect of the Senate's action was to create an entirely new situation in Europe which properly required a completely new settlement.

The treaty was never enforced in its entirety, and as the years passed it was eaten into clause by clause. Few people had sufficient faith in it to wish to defend it. France and Italy both felt cheated. Germany felt humiliated. Britain felt uneasy. Russia had been left out of it. The United States had disowned it. If we wish to discover why Versailles failed to produce a lasting settlement, we must look at the conduct of the nations rather than at the terms of the treaty. In spite of the abuse that has been heaped upon the settlement, it bears the stamp of goodwill and justice which Wilson gave it. His noble phrase 'Peace without Victory' remains unburied.

Many lessons may be drawn from the Versailles settlement. One at least is unquestionable. As Sir Harold Nicolson has observed, after a long war it is impossible to make a quick peace. The age of the great Peace Conference had passed.

## 11  The League of Nations

The first twenty-six articles of each of the peace treaties forming the Versailles settlement set out the aims and organization of the League of Nations. These articles formed the Covenant, or the written Constitution, of the League. Wilson insisted that the Covenant should form an inseparable part of the treaties so that none of the signatories could set aside the League without also setting aside the other provisions. His own country had, in fact, to abandon the whole settlement in order to avoid joining the League.

The Covenant set out the rules which each member had to observe. The League was open to any independent state. Members undertook 'to respect and preserve against aggression' the territory and independence of all the other members. They undertook not to make war on each other until they had first submitted their dispute to the League, and even if this method failed to find a settlement after six months, the disputing states undertook to give three months' notice before declaring war. Article 8 of the Covenant called for the reduction of armaments 'to the lowest point consistent with national safety and the enforcement by common action of international obligations'. Any state which violated the Covenant was liable to have 'sanctions' imposed on it, that is to say was liable to face joint economic or military action, or both. Article 18 required that every treaty or international agreement entered into by a member should be registered by the League Secretariat and published. Article 19 provided for the revision of treaties which had become outdated or which endangered peace.

THE MACHINERY OF THE LEAGUE

The League functioned through a General Assembly and a Council. The Assembly met annually and was made up of representatives, usually the Foreign Ministers, of all the member states. The Council, which was to carry out much of the executive work, met three times a year. The Council at first consisted of four Permanent members, Great Britain, France, Italy, and Japan, and four Non-Permanent members. The Permanent seats were given to the most powerful countries on the realistic understanding that strong countries have the dominating influence on international affairs. The framers of the Covenant intended the Permanent members to outnumber, and thus to be able to outvote, the non-Permanent members, but the failure of the U.S.A. to join the League made the numbers equal. Later the Permanent members were heavily outnumbered, for although Germany joined the Council as a Permanent member in 1926 and the U.S.S.R. in 1934, the number of Non-Permanent members was increased by stages to eleven by 1936. It must be remembered, too, that Germany left the League in 1933, Japan in 1934, and Italy in 1936. However, in certain cases it was possible for a Non-Permanent member to be re-elected and in fact Poland served on the Council from 1923 to 1938. One serious obstacle to action both in the Council and in the Assembly was the ruling that decisions on all except a few particular cases had to be unanimous. It is one thing to allow a powerful state to 'veto' the proposals of its fellow powers, as is possible on the Security Council of the United Nations. It is quite another matter to allow a minor state the right to thwart the action of major powers.

The Council and the Assembly provided the Executive and the Legislature, the Cabinet and the Parliament as it were, of the League. The Judiciary was provided by the Permanent Court of International Justice which was set up at the Hague to deal with legal disputes between nations, as opposed to political disputes, which were to be dealt with by the Council and the Assembly. The Court consisted of fifteen judges chosen, theoretically at least, on their merit, from various countries. The idea of a World Court, unlike the idea of a World Government, was popular in the United States, and in 1926 the Senate agreed to join, on condition that the Court did not sit in judgment on matters concerning the United States without their permission.[1] On these terms, the other signatory states declined to accept the membership of the United States.

The day-to-day business of the League was conducted by the Secretariat, an international civil service, working under the Secretary-General.

[1] Just as today the United States excludes from the jurisdiction of the International Court of Justice 'disputes which are essentially within the jurisdiction of the United States, *as determined by the United States*', though such a reservation conflicts with the Court's Statute.

## THE SPECIAL COMMISSIONS

The most valuable work of the League was done not by the Council or by the Assembly but by the numerous commissions and committees which were appointed to deal with specific and limited matters. Some governed the League territories such as Danzig and the Saar. Others like the Mandates Commission, the Minorities Commission, and the Disarmament Commission were set up to supervise the observation of treaty obligations. Other bodies dealt with such a wide range of matters as refugees, drugs, health, forced labour, transport and communications, and intellectual co-operation. Because they were limited in their scope these committees dealing with economic and social problems were able to achieve much and a great deal of valuable experience in international co-operation was gained. Easily the most successful organization associated with the League was, however, the I.L.O.

## THE INTERNATIONAL LABOUR ORGANIZATION

The Constitution of the International Labour Organization was separate from the Covenant of the League but was included in the peace treaties in the same way. The object of the I.L.O., as set out in its preamble, was to secure social justice on which a universal peace could be established. Injustice, hardship, and privation cause threats to peace, and the failure of one nation 'to adopt humane conditions of labour is an obstacle in the way of other nations which desire to improve the conditions in their own countries'. The I.L.O. was founded, therefore, to fix a maximum working day and week, to take measures against unemployment, to provide an adequate living wage, sickness and injury benefit, and old age pensions, to ensure freedom of union organization, and to take whatever other measures would be required to realize its aims.

All members of the League were members of the I.L.O., but other nations could join, and the United States did so. The I.L.O. had its own secretariat, the International Labour Office. One of the most interesting features of the I.L.O. was the composition of the delegations to the annual conference. Each member state sent four representatives, two representing the government, one the employers, and one the employees. These delegations had to report to the conference on how far previous resolutions had been put into effect. Much of the success of this body must be attributed to the driving personality of its first director, the Frenchman, Albert Thomas, under whose guidance a great deal of information on a wide range of labour matters was collected and published.

## THE IDEAS BEHIND THE LEAGUE

Wilson aimed in the Versailles settlement, including the League, to ensure a lasting peace by dealing with the causes of war as he saw them.

The desire of peoples for national self-determination was largely met by the territorial arrangements in the treaties. The inevitable minorities which remained were to have their interests looked after by a special commission. Colonial rivalry would become meaningless as the mandates system developed. By the Covenant of the League, nations agreed to disarm and thus the dangers of an arms race would be avoided. Nations also agreed not to conclude secret alliances. Unfair treaties were to be revised. Economic and social inequalities and grievances were to be dealt with by the I.L.O. and various committees. All was provided for. Even German militarism was guarded against specifically by the disarmament clauses of the treaty. The supporters of the League, and they were many in many countries, saw in it the means by which disputes between nations could be settled like disputes within civilized nations, not by violence, but by discussion, compromise, and above all by respect for law. This did not seem an impossible ideal. Indeed, after four years of terrible warfare, it seemed essential. But the supporters of the League were destined to disillusionment. The League failed to keep the peace.

### THE LEAGUE IN ACTION

The first dispute which came before the League concerned the Aaland Islands. When Finland declared its independence from Russia in 1917, the inhabitants of the Aaland Islands which command the entrance to the Gulf of Finland asked to be united to Sweden. Finland refused to consider their request, but the matter came before the Council of the League in 1920. A committee of inquiry reported in favour of Finland and the dispute was settled.

The next dispute was between Poland and Lithuania over the town and district of Vilna. The frontier of Poland in the east had not been finally settled by the Treaty of Versailles. Meanwhile a provisional frontier was fixed along what was known as the Curzon line. The Poles, however, never felt bound to remain west of this line and in 1919 they seized Vilna from the Russians. The following year the Bolsheviks recaptured the district and handed it over to Lithuania. The Poles asked the League to intervene and at the same time a Polish general, ostensibly acting on his own initiative, seized Vilna. This aggression was allowed to stand and the matter was finally taken out of the hands of the League and settled by the Conference of Ambassadors in 1923, which recognized Poland's sovereignty over the region.

Undoubtedly, the League's action in this matter was largely determined by the hostility of the Allies to the Soviet régime, and by the anxiety of France to bolster Poland as her ally in the East, rather than by the merits of the situation. This was not the last time that the League was to act according to the apparent interests of Britain and France, rather than in the interests of international justice.

The League was again side-stepped and the dispute settled by the Conference of Ambassadors in the matter of the Corfu case. In 1923 an Italian general, with three other Italians and an Albanian driver, was ambushed and murdered on Greek territory while engaged on drawing the line of the frontier between Greece and Albania. Two days later the Italian Government sent the Greek Government a note demanding an indemnity of 50 million Italian lire within five days. The Greek Government agreed to pay fair compensation to the families of the victims but not the indemnity. Accordingly the Italian Government bombarded and occupied the Greek island of Corfu. Greece raised the matter with the Council of the League, but Italy refused to recognize the competence of the League to deal with the matter. The Conference of Ambassadors ordered Greece to pay the 50 million lire and Corfu was evacuated. Again force had triumphed.

In 1925 Greece was involved in a dispute with Bulgaria. A series of border incidents culminated, after the shooting of a Greek soldier who was trying to mediate under cover of a white flag, in a Greek invasion of Bulgaria. The League ordered Greece to withdraw her troops and to pay Bulgaria £45 000 in reparation, and the Greeks obeyed. In this dispute, the League acted promptly, rightly, and successfully. But Greece was only a small nation.

In the early years of its existence, when it was clearly subordinate to the Conference of Ambassadors, the League had little chance to be effective. In 1923 a resolution was passed to the effect that each member state would decide for itself whether or not to fight in any crisis. This made nonsense of the League as a means of guaranteeing collective security. Nations now sought to achieve security by regional agreements.

## LOCARNO AND THE PROSPECT OF PEACE

1925 brought the signing of the Locarno Pact. This consisted of a treaty of mutual guarantee of the Franco-German and the Belgo-German frontiers, signed by Germany, France, Great Britain, Italy and Belgium, and a Franco-Polish and a Franco-Czech treaty of mutual assistance in the case of aggression by Germany. Locarno brought about a great relief in international tension. The British guarantee gave France reassurance for the first time since the United States rejected the Anglo-American guarantee signed by Wilson. Furthermore, Locarno was no *diktat*. The Germans had signed the treaty voluntarily and could therefore reasonably be expected to honour it. However, it contained no German acceptance of any but her western frontiers, and by reaffirming some parts of the Versailles settlement, Locarno weakened the authority of the other clauses.

However, the immediate atmosphere produced by Locarno was one of optimism. In 1926 Germany was admitted to the League. In 1928 the Kellogg-Briand Pact was drawn up renouncing war as an instrument of diplomacy, and by 1930 it had been signed by all major Powers. But, apart from the Washington Conferences of 1921–22 and 1930 at which Britain, the United States, France, Italy and Japan agreed to the limitation of their navies, and in spite of endless discussion, no advance was made towards the crucial matter of general disarmament.

## THE LEAGUE DEFIED

In September 1931 an explosion occurred on or near the South Manchurian Railway which was owned and guarded by the Japanese. The passage of trains was conveniently unaffected. The Japanese accordingly proceeded to occupy the Chinese town of Mukden and they also made other well-prepared attacks against the Chinese elsewhere in Manchuria within an astonishingly short time of the explosion. Within seven months the whole of Manchuria was in Japanese hands. The Chinese Government appealed to the League Council and after much delay a Commission of Inquiry was appointed. The League did not insist on the withdrawal of Japanese troops as a preliminary to investigations and consequently the Commission had to carry out its duties in a country overrun by Japanese. Nevertheless, although the Commissioners in their report were oddly sympathetic to Japan's ambitions in the area and although they recommended concessions to Japan, the evidence they collected showed clearly that the people of Manchuria had no desire to be connected with Japan. The report condemned Japan's action and recommended that Manchuria should be an autonomous state. Japan, however, in open defiance of the League, created a puppet government in Manchuria which was henceforth to be called Manchukuo. Having done that, they invaded more Chinese territory and gave notice of withdrawal from the League. The Manchurian incident is now clearly seen to have been the crucial test of the League's ability to stop aggression. No one was prepared to help China effectively, because no one was prepared to risk war with Japan. Excuses for inaction were not lacking. Japan was regarded by some as a restorer of law and order —a civilizing influence. Those who hoped that Japan might expand in the East at the expense of Soviet Russia were not displeased by events. In any case, the Manchurian affair was not a 'war', merely 'an intervention'. It was also taking place a long way from Europe. The League was henceforth frightened to do anything which might be contrary to Japan's wishes and interests. Other nations were not slow to observe the moral.

The coming of Hitler to power in 1933 made Britain and France even less enthusiastic about disarmament than they had been before. Germany used this as her excuse to withdraw from the League and in 1935 she broke the Treaty of Versailles by beginning open rearmament and by introducing conscription. Of the League members only Britain took action. She underlined this repudiation of Versailles by concluding a naval treaty with Germany (see p. 148).

On October 3rd, 1935, Italy attacked Abyssinia. The Emperor of Ethiopia, Haile Selassie, appealed to the League, and four days later the Council branded Italy as an aggressor. Sanctions were imposed but coal, oil, iron and steel were specifically excluded, and the Suez Canal was not closed to Italian warships or transports. Such was the anxiety of Britain and France not to annoy Mussolini that Sir Samuel Hoare, the British Foreign Secretary, and Pierre Laval, the French Premier, drafted a scheme known as the Hoare-Laval Pact by which Mussolini was to be allowed to have some two-thirds of Abyssinia. The plan leaked out prematurely and Hoare was obliged to resign in face of the indignation it aroused. Nevertheless, by May Italy had conquered the whole country and in July the sanctions, such as they were, were called off. Italy had walked out of the League in May 1936 and in 1937 gave notice of her withdrawal.

In March 1936 Hitler marched into the demilitarized zone of the Rhine, and thus broke the Locarno Pact as well as the Treaty of Versailles. Britain and France took no action. In July General Franco led a rebellion against the government of the Spanish Republic. Britain and France vigorously pursued a policy of 'Non-intervention' while Italy equally vigorously, and Germany to a lesser degree, pursued a policy of active support for Franco. The only setback suffered by the aggressors was achieved in their absence at the Nyon Conference in September 1937. 'Unknown' submarines operating in the Mediterranean had been attacking shipping bound for Spanish Republican ports. At Nyon, Britain and France resolved on joint naval patrols with instructions to attack any submarine, aeroplane, or surface vessel attacking ships other than Spanish ships. The mysterious attacks mysteriously stopped, but the Nyon agreement was little comfort to the Spanish, particularly as it showed that firm action could immediately call the bluff of the bullying dictators.

Meanwhile, in July 1937, the so-called 'China Incident' began: that is to say, Japan launched the second stage of her attack against China. China's appeals to the League brought sympathy but little else. The United States, which had applied the Neutrality Act (see p. 194) in the Spanish war failed to do so against Japan, so she was able to buy much of her arms and raw materials from America. Britain and France from 1937 onwards were more than ever concerned with events in Europe.

THE LEAGUE IGNORED

For all matters of importance, the League was usually ignored in the years immediately preceding the Second World War. Germany, Japan, and Italy, all ex-Permanent members of the League Council, were in alliance by 1937. In face of this growing threat, Britain and France began to rearm. When Austria, Czechoslovakia, and Memel were seized by Germany, and when Albania was invaded by Italy, the League was not consulted. Britain and France were, apart from the Soviet Union (with whom they felt rather ashamed to be associated), the only major Powers in the League. It was only sensible to by-pass its machinery. Certainly, the result in terms of action, or rather inaction, was the same. When Danzig and Poland were invaded in September 1939, Britain and France went to war in fulfilment of private guarantees to Poland, not in pursuance of their obligations to the League.

Even so, the League was not quite dead. Having endured the humiliations heaped upon it by Japan, Italy, and Germany, all of whom it had meekly allowed to resign, the League, witnessing by now the early stages of a war which was to shatter the world, rightly took note of the aggression committed by Russia against Finland in November 1939. On December 14th, 1939, Russia was expelled from the League. The only effect of this act was to ensure that the League would not survive the war, for neither of the two great Powers to emerge victorious from the conflict was a member.

### THE FAILURE OF THE LEAGUE

The main causes of the failure of the League are evident from what has been written of its history. The complete absence of the United States, and the absence from time to time of Germany, Russia, Japan, and Italy, made the League too much of an Anglo-French alliance. An Italian once remarked that the League was a place where English and French was spoken in all languages. The statesmen of both these countries always had more faith in the 'old diplomacy' than in the open covenants of the League. Nevertheless, as an organization to deal with genuine grievances the League was well-equipped. It was less well-equipped to deal with naked aggression. It was designed primarily to act in civil rather than in criminal cases. One very serious weakness was the great difficulty involved in bringing about an amendment to the Covenant. It was therefore difficult to make adjustments in the light of experience.

However, none of these objections was insuperable. The League failed because its members failed to keep the rules and fulfil their obligations. Had the League condemned, and expelled, those members which committed aggression, and had it imposed economic, and if necessary military, sanctions against them, the League would have proved the valuable instrument for civilized conduct its supporters believed it would be. But the members of the League were too anxious for peace to take the necessary steps to ensure it, and in this mood they were widely supported by the people they represented.

The only valid reason for the failure of the League is a very simple one. No organization can maintain the peace while any Power which is *able* to make war is *willing* to make war. Firm, united action on the part of other states can, of course, do much to persuade an aggressively-minded state to think again. But, if the determination to resort to force remains, no resolution will prevent war. Too many people regarded the League as an organization distinct from nations. They expected 'the League' to take action while they themselves were not prepared to act. National interests were too strongly rooted in Europe after the war to allow the measures necessary for the implementation of collective security to be taken. As has been said before, it was not the League that failed but the Nations.

In viewing the conduct of the League members, and of Britain and France in particular, it is very tempting to be wise after the event. Because Britain and France eventually went to war against Germany, Italy, and Japan it is easy to see why they should have risked war against them much sooner. But the temptation to believe their own excuses for inaction and to remain at peace was very strong. It was very easy to understand Germany's grievances, to see the shortcomings of Chinese and Abyssinian government, and to recognize the civilizing qualities of the Japanese and the Italians. The real issue in these cases was not, of course, whether Japan had any rights in Manchuria, or Italy in Abyssinia, or Germany in Czechoslovakia, but whether such questions should be settled by force. But when events occur in far distant countries, which seem to have no immediate influence at home, and which may even seem to produce advantages by engaging the attention of an enemy, only a very clear and unprejudiced mind can see the issues clearly, and there are few such minds among statesmen and few among electors.

# 12 Europe between the Wars, 1919-1939

The story of Germany, Italy and Russia, and of the diplomacy of the inter-war years is told in other chapters. We are here concerned with a survey of the internal affairs of some of the other continental countries, including those newly created in 1919.

## FRANCE

France had suffered terribly in the war. Her land, including the industrial and mining area in the north-east, had been devastated and she had lost well over a million men. The task of reconstruction was immense, but what haunted Frenchmen in 1919, as we have seen in the previous chapter, was the fear that Germany, with its greater industrial potential and its larger population, would arise from its defeat to threaten France again. All the problems which had prevented good government in the Third Republic before 1914 emerged after the war. Not even fear of Germany had been removed.

During the war, the rival political groups in France had largely sunk their differences in facing the common foe. This spirit of national unity survived in the government which was formed in 1919. Aided by a new electoral law, the *Bloc National*, a coalition of conservative groups, won a sweeping victory at the polls. French dissatisfaction with the Treaty of Versailles was apparent in the new government's foreign policy and when

Millerand, the ex-Socialist, became President in 1920, he provided a strong lead. Alliances were concluded with Poland in 1921 and with Czechoslovakia in 1924, and France entered into a military understanding with the so-called 'Little Entente' which had been formed in 1920–21 between Czechoslovakia, Rumania and Yugoslavia. In 1922 Millerand called upon Poincaré, who had been the war-time President of France, to become Prime Minister, and it was Poincaré who ordered the occupation of the Ruhr in 1923 (see p. 137) when Germany defaulted in the payment of reparations.

At home, however, the Government was unable to cope with the financial situation. Taxes were increased, but still the budget did not balance; prices were rising and the franc fell in value. The Ruhr occupation was an additional expense and it failed to make the Germans pay. The Radicals who had joined the *Bloc National* left the coalition and in the elections of 1924 the Government was defeated.

The *Bloc National* was replaced by a coalition of Radicals and Socialists called the *Cartel des Gauches*. This group remained in office until 1926, and there was a marked change in French foreign policy. The Ruhr was evacuated and the Dawes Plan for reparations payments was accepted. In 1925 the Locarno treaties were signed. Again, however, the new Government met disaster at home. Anti-clericalism, which had largely been buried after the valour displayed by Catholic priests and laity in the war, was now resurrected when the Government tried to impose the pre-war anti-clerical legislation on the restored provinces of Alsace and Lorraine. The policy failed but it needlessly created much ill-will. The main factor, however, in the collapse of the *Cartel des Gauches* was its failure to avoid a financial crisis. The value of the franc, which in 1924 stood at 70 to the pound, had dropped by July 1926 to 250 to the pound. The Radicals once more deserted the Government and joined with Poincaré, who was summoned back to save the franc in a new coalition called the *Union Nationale*.

The new Government was given emergency powers to rule by decree. The franc was revalued and stabilized, and public confidence was restored. With the immediate crisis over, the Radicals left the coalition in 1928. Poincaré retired through ill-health in the same year and was succeeded by Briand, but faced with a new economic crisis, following the depression which hit the United States in 1929, and with a sharp deterioration in the political situation, following the rise of the Nazis in Germany, the *Union Nationale* fell in December 1932.

In 1933—the year in which Germany left the League—France was politically paralysed. There were four Cabinets between December 1932 and February 1934. In the winter of 1933–34 the Stavisky scandal, comparable to the Panama scandal of 1892, swept France into turmoil. Stavisky, a crooked financier, was found by the police dead with a bullet through his head. It was widely believed that the 'suicide' had been arranged by the police to protect people in high places. Certainly his career and the freedom he had apparently been allowed to enjoy to carry out swindle after swindle gave grounds for suspicion. Royalists seized this new opportunity to discredit republican government. On February 6th, 1934, Right-wing demonstrators clashed violently with the police in and around the Place de la Concorde. Eleven were killed and three hundred wounded. The Prime Minister, Daladier, although supported in the Assembly, resigned and his place was taken by Doumergue, who was supported by the Right-wing press. On February 9th there was more violence when the Communists staged a counter-demonstration in the Place de la République and three days later the Socialists called a one-day general strike. Once again the barricades had been raised in Paris and France seemed close to yet another revolution. However, the new Government of the *Union Nationale*, to which the Radicals gave their support, was able to restore confidence and order, but it did so by increasing use of the dictatorial powers which the Assembly had despairingly given it.

French foreign policy under the new Government entered a disastrous phase after Pierre Laval took office in 1934. He sought to isolate Germany by concluding a pact of mutual assistance with Russia and by giving Mussolini a free hand in Abyssinia (see p. 107), but the disclosure of the Hoare-Laval pact brought about a wave of anti-Government and anti-British feeling in France—a favourable atmosphere for Hitler when he reoccupied the Rhineland in 1936.

In 1936 a *Popular Front* (see p. 125) Government was formed under the Socialist, Léon Blum. This Socialist-Radical coalition had the nominal support of the Communists, but they declined to join the Cabinet and a wave of strikes broke out. Although many measures were introduced which improved working conditions—higher wages, holidays with pay, and the forty hour week—unemployment remained a problem and the general economic state of the country did not improve. Moreover, extreme Right-wing groups, strongly anti-semitic, grew in strength.

By 1938 the Popular Front had broken up and the Government again lived from hand to mouth, ruling almost entirely by decree. France was by now quite incapable of taking a firm line in foreign affairs and she followed Britain blindly. When war came in 1939, France, bitterly divided internally, was unprepared militarily and psychologically to fight. After the Russian attack on Poland, the Communists denounced the war against Germany as an imperialist adventure and set about undermining the morale of servicemen and civilians alike. The non-appearance of the expected German attack in the west brought to the surface a strong peace party, of whom Laval was one, which advocated a deal with Germany, now that Poland had fallen. The collapse of the Third Republic came rapidly when the attack finally came. It was a wonder to many that it had lasted so long.

## POLAND

The state of Poland as it existed between the wars was largely the creation of Marshal Pilsudski, who, born in Russian Poland, had fought with the Central Powers in the war in the hope that his country's freedom would come with Russia's defeat.

Pilsudski became the head of Poland in 1918 and, having failed to get all he wanted for his country at the Peace Conference, he set about enlarging it by force. He attacked Russia and secured a large part of the Ukraine, and he seized Vilna from Lithuania. These gains he was allowed to keep and Poland became by far the largest of the new post-war states in Europe, but it had enemies on all sides. Germany resented the loss of the Polish Corridor and Danzig, Russia the loss of the Ukraine, Lithuania Vilna and Czechoslovakia Teschen. Lying as she did in the east European plain without obvious geographical boundaries, Poland was in no position to fulfil the role demanded of her as a bulwark against Communist Russia and as a safeguard against the re-emergence of German militarism.

Internally, too, Poland was weak. Coming as they did from three different empires, the people had quite different traditions and no common loyalties. The large minority groups, Russians, Germans and Jews, presented grave problems. After an attempt at parliamentary government with Paderewski (the pianist) as Prime Minister, Poland relapsed after 1926 into a dictatorship (in everything but name) under Pilsudski. When he died in 1935, Poland was left with neither parliamentary government nor strong leadership.

## AUSTRIA

The new Austria, a fragment only of the old Habsburg Empire, faced great economic distress after the war, but nevertheless managed to maintain a democratic form of government for several years. Politically the country was divided between the Social Democrats and the conservative and Catholic Christian Socialists, but the economic crises which followed the slump of 1929 increased the following of a third party—the Austrian National Socialists (Nazis). In 1932 there were clashes between the private armies of all three groups and trouble increased after the Nazis came to power in Germany in 1933 (see p. 141f ). Dollfuss, the Christian Socialist Chancellor, established a dictatorship and dissolved the Social Democrat forces and the Austrian Nazi party, but in July 1934 he was murdered when the Nazis tried unsuccessfully to seize power. Dollfuss was succeeded by Kurt von Schuschnigg, who, under the protection of Mussolini, was able to continue the dictatorship for four more years, by which time Hitler was ready to strike again.

## CZECHOSLOVAKIA

Czechoslovakia, like Poland, was largely the creation of one man. Thomas Masaryk seized the chance offered by the First World War to win sympathy among the Allies for the cause of Czech independence and he took the practical step of organizing a Czech army in Russia in 1917 (see p. 116). He became the new nation's first President.

Czechoslovakia was not without problems. First there were divisions internally. The Slovaks, mainly peasants, resented the power which was wielded in the new state by the Czechs, who were more numerous and more experienced politically and who had a stronger tradition of national feeling. In addition there were other minorities, Germans, Hungarians, and Poles. Second, Czechoslovakia was weak strategically. It had no access to the sea and, even with the Bohemian mountains, it was not an easy country to defend. Nevertheless, the new country was self-sufficient in agriculture and it had great industrial power, based on its deposits of coal and iron.

Masaryk retired through ill-health in 1935 and he was succeeded by Edward Benes, who had worked closely with Masaryk in the foundation of the state. Between them they established and maintained stable and liberal government. Masaryk died in 1937 before his country was betrayed by the friends in whom he had placed his trust.

## THE BALKANS AND THE BALTIC STATES

The history of the reshaped Balkan countries and of the newly created Baltic States is one of the establishment of dictatorships following the failure of democratic government.

In Hungary the Communist leader Bela Kun overthrew the Government as early as 1919. He in turn was overthrown in the same year by Admiral Horthy, who set up a dictatorship which destroyed Communism and Liberalism alike. In Yugoslavia quarrels between the Serbs and the Croats led to the establishment of personal rule by King Alexander in 1929. When Alexander was assassinated in Marseilles in 1934, a Regency was established to rule in the name of his son Peter II. Rumania never satisfactorily established a democratic government and after King Carol came to the throne in 1930, absolute rule prevailed. In Bulgaria a dictatorship was established first by army officers in 1934 and then by King Boris in 1935. Albania fell under the control of Ahmed Zog who became President in 1925 and King in 1928. Greece tried to maintain a republican government between 1925 and 1935 but the return of King George II in that year heralded a dictatorship under General Metaxas.

The Baltic States, faced with economic difficulties and with the growth of Communism, lapsed into dictatorship too—Lithuania in 1926, Estonia in 1934 and Latvia in 1935. Finland alone managed to maintain stable democratic government.

Political inexperience, a heritage of bad government and complex problems, and the world economic crisis of the early 1930's combined to defeat the democracies created so hopefully after the First World War.

TURKEY

In 1919, after the defeat of Turkey, an army officer called Mustafa Kemal, went into the heart of Asia Minor and gathered round him a band of patriotic Turks. He drew up a policy statement called the 'National Pact' which accepted the loss of the Arab provinces of the old Empire but which asserted the independence and unity of Turkey proper. This conflicted with the Treaty of Sèvres (see pp. 95–96) and Allied troops were sent to Constantinople to dissolve the parliament which had accepted this document. Kemal then established his own government in Angora (Ankara) in rivalry to the Sultan and in defiance of the Allies. The Sultanate was abolished in 1921 and Kemal, who took on the name Kemal Atatürk, became President of the Turkish Republic. He expelled the Greeks from Asia Minor and secured a new peace treaty at Lausanne in 1923. Then, armed with dictatorial powers, he revolutionized the life of Turkey.

First he attacked Moslem practices and customs. Religious toleration was introduced and Islam was no longer the state religion. Education was taken out of the hands of the religious leaders and placed under the control of the state. The fez, the Moslem headdress, was declared illegal. Women were forbidden to wear veils and they were encouraged to take up careers. They were given the vote. Western handwriting replaced the Arabic. Furthermore, he carried out a great industrial and agricultural revolution designed to develop Turkey's resources, which had long been neglected. Coupled with this went the construction of new roads and railways.

In 1930 Kemal, who ruled his country like a father, tried to educate his people politically by creating an opposition party in parliament, but the experiment failed and he was forced to resort to dictatorship.

Not all of his social policy succeeded at once. The changes were too violent to be accepted happily by all the Turks. Nevertheless, his achievement in creating a modern state out of the crumbled ruins of the Ottoman Empire was quite remarkable. Kemal died in 1938, but his successor Inönü continued his work to the point where in 1950 he was able to resign in favour of the opposition party he had created.

SPAIN

In Spain, which had remained neutral in the First World War, the story is less happy. In theory, the Government was a constitutional monarchy, but in practice the poverty, backwardness and the political disunity of the country made this a rather meaningless term. In 1923 a right-wing dictatorship was established under General Primo de Rivera. He fell from power in 1930, having lost the support of the Army, and the constitution was restored, but unrest continued and in 1931 King Alphonso fled and a republic was proclaimed.

From the beginning the new republic faced determined opposition from right-wing elements and an organization called the Falange Española, largely made up of army officers and university students, was formed in 1932 to exploit the Government's difficulties. When the Left-wing parties won the elections of 1936 and formed a Popular Front Government, civil war broke out.

The rebellion was led by General Franco who crossed with an army from Spanish Morocco. Most of the army officers joined him, though the navy was divided. The Republican forces were backed by the Soviet Union and an International Brigade. Franco had the support of Hitler and Mussolini, although only Mussolini committed himself heavily. Britain and France remained severely neutral.

The war dragged on until March 1939, when Madrid fell to Franco, and by then the fighting had brought great misery to the Spanish people and had lain waste much of the land. The war has been variously regarded as a clash between democracy and totalitarianism, or between the rival extremes of Fascism and Communism. Certainly the conduct of the Communists, who appeared to be more anxious to consolidate their own position in the Republican forces than to defeat Franco, did much to disillusion many left-wing sympathizers who went to Spain. Perhaps the truth is that neither side was right or worthy, and that Spain neither lost nor gained good government through the war.

Franco established a military dictatorship on the Nazi and Fascist model and adopted the title *Caudillo* (leader), but he followed neither the lead nor the example of Hitler and Mussolini in foreign affairs. In the Second World War he remained neutral. With repression at home, but caution abroad, he was able to survive his patrons.

# 13  The U.S.S.R.

As a good Marxist, Lenin had never, until 1917, regarded Russia as a suitable country for a Communist revolution. The capitalists, or bourgeoisie, could not be overthrown by the proletariat, or industrial workers, in a country where a bourgeoisie and a proletariat scarcely existed. In 1917 Lenin changed his mind, but he still regarded the October Revolution as a mere prelude to the more important revolution in Western Europe. His first act was to call upon soldiers everywhere to stop fighting and to overthrow their governments.

Lenin had been able to seize power in Russia because he promised the people peace and food. He could not begin to provide food until he had concluded a peace, and this task assumed first priority. He had to have peace. The price he had to pay for it was of little importance to him. What did it matter how harsh the terms were if, in a few months at most,

Germany, and probably the whole of Europe, would be swept up in a Communist revolution after which Imperial treaties would be so much waste paper?

The terms the Germans imposed were harsh indeed. Trotsky, the Commissar of Foreign Affairs, who was in charge of the negotiations, was so appalled by the German demands that at one stage he walked out of the talks and declared that Russia would neither fight the Germans nor make peace with them ('No peace, no war'). But in the face of a further German advance, the Bolsheviks were forced to come to terms. By the Treaty of Brest-Litovsk of March 1918, Russia ceded Poland and her Baltic lands to Germany and Austria-Hungary, recognized the independence of the Ukraine and Finland, and agreed to pay an enormous indemnity. Only on Lenin's insistence were these harsh terms accepted.

## CIVIL WAR AND FOREIGN INTERVENTION

Having made peace with the Germans, the Bolsheviks found themselves faced with civil war at home, backed by armed intervention from foreign countries. The Russian counter-revolutionaries, or 'Whites', were not supporters of the Czarist régime. They were opponents of the Bolsheviks. Some were ex-officers who were embittered by the peace terms, but the main support came from the Social Revolutionaries (the peasant party), from the Mensheviks, and from those who were disillusioned by the early measures of the Bolshevik government. In Siberia a White government was set up under Admiral Kolchak, and the trans-Siberian railway was seized by a Czech army. These Czechs, who were ex-prisoners and deserters from the Austro-Hungarian army, had fought against the Germans under the Kerensky government. After peace had been concluded, the Bolsheviks first gave them permission to leave for the western front via Vladivostok to continue their fight for national independence, but then tried to disarm and intern them. The Czechs successfully resisted the Bolsheviks and formed a powerful nucleus for the White Army in Siberia. Another White Army under General Denikin was formed in the Caucasus. To add to their numbers came armies from the Allied countries.

While the war with the Central Powers continued, the Allies were anxious, if not to reopen the Eastern front, at least to stop Germany from receiving any aid from Russia. When the European war ended the Allies intervened on a greater scale, and for rather different reasons. They were out to destroy the Bolsheviks, who, besides negotiating a separate peace, had confiscated property, repudiated foreign debts, and preached world revolution. Landings were made at Archangel and Murmansk in the north, while Japanese and American troops entered Siberia through Vladivostok. In the summer and autumn of 1919 White attacks from Siberia, from the Caucasus, and from the Gulf of Finland, greatly threatened the Bolsheviks, but the newly-formed Red Army—led by Trotsky from a railway train— was able to deliver unified blows against its divided opponents. The armies of intervention were small; they lacked popular support at home, and they were half-hearted in their fighting. The Russian people suffered terribly from the appalling atrocities committed by both Reds and Whites,[1] but their sympathies turned increasingly to the Bolsheviks. The organized workers had been behind the Bolsheviks to a man since 1917, but they were in the minority. The peasant feared a return of the landlords, which was a likely result of a victory for the Whites, and although they were treated harshly by the Bolsheviks, who desperately needed their produce, they dreaded the landlords even more. But the main reason why the Bolsheviks were able to survive these perilous years and increase their slender hold on the country was the patriotism which intervention provoked. The Reds were Russians. The Whites were identified with foreigners. For many, Russians, even Red Russians, were preferable to foreigners.

## THE POLISH WAR 1920–21

The main threat from the Allied Forces was over by 1920, but then the Poles, helped by the French, launched an attack in the Ukraine. The eastern frontier of Poland had not been finally settled by the peacemakers at Versailles, and the Poles were anxious to draw it as far to the east as they could. France supported her in this endeavour in order to keep Bolshevism out of Eastern Europe. Lord Curzon, the British Foreign Secretary, suggested, in September 1920, that an armistice should be concluded on the basis of what was called the Curzon line (see Map p. 97). Neither side would agree to this, but the Poles, who had advanced as far as Kiev, were driven back by the Red Army to the gates of Warsaw. General Weygand was sent from France to reorganize the Polish armies, and they were able to throw the Russians back. Peace was concluded by the Treaty of Riga (1921) by which Poland acquired a large slice of the Ukraine and White Russia (see Map p. 97).

## WAR COMMUNISM AND THE NEW ECONOMIC POLICY

When Lenin seized power in Russia the whole means of production, distribution and administration had already broken down. Since he was faced immediately with civil war and foreign war, he was forced to adopt a sweeping programme of State control and direction long before he wanted to. This programme was known as 'War Communism'. In June 1918 large-scale industrial enterprises were nationalized, and this law was followed in December 1920 by the nationalization of all factories employing more than ten workers. To feed the hungry town-dwellers and the armies, the Government ordered that all surplus grain must be sold to the state at fixed prices. 'Committees of Poor Peasants' were set up to seize stocks from their richer neighbours, and foraging parties descended on the countryside from the

[1] *Dr Zhivago*, by the Soviet novelist and poet Boris Pasternak, gives a gripping picture of the terror and helplessness of this period.

towns. The peasants replied to these confiscations by producing only enough for their needs. When their stocks were discovered and seized, peasants were left to starve. Money became valueless, and trade was carried on exclusively by barter. Factories stopped working and, except for military needs, transport broke down almost entirely. Sickness and famine swept the country. When the fighting ended in 1921 Russia was in economic ruins, and groups of peasants, town dwellers, and demobilized soldiers, were roaming the country for food.

An unsuccessful mutiny by troops at Kronstadt in March 1921 convinced the Bolsheviks of the need to accept Lenin's plan to replace 'War Communism' by his 'New Economic Policy'. The basic aim of the N.E.P. was to secure the support of the peasantry so that food supplies could be ensured. Peasants no longer had to surrender their surplus crops. After paying a substantial tax in kind, they were free to sell their remaining products. Private trading, which had been abolished under 'War Communism', was restored, and some small factories were even restored to private ownership. Piece-work rates, preferential rations, and bonuses were introduced to provide incentives for workers. Many Communists were horrified by these retrograde proposals, but Lenin was a realist, and he had the authority to prevail over the party. It was clear by then that the revolution was not going to spread to other countries. It was equally clear that Communism could not be made to work in Russia as it was then. If the Bolsheviks were to remain in power they had to adopt a system which would work whether it conformed to their ideals or not.

An important part of the N.E.P. was the re-establishment of foreign trade, which had ceased altogether after the revolution. Once trade had resumed, diplomatic recognition of the Soviet government soon followed. Already in 1920 Russia had signed treaties with Finland, Estonia, Latvia, and Lithuania, recognizing their independence. Then in 1921, at the same time as she made peace with Poland, she concluded a commercial treaty with Britain. By 1924 the Soviet government was trading with, and had been recognized by, most European countries, but they were still very suspicious of her, and they were positively alarmed by the good relations established between Russia and Germany, which were expressed in the Treaty of Rapallo (1922). The chain of states created at Versailles between Germany and Russia had come to be regarded as a barrier against Bolshevism as well as a containing ring round Germany. Rapallo, by drawing together in friendship the two disgraced nations of Europe, seemed to threaten the protective chain.

In 1922 Lenin had a stroke, and he was thereafter fit to play little part in government. After two more strokes, he died in January 1924 at the age of fifty-three. He was a great leader, and his death was greatly mourned in Russia. Petrograd was renamed Leningrad in his honour. His body was embalmed, and millions have filed past his tomb in veneration. While facing reality sternly, he had given the Russian people the vision of a new and infinitely better life. He was their saviour.

STALIN

Joseph Stalin was the son of a Georgian cobbler. His real name was Joseph Djugashvili. 'Stalin', which is derived from the Russian word meaning 'steel', was one of the many names he found it convenient to use in the days when he was wanted by the police. His mother intended him for the priesthood, and he spent several unhappy years at the Orthodox Theological Seminary at Tiflis. In 1898 he entered upon his career as professional revolutionary. One of his duties was to obtain funds for the party by bank robberies. He was imprisoned five times, and four times he escaped. During the October revolution of 1917 he was in exile in Siberia, within the Arctic Circle.

Stalin was made a member of the Politbureau (the Political Bureau of the Communist Party) as soon as it was formed in 1917. His first post under Lenin's government was that of Commissar of Nationalities. Russia was an empire of which the Russians formed merely the dominant national group. Other groups, which together formed about half the population, such as the Ukranians and the Georgians, had been treated as subject peoples by the Czars. The Communists determined to halt this process of Russianization, and to accord the different nationalities their individual rights. Stalin's post was useful to him as a means of gaining universal recognition. The other post he held was that of Commissar of the Workers' and Peasants' Inspectorate, which was set up to eliminate inefficiency and corruption. This office gave Stalin the chance to wield considerable power. However, his real chance came in 1922, when he was made General Secretary of the Communist Party. This post was not regarded as being of any great importance at the time, but Lenin's ill-health left Russia without a firm ruler, and Stalin exploited the situation to the full. As Secretary, he knew better than any other one person what was going on in all departments of government. This knowledge gave him power. His advice became indispensable, his influence in appointments overriding.

The work of Stalin first appeared in the new Constitution of 1923. By this, Russia took the title of 'Union of Soviet Socialist Republics'. The new union was in fact a federation of four republics, Russia, Transcaucasia, the Ukraine, and Byelorussia.[1] Each republic was to have its own government and to maintain its own culture, language, and traditions. The sovereign power in the union was vested in the All Union Congress of Soviets.

THE STRUGGLE FOR LEADERSHIP

When Lenin died, effective power passed into the hands of a triumvirate consisting of Stalin, Zinoviev (president of the Comintern[2]) and Kamenev. Their object was to prevent Trotsky from becoming leader. In many ways

[1] These have subsequently been increased to fifteen.
[2] Communist International, the body to which all Communist parties are affiliated.

Trotsky was the natural successor to Lenin. Although he had been a Menshevik up till the revolution, he quickly became, next to Lenin, the leading party member. As Commissar for Foreign Affairs he had negotiated the Brest-Litovsk Treaty, and as Commissar for War he had organized and led the Red Army in the civil war and intervention. The struggle for leadership between Stalin and Trotsky which followed Lenin's death marked a clash of personality as well as of principle. Stalin was cautious, patient, silent, a master of committee work, at his best behind the scenes. He was of peasant stock, and uncouth. Trotsky was vivacious, impetuous, a fiery orator, an open individualist. Like many of the Bolshevik leaders, he was a middle-class intellectual. Stalin and Trotsky detested each other, and Trotsky lost no opportunity to insult Stalin.

They quarrelled on principle over the question of the future course of the revolution. Trotsky, having spent much of his life in exile in Europe, thought, as Lenin had, of the Russian revolution as a mere starting point for the important European, and then World, revolution. His policy was one of 'permanent revolution'. Communism, he preached, could only succeed in Russia if it were accompanied by international revolution. No effort should be spared to foster and organize this end. Stalin, on the other hand, who had scarcely left Russia, saw that the attempts to spread the revolution had failed. Communism, in fact, had failed even in Russia. What was needed was a period of consolidation so that a socialist system could be made to work in Russia. His policy was summed up in the slogan, 'Socialism in one country'. Stalin's was a national programme; Trotsky's international. Weary of want and suffering, and proud of their national achievement, the mass of the Russian people found Stalin's policy the more appealing.

From his position of power Stalin quickly won the support of the majority of the party and emerged supreme. In 1925 Trotsky was dismissed from the War Commissariat, and Kamenev and Zinoviev, who were sufficiently alarmed by Stalin's power and his policy to attack him at the Party Congress of that year, were removed from power. After the failure of the General Strike in England in 1926, Zinoviev was dismissed from the leadership of the Comintern, and in 1927 both he and Trotsky were expelled from the Party. In 1929 Trotsky was expelled from the Soviet Union, but in exile he carried on his struggle until in Mexico, in August 1940, a Russian smashed his head in with an axe while he was writing a biography of Stalin.

THE FIVE YEAR PLANS

By 1928, Stalin, although officially only the Secretary of the Communist Party, was the supreme ruler in Soviet Russia. His first task was to prove the correctness of his policy of consolidation by putting the country on a sound economic footing. The drive for greater industrialization was inaugurated by the first Five Year Plan, which began in 1928. The scope of this immense piece of State planning was staggering, particularly as it involved the creation of a whole new class of technicians and administrators, which Russia had so conspicuously lacked in the past. Foreign capital and technical help were forthcoming and indispensable. Although many mistakes were made, sabotage was quite widespread, and compulsion was ruthlessly employed, nevertheless production soared. New towns and factories sprang up. New areas were developed. At a pace that would have seemed reckless had the urgency not been so great, Soviet Russia laid the foundations of her industrial might.

The first Five Year Plan, like the succeeding ones, was declared completed in four years. The concentration was on goods to promote more production, e.g. machinery, power stations and tractors, rather than on consumer goods to raise the standard of living of the people. In the second Five Year Plan, compulsion was tempered by greater incentives. Good workers who exceeded their targets were rewarded with progressively rising pay. Honours Boards appeared in factories and decorations such as 'Hero of Socialist Labour' were awarded. Competition between factories was encouraged, and as these schemes developed the government was able to raise the targets. Communist internationalism had already been replaced by Soviet nationalism. Now co-operation was replaced by competition. Other early Communist ideas faded. School uniforms were reintroduced, and strict discipline—though not corporal punishment—was enforced by parents and teachers. Peter the Great was honoured as a national hero.

### COLLECTIVIZATION

Lenin's 'war communism' had been broken by the peasants. Shortage of grain was still the crucial danger in the early years of Stalin's rule, but Stalin was not defeated by it. He broke the peasants. He was not called the 'Man of Steel' for nothing.

Stalin badly needed grain, not only to feed the people, but also to sell abroad in exchange for machinery. He was determined that his power and the Soviet economy should not be at the mercy of the peasants. Accordingly he planned to destroy the *Kulaks*, the more prosperous peasants, who had machines and employed labour, and who were, therefore, the biggest producers of grain for export, and to substitute a system of collective farming. Collective farms were to be large units in which machinery could be employed efficiently. Peasants were to own and work them jointly under State direction. At first the Government tried to persuade the peasants into the collectives by such measures as increased taxation for private farmers, but the peasants fought bitterly, as they had before, against state control.

In the winter of 1928-9, the war between the Government and the peasants was fought in earnest. Thousands of peasants were killed, thousands were sent to forced labour in Siberia, and thousands were left to starve. The utmost ruthlessness was employed. The *Kulaks* were wiped out, and their grain confiscated. For a while this enabled grain exports to be increased, but in 1932, with the breakdown of farming, widespread famine reappeared, and grain had to be imported. Worse still, the peasants had slaughtered a vast number of animals, for they were determined that if they must enter a collective farm they should do so empty-handed. The effects of this loss of livestock were felt for more than twenty years afterwards.

Faced with the complete ruin of agriculture, Stalin called off forcible collectivization in March 1930, but life was made progressively more difficult for the individual farmer, and easier for the collective farmer. In the next few years most of the best arable land in Russia was collectivized. For a few years the fate of the Soviet Union had hung in the balance. At a terrible cost Stalin had beaten the peasants. They had cracked; he had remained unmoved. But in November 1932 his wife committed suicide.

## THE PURGES

Although Stalin had established himself in power, the Old Bolsheviks (those revolutionaries who had been active before 1917 and who had worked alongside Lenin in the early days) were still at large. Many of these resented Stalin's abandonment of Communist ideas. Many feared his power. While they remained alive, Stalin could not feel secure. In 1934 he began to get rid of them.

The first move was occasioned by the assassination in December 1934 of one of Stalin's right-hand men, Kirov, who had replaced Zinoviev as party boss in Leningrad. The assassin was a Communist, and Stalin seized the chance to execute over a hundred Bolsheviks who were already in prison on various charges of conspiracy or espionage. This was followed in the next few years by a series of sensational trials in Moscow which resulted in the extinction of most of the Old Bolsheviks.

In 1936 Kamenev and Zinoviev, with fourteen others, were tried and executed. The trial of distinguished Army Officers and more former Bolshevik leaders followed in 1937 and 1938. The pattern of all these trials was the same. The accused were charged chiefly with being in league with Trotsky, and with having plotted to assassinate Stalin, but other charges were made, including those of sabotage and espionage. The chief evidence produced was the confessions of the prisoners, who publicly blackened their own names and freely testified against each other. The sentence was usually death. Subsequent trials in Communist countries have adhered to this pattern. The procedure is one which has always astonished people in non-Communist countries. How is it that prominent men and ex-heroes can be brought to confess to the most outrageous crimes against the State, and go quietly to their deaths? This phenomenon has been attributed variously to torture, drugs, elaborate and persistent interrogation (which is now termed brain-washing), even to impersonation.

Whatever may be true of later trials, the Moscow Trials were probably

**The Nazi Revolution.** The two courses open to Hitler in 1934 are clearly portrayed in this picture. In the centre is the ex-Crown Prince, symbol of Imperial Germany; on his right is Röhm, leader of the Nazi S.A. Hitler decided to turn his back on social revolution. A few days after this picture was taken, Röhm and his associates were murdered (see p. 143).

**Munich.** Chamberlain and Mussolini in earnest conversation at the meeting which led to the destruction of Czechoslovakia.

**Hitler.** This still from a newsreel was used by the Allies for propaganda purposes during the war. It was claimed that it showed Hitler dancing for joy on receiving the news that Paris had fallen in 1940. In fact, as the complete film shows, he was merely walking towards the group on the left.

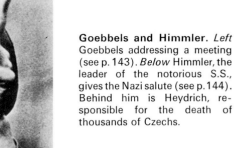

**Goebbels and Himmler.** *Left* Goebbels addressing a meeting (see p. 143). *Below* Himmler, the leader of the notorious S.S., gives the Nazi salute (see p.144). Behind him is Heydrich, responsible for the death of thousands of Czechs.

conducted as straightforwardly behind the scenes as they undoubtedly were in public. What brought these Old Bolsheviks to behave in the way they did was probably their own attitude of mind. For them the Party was everything. Most of them probably had wished to get rid of Stalin. Some of the generals may have thought in terms of a military coup with the support of their opposite numbers in Germany. In the Rapallo period of friendship between Germany and Russia from 1922 to 1930, the Red Army had very close links with the German Army. These Old Bolsheviks opposed Stalin because they thought he was endangering the future of the Party. When they were arrested, it would not have been very difficult to persuade them that they could best serve the Party by confessing their mistakes, and that the Party's unity could be reinforced if they obliterated any sympathy that might be felt for them, any lingering memories of their past services, by confessing to terrible crimes which in fact they had not committed.[1]

The trials of the leaders were the public part of a widespread purge of government and party officials, and of army officers, who were suspected of disloyalty. Thousands were shot. The break with the past was now complete. The country was now run by Stalin's creatures.

## THE STALIN CONSTITUTION OF 1936

In 1936 Stalin introduced a new Constitution. The Supreme Soviet was reorganized into two Houses of equal authority: one, the Soviet of the Union, with representatives elected on a population basis over the whole country; the other, the Soviet of Nationalities, with representatives of the various nationalities of the Union. These two Houses are comparable (in what they represent) with the House of Representatives and the Senate of the United States. Candidates could be nominated by any association, e.g. the Communist Party, trade unions, co-operatives. All citizens over the age of eighteen could vote. Voting was to be by direct and secret ballot. The only flaws in this admirably democratic procedure were that citizens had only one candidate to vote for in each constituency, and that each candidate, whether a Party member or not, was a supporter of the régime.

The Constitution, with its guarantees of the liberty of the individual, is hardly worth studying in detail, since it would give a highly misleading idea of how the Soviet Union was governed under Stalin. The real power rested with the Party, and the real power in the Party, in spite of the existence of an elaborate chain of elected bodies, rested with the Central Committee and the Politburo.[2] As Secretary of the Party, Stalin was supreme. Not until 1941 did he become Premier. Hardly any one remembers the names of the Presidents or of the other Premiers.[3]

[1] Arthur Koestler, in his novel *Darkness at Noon*, throws interesting light on this aspect of the Moscow Trials.

[2] Just before Stalin's death in 1953 its name was changed to the Presidium.

[3] The correct titles for these offices are: (a) Chairman of the Presidium of the Supreme Soviet (President and official Head of State), (b) Chairman of the Council of Ministers (Premier).

It would be foolish to end this account of the home affairs of the Soviet Union without stating quite clearly that the mass of the Russian people enjoyed under Soviet rule benefits and opportunities which were undreamed of in Czarist days. Social services, education, recreational facilities, were available for all citizens. For many years after the Revolution conditions were terrible in Russia, and even when economic recovery came, the material comforts of the individual were placed after the needs of the State. But even in the worst hours, things were better than they had been for most people. There was hope of a bright future—not in their time, perhaps, but in their children's or their grandchildren's time. This buoyantly optimistic outlook runs through the period covered by this chapter. It was totally absent under the Czars. Then the people hoped for a better time in the world to come. The Soviet régime under Lenin and Stalin was a dictatorship. Russia was a police-state. It had been both these things under the Czars, but whereas the Communists gave hope to the people in return for their liberty, the Czars gave nothing.

It would be wrong, of course, to assume that had the Bolsheviks not seized power, Russia would not have made great advances in the 20th century. Before 1914 Russia was already making rapid industrial progress, and a modest start had been made towards representative government. These movements might well have continued and grown, though it would have been very difficult, even with widespread goodwill, to introduce rapidly into Russia a democracy on the western pattern, and to make it work. History does not concern itself with what might have happened. Nor does the U.S.S.R. The Russian people now have new opportunities. Their country is a richer, mightier, land. It would be difficult to persuade them that the Communists were not responsible for the transformation.

## FOREIGN POLICY

### ISOLATION

The success of Stalin's policy of 'Socialism in one country' depended on Russia's becoming a strong Power again. The aim of the Five Year Plans was to build up Russia's defensive strength, but this could not be achieved overnight, and Stalin could not remain unconcerned by events in foreign countries in the 1930's.

In 1931, Russia's eastern neighbour, Japan, invaded Manchuria, and proceeded in the following years to extend her power on the Chinese mainland. To the west, Russia was threatened by Germany after the accession of Hitler in 1933. Hitler, sworn enemy of Communism, made no secret of his aim to give the German people living-space in the east. Poland, which had been largely formed from ex-Russian land, remained hostile and, in fact, busily cultivated good relations with Hitler. The U.S.S.R.'s admission to the League of Nations in 1934 (eight years after Germany had become a Permanent Member of the Council) was a sign that Stalin wanted friends abroad, but he found them difficult to come by.

Although the U.S.S.R. had been recognized by most European countries by 1924,[1] and although trade and diplomatic relations had been resumed, there was no close, friendly, contact between Russia and foreign countries throughout the whole period from the 1917 revolution until Hitler's invasion of Russia in 1941, except, perhaps, for the brief honeymoon with Germany for a few years after 1922. Neither Britain nor France, the two countries which dominated the League, regarded Russia as respectable, nor, indeed, of very great importance once the threat of the spread of international Communism had passed. Russia's isolation was partly due to her internal problems. She could not play a vigorous part in foreign affairs until her government and her economy were firmly established. But her isolation was chiefly due to the suspicion and hostility of the other Powers. Only the growing fear of Germany led Britain and France to speak to Russia at all.

## THE THREAT FROM GERMANY

In 1935 Britain, France and Italy formed the Stresa Front (see p. 148), but Russia was not invited to join them, though her interest was no less than theirs. Mussolini, who was as hostile to Communism as Hitler, would not ally himself with Stalin, and Britain and France, with justice at that time, regarded Italy as a more formidable ally than Russia.

Nevertheless, France concluded a pact of mutual assistance with Russia to replace the non-aggression pact which the two countries had signed three years earlier, in 1932. It was a long-standing French policy to have an ally to the east of Germany. After 1919 that ally had been Poland, but after Hitler's treaty with Poland in 1933, the French sought extra security. Russia also concluded in 1935 a similar pact of mutual assistance with Czechoslovakia.

## THE POPULAR FRONTS

In 1935, at the Congress of the Third Communist International, a new policy was approved of socialist co-operation. This was known as the Popular Front. The idea was that the spread of Nazism and Fascism threatened all liberal and left-wing forces everywhere, from moderate reformers, Socialists and trade-unionists, to extreme Communists. Therefore, despite their individual differences, they should unite to defeat those forces which would destroy them all. In France in 1936, the Radicals, Socialists, and Communists, together with the leading trade unions, gave their support to this policy, and won a large majority at the elections. A Popular Front government was formed under Léon Blum, but the Communists refused to join it, and in fact continued to stir up industrial unrest. The government fell within two years. Another Popular Front coalition won the elections in Spain in 1936 and it was against this government that

[1] The United States did not grant recognition until 1933.

General Franco led a military revolt, supported by Italy and Germany in July of that year.

Faced with the rising success of anti-democratic forces, many liberal and left-wing people found the idea of a Popular Front attractive. But suspicion of Communists was strong amongst trade-unionists and moderate Socialists, and the behaviour of the Communists in France and Spain confirmed their suspicions. The British Labour Party rejected the idea of an alliance. The Communists never abandoned their aim of dominating the Left, and there seemed little point in submitting to one dictatorship in order to ward off the threat from another.

### PREPARATIONS FOR WAR

In November 1936 Germany and Japan signed an Anti-Comintern Pact. A year later Italy joined them. In 1937 Japan launched her attack on China; in 1938 Hitler absorbed Austria. The enemies of the Soviet Union were on the march. In 1938 Hitler sought to dismember Czechoslovakia. Russia renewed her pledges to that country, but the Czechs, abandoned by France and Britain, declined Russia's help.

When, in March 1939, Hitler completed the dismemberment of Czechoslovakia, and Chamberlain saw that he had not bought 'peace in our time' at the Munich talks, from which Russia had been excluded, Britain prepared to check the eastward expansion of Germany. In March and April, Britain gave guarantees for the independence of Poland, Greece, and Rumania. No guarantee for Poland or Rumania could be effective without Russian support. The British government, therefore, reluctantly entered into negotiations with Russia. Talks dragged on from May to August. There were endless difficulties, among them the refusal of the Poles to have Russians on their soil, even to rescue them from Hitler.

In August the situation was transformed. Russia concluded a non-aggression pact with Germany, by which both countries secretly agreed to partition Poland. It was a cold-blooded treaty. Hitler was given security from interference in the east when he attacked Poland. Britain and France would declare war, but there seemed a good chance that they would agree to peace once Poland, whom they were powerless to help, had fallen. Stalin, on the other hand, was assured of a large slice of territory which would have to be fought over when Hitler eventually attacked Russia. Furthermore, Russia was secure from having to fight a war against Hitler alone. By helping Hitler to attack Poland, Stalin made sure that Britain and France would fight Hitler first. Russia had everything to gain from both sides exhausting themselves. Stalin bought valuable time to complete his preparations to defend his country.

The agreement was entered into cynically, and neither side had any illusions about the other. France, which was in alliance with Russia and Poland, had perhaps some grounds for feeling aggrieved. Britain had none. Stalin had nothing to thank either country for.

In September Hitler invaded Poland, and Britain and France declared war. The Russians marched in from the east, and the country was divided roughly along the Curzon line. In September and October Russia demanded and secured naval bases in the Baltic States of Estonia, Latvia, and Lithuania, and by June 1940 the three states were incorporated into the Soviet Union. In November 1939 Russia attacked Finland. The Finns resisted fiercely, but in March 1940 peace was concluded, and the frontier was pushed back to give greater protection to Leningrad.

While Hitler was occupied in the west, Stalin made these strategic moves in preparation for the attack which was bound to come. Hitler was not occupied for long. By March 1941 he was master of Europe. Only Britain and her Commonwealth stood against him. He was now ready to fulfil his life's ambition in the east. On June 22nd, 1941, he struck. The Great Patriotic War, as it is called in Russia, began. The success of 'Socialism in one country' was put to the test.

# 14   Italy, 1870-1940

The movement for Italian unification excited the imaginations of the 19th-century liberals everywhere. It was seen as the spiritual resurgence of a people subdued for generations beneath the yoke of tyrants and foreign princes. The very name given to the movement—the *Risorgimento* (the rebirth)—was rich in romantic associations. Certainly the phrases of Mazzini, founder of the 'Young Italy' movement, and the exploits of Garibaldi, who invaded Sicily with a thousand volunteers and drove the Bourbon forces from the island, were stirring enough. 1870 brought the climax of the movement. Rome, which since the 1848 revolutions had been occupied by French troops, was left undefended when the French returned home to face the Prussians. The city then became the capital of the Kingdom of Italy.

The Risorgimento had ended and so had the period when Italian patriots and their admirers abroad could ignore the realities of the unified state which had been brought into being. From the first, the Italian patriotic movement had never enjoyed wide popular support amongst Italians themselves. It was a movement of a small group of middle-class liberal intellectuals and it owed its success chiefly to the aid it received from France, Prussia and Britain. In consequence the Italian people did not regard their new state fondly as their creation. For them it was a change of government and it was to be judged solely on how well it governed. The immediate problems of government sprang from the fact that Italy was united in name only. The country was deeply divided within itself.

First there were the divisions between the north and south. Italy was a poor country, chiefly agricultural, with a large backward and illiterate peasantry which could barely be supported by the country's resources. The north, however, had by far the greater share of what raw materials and industry there were, and it also had the best agricultural land. The mountainous south was desperately primitive and poverty-stricken, bled by absentee landlords, and riddled with brigandage and secret societies. Many people in the south feared, with justice, that the union would bring about a rise in their taxes, while the north enjoyed the benefits.

Then there was the problem of the Church. The Papacy, which had been robbed of all its lands, refused to recognize the Kingdom of Italy. As a gesture of goodwill, the Italian Government passed in 1871 an act called the Law of Guarantees by which the Pope's status was recognized, his palaces exempted from taxation, and an annual income allotted to him by the State. Pope Pius IX, however, refused to accept the income, and ordered Roman Catholics not to participate in the political life of the nation or to vote in the national elections. Not until 1905, after the accession of Pius X, and in the face of growing Socialism, did the Church allow Catholics to vote, although in practice many had done so. Even then, the bitter rivalry between Church and State continued to be a disturbing factor in Italian life.

Finally, there was the problem of political inexperience. Although Piedmont in the north had had experience of working a parliamentary form of government, no other part of the country had. The vote in 1870 was given to only some 2 per cent of the population, but even so numerous party groups arose and stable government was achieved only by manipulating the elections and by bribing members of parliament either directly or with office, honours and favours for their constituents. Politics became not matter of principles but of the maintenance of personal power.

Three men dominated Italian political life in the period before the First World War: Depretis from 1876 to 1887, Crispi from 1887 to 1896 and Giolitti from 1903 to 1915. Depretis and Giolitti were experts in parliamentary corruption. Crispi sought to restore national life to an honourable level and to maintain himself in power by sheer leadership. But his ambition for Italy as a great power exceeded the country's resources and the Italian failure in Abyssinia brought his downfall.

## COLONIES

Italy, frustrated in her first colonial ambition by the French occupation of Tunis in 1881, turned her eyes to East Africa and by 1885 had established a colony in Eritrea. Further expansion in the next few years under the guidance of Crispi brought about the creation of the new colony of Italian Somaliland. In 1889 the African kingdom of Abyssinia concluded a treaty with Italy, but a dispute between the two countries resulted in the Abyssinians inflicting a crushing defeat on the Italians at Adowa in 1896.

The Italians retained Eritrea and Somaliland, but acknowledged Abyssinian independence.

Not until 1911 did Italy renew her colonial activity. By then France was in control of Morocco, Algeria and Tunis; Britain occupied Egypt. Tripoli, with Cyrenaica, was the only stretch of the North African coastline left in the Turkish Empire. Italy took advantage of a favourable diplomatic situation (see p. 62) to go to war with Turkey. In 1912 Tripoli and Cyrenaica were formed into the Italian colony of Libya, and Italy also acquired Rhodes and the Dodecanese.

## SOCIALISM

Socialism arose in Italy chiefly because of the widespread poverty in the country, but its growth as a movement was aided by the disgust men felt for their existing form of government. In 1894 Crispi, like Bismarck in Germany, sought to crush Socialism by repression. He banned Socialist organizations and newspapers. But Socialists increased their representation in parliament and they gained the alliance of other political groups. After the failure of a general strike in 1904, Giolitti tried to win the support of moderate Socialists. Moderate reforms in the way of factory legislation and national insurance were introduced, and in 1912 a new electoral law greatly widened the suffrage. Italy undoubtedly made economic progress in the Giolitti era, but the basic causes of unrest were not removed. Giolitti's policy was never much more than a part of his elaborate machinery for maintaining himself in office.

## FOREIGN AFFAIRS

The part played by Italy in international affairs in this period is dealt with in other chapters. All that need be noted here is that the new Italian Kingdom was never treated by the other Powers as their equal. Bismarck aptly summarized the situation when he remarked: 'Italy has such poor teeth and such a large appetite.' Italy joined in the Triple Alliance with Germany and Austria-Hungary in 1882, but the alliance was never very convincing. Austria was the traditional enemy of the Italians and Italy regarded her unification as incomplete while Austria retained the South Tyrol and Istria—*Italia Irredenta* (unredeemed Italy). When war broke out in 1914, Italy, weak and with no interest in fighting alongside Austria-Hungary, declined to join the Central Powers. When Italy did enter the war, in 1915, it was on the side of the Allies and she did so with the promise that *Italia Irredenta* would be hers on the defeat of Austria-Hungary. But as well as material gains, the war also offered Italy—in the eyes of some Italians—the chance to achieve greatness and recognition at last.

## ITALY AFTER THE FIRST WORLD WAR

Italy emerged from the war victorious but humiliated. Her allies were contemptuous of her fighting record and they treated her with scant respect at the Peace Conference. Although she was given *Italia Irredenta*, she failed to get Fiume and she was not granted a mandate over any of the former German colonies. The war had strained the slender resources of Italy to breaking point, and the people felt that they had been cheated of a just reward for their sacrifices. For over forty years the Italian people had suffered corrupt government, poverty, heavy taxation, budget deficiencies, social unrest, military defeats, the contempt of other Powers. Now they had suffered defeat at the conference table. Their wrath turned against their system of government.

In 1919 lawlessness broke out in the south and there were strikes in the north. Gabriele D'Annunzio, the nationalist poet who for years had been flamboyantly urging Italians to re-enact the glories of their past, marched on Fiume with a band of volunteers and seized the city. Giolitti, who returned to office as Premier in 1920, had the task of driving D'Annunzio out, and Fiume became a Free City. In 1920 workers' soviets were set up in a large number of factories. Frequent clashes occurred between Socialist and Communist workers and the Fascists, the *Fascio di combattimento* who had been formed by Mussolini in 1919, and who secured the backing of the middle classes and the industrialists who feared Communist revolution, of the nationalists who were disgusted with the weakness of their parliamentary government, and of thugs who donned the black shirt merely to revel in lawlessness for its own sake. In the elections of 1921 the Fascists won parliamentary representation for the first time—35 out of the 535 seats. The divisions, however, among the other parties made stable government impossible. Giolitti resigned, and, as disorder grew, the Fascists by violence and intimidation increased their hold on the country. In October 1922 the Fascists felt strong enough to seize power. Mussolini himself went to Milan while his followers organized the famous 'March on Rome'. The King, Victor Emanuel III, refused to sign a decree drawn up by the Prime Minister proclaiming martial law, and Mussolini arrived in Rome by train (as indeed many of the other 'marchers' did) and was asked by the King to form a government.

## MUSSOLINI

Benito Mussolini was born in 1883, the son of a village blacksmith who was also an ardent Socialist. He was by nature a revolutionary and he at first found an outlet for his instincts in Socialism. He ran away to Switzerland in 1902 to escape military service, but later returned to do it and became by turns a teacher, a journalist and an agitator, and was frequently imprisoned for lawlessness. He became the editor of the Socialist paper *Avanti!* but was expelled from the party in 1914 because he advocated Italy's entry into the war. He then ran his own paper *Il Popolo d'Italia*, which was financed, it is believed, by French funds, and played an effective part in mustering popular support for war. He fought in the war and was wounded.

In 1919, when he founded the Fascist party, he still regarded himself as a Socialist and he hoped to be the Lenin of Italy. The change in his thinking came in 1921 when he saw that his only way to power was with conservative support. Here was his chance. He would become the saviour of Italy from Bolshevism.

## THE ESTABLISHMENT OF FASCIST RULE

When he became Prime Minister, Mussolini had nothing like a majority of his own party in parliament. Nevertheless he demanded 'full powers' and was granted them by an overwhelming majority. He next proceeded to crush opposition in the country by violence and intimidation. One of the favourite Fascist techniques was to make opponents swallow a pint or two of castor oil. During the next three years all opposition organizations were crushed and the electoral laws were arranged to ensure a Fascist majority. In 1925 Mussolini, having cleared the ground, embarked upon the creation of the Fascist state. Newspapers were censored and editors who did not support the régime were replaced by Fascists. Local elections were abolished and towns were run by government officials. Political crimes were to be tried by special courts from which there was no appeal. The government was given the power to issue orders-in-council which enabled it to by-pass even the rigged parliament. Schools and universities were brought under Fascist control. Teachers were put into uniform and text-books had to follow the party line. Fascist youth organizations were established. The framework of the constitution, King, Prime Minister, Cabinet and Parliament, was retained, but the real executive body was now the Fascist Grand Council. Mussolini remained Prime Minister, but it was as a member of the Fascist Grand Council that *Il Duce* (the leader), as he insisted on being called, wielded his power. The similarity in organization between the Fascist state and its arch-enemy the Communist state in Russia is worth noting.

## THE CORPORATE STATE

The economic life of the country was brought under Fascist control by the formation of unions for the employers and for workers. These were grouped into National Confederations and put under the direction of a Minister of Corporations. Strikes and lock-outs were forbidden and disputes were settled by compulsory arbitration. The structure was evolved over several years and was not completed until 1934, but already in 1928 the unions had been handed the responsibility of submitting names of candidates for parliamentary elections to the Fascist Grand Council which then drew up the final single list for the electors to approve. The final stage in the creation of the Corporate State came in 1939 when the Chamber of Deputies, the lower house of parliament, was abolished and replaced by a Chamber of Fasces and Corporations, made up of party leaders and representatives from the various corporations. Like the one it replaced, the new Chamber had no power.

## FASCISM IN ACTION

1. *Economic life.* The basic economic problems of Italy were not solved by Mussolini's seizure of power nor by his propaganda machine, which presented him as a miracle-man. Indeed, some of the safety-valves which had operated before the First World War—mass emigration to America and elsewhere and the regular despatch by emigrants of allowances to their relatives at home—had gone. Moreover, the world slump in trade in the 1930's added a new problem. Mussolini aimed to make Italy self-supporting and directed his vast control of the economic life of the nation to that purpose. A 'Battle of Wheat' was launched and farmers encouraged to increase productivity. New industry was promoted and heavily protected by the State. Mussolini sought, unsuccessfully, to deal with the problem of unemployment by a huge public works programme. New roads were constructed, including great motor-ways called *autostrada*; hydro-electric schemes were developed (to save importing coal) and the railways electrified. Impressive blocks of flats, railway stations and stadiums were built. Perhaps Mussolini's best-known achievements in this field were that he drained the Pontaine Marshes and that he made the trains run on time. Both these achievements were special items of window-dressing designed to impress tourists and to hide the barrenness of Fascist economic ideas. It should also be remembered that only the main line trains ran on time and that this phenomenon was achieved in free countries no later. Mussolini failed to solve Italy's problems. He had no answer to the shortage of raw materials, and even Fascist ruthlessness did not root out inefficiency. Indeed, nowhere was inefficiency greater than in the Fascist machine. When war came in 1940, Italian industry was hopelessly unprepared to meet the demands made upon it.

2. *The Concordat with Rome 1929.* By the Concordat of 1929, the Pope recognized the Kingdom of Italy, while Mussolini recognized the Pope as head of the Vatican State and guaranteed the position of the Roman Catholic faith as the sole religion of Italy. Mussolini thus healed the breach between Church and State which had existed since the foundation of the Kingdom. The Pope, for his part, had given the Fascist régime a cloak of respectability.

3. *Foreign Affairs.* Mussolini sought to make Italy a great Power. As we have already seen, he failed to conjure up industrial riches on which military power could be based, but he nevertheless pursued a vigorous foreign policy throughout his rule. To give him credit, he managed for years to fool

the rest of Europe into believing that he was strong. Even Hitler was taken in. His downfall came partly because he fooled himself; but it would have come in any case. He remained in power, surrounded by hero-worshipping incompetents, only while bluster was enough. When great deeds were required he was unable to perform them.

Most of Mussolini's foreign policy is dealt with in other chapters. Here it is only necessary to summarize the main incidents. In 1923 he provoked the Corfu Incident (see p. 105); in 1924 he acquired Fiume by treaty with Yugoslavia; in 1926 he began a policy of infiltration into Albania by making loans, receiving oil concessions and sending military advisers to organize the Albanian Army. This process culminated in 1939 in Italy's invasion and conquest of Albania. In 1935 Mussolini attacked Abyssinia (see p. 106) and avenged Adowa with the use of poison gas and aircraft against almost unarmed Africans. From 1936 to 1939 he gave considerable support to Franco in Spain (see p. 115). In 1936 he formed the Rome-Berlin Axis with Hitler (see p. 149) and in 1940, thinking the war was nearly over, he launched his spectacularly unsuccessful attack against France and Britain. At last, he was faced with the terrible realities of his country's weakness and of the incompetence of his rule. His armies were defeated by the Greeks when he attacked them in 1940, by the British in North and East Africa, and finally his country was overrun and fought over by friend and foe alike. He could not even capture Malta, isolated in the middle of what he was pleased to call *Mare Nostrum*.

Fascism in Italy was almost wholly concerned with appearances. Violent speeches were made, wild demonstrations organized and lavish uniforms created. Handshaking was forbidden as un-fascist. But behind this trivial façade there was nothing—except violence. Fascism did not go down to the roots of the Italian people as Nazism did in Germany. Nor did it perpetrate mass atrocities like those which were committed by the Nazis. Basically, Mussolini was a politician of the old Italian type—an opportunist intent on maintaining himself in power by any makeshift means. His last dramatic appearance—dead, and strung up by his heels in a square in Milan—contrasted sadly with the high hopes that had been entertained for Italy in 1870.

# 15   The Weimar Republic

## THE NOVEMBER REVOLUTION 1918

In November 1918 revolution broke out in Germany. The country was in a state of military and economic collapse. The armies were incapable of further effective resistance, and their capitulation could be only a matter of time; internally the means of communication and distribution had broken down; the people were starving. Moreover, they were bitterly disillusioned. A few months earlier, when Ludendorff had launched his spring offensive, they had believed that victory was within their grasp. Now came defeat, and the Germans were utterly unprepared for it psychologically. The November revolutionaries had one common aim—to be rid of the war and the Kaiser who had led them into it. Their weakness lay in the fact that this negative aim was all they had in common.

The three centres of the revolution were Kiel, Munich and Berlin. Sailors at the naval bases of Wilhelmshaven and Kiel mutinied and the movement spread in the northern coastal area. Workers' and Soldiers' Councils (soviets) were set up and these assumed the task of local government. In Munich, Kurt Eisner, the Jewish leader of the Independent Socialists, was proclaimed head of the new Bavarian Republic, while in Berlin, on November 9th, the Chancellor, Prince Max of Baden, announced that the Kaiser and the Crown Prince would abdicate.[1] The Chancellor then handed over his office to Ebert, leader of the Social Democrats, who became head of the provisional government, which immediately faced a challenge to its authority.

## THE SPARTACIST RISING

At the end of the war there were three groups in the German socialist parties, the Social Democrats, the Independent Socialists, and the Spartacists. The Social Democrats wanted a parliamentary democracy. Their socialism was moderated by a strong regard for Germany's national heritage and for this reason they had supported the war, which had been condemned as an imperialist adventure by other socialists all over Europe. Above all, they hated violent revolution, and they had no wish to see German socialists behave like Russian Bolsheviks. The Independent Socialists, who deplored German militarism, had opposed the war. They favoured democratic institutions, but, since the German people lacked the experience to work them properly, they felt that it would be better to delay their full introduction until the people were more ready to use them. Dictatorship, they felt, might be necessary for a time, but it should be a dictatorship based on the will of the majority of the people. The Spartacists, who in December 1918 formed themselves into the German Communist Party, had no such scruples. For them the Russian Bolshevik revolution was a model. If the Germans were not ready to set up a socialist state, then it should be imposed on them forcibly and violently by the minority that advocated it.

The Spartacists, led by Karl Liebknecht and Rosa Luxemburg, planned to undermine the new government by all possible means. They provoked strikes, street fighting and armed insurrections. Although the Spartacists represented but a fraction of the German working population, they could count on some support from the Independent Socialists, and also from

[1] The Kaiser actually abdicated on November 28th after he had fled to Holland. Most of the princes who ruled the states abdicated, too.

many others who, for various reasons, were disgruntled. The three Independent Socialist ministers did in fact resign in December 1918 rather than be associated with the Government's efforts to keep order. Their resignation removed from the Government the only element which stood for a complete break with Imperial Germany. The Social Democrats had now no alternative but to call on the Army for help. After several days' bitter fighting, the revolt in Berlin was crushed on January 13th, 1919. Liebknecht and Rosa Luxemburg were murdered. The Social Democrats had won, but at the cost of resurrecting the Army as a dominant political factor in Germany.

## CIVIL WAR IN BAVARIA

In Bavaria, the elections at the beginning of 1919 brought about the decisive defeat of Eisner, and on February 21st he was assassinated. In the confusion that followed, civil war broke out, and between April 30th and May 8th Munich was the scene of indiscriminate brutality on the part of the extreme socialists and their opponents. Again the Social Democrats were forced to lean on the Army to restore order. It is scarcely surprising that increasing numbers of people turned from the apparently weak republicans of the Government to the nationalist groups of the Right which had close links with the Army. Anti-semitic feelings grew, too, partly because of the large numbers of Jews among the Spartacists and the Independent Socialists. Munich, where Hitler's Nazi party was later to be formed, was already becoming a centre of opposition to the new Republic even before its constitution had come into operation.

## THE CONSTITUTION

The National Assembly which was to draw up a constitution for Germany met at Weimar in February 1919. On paper, the delegates created the most perfect democracy of modern times. At the head of the Republic was a President who was to be elected by popular vote every seven years. His position was similar to that of the French President, or the British Sovereign. For instance, it was his duty to choose the Chancellor (or Prime Minister), but he had to choose someone who could command a majority for himself and his Cabinet in the Reichstag. One important power the President had was the right to suspend constitutional privileges and rule by decree, when he considered a crisis existed. A majority demand in the Reichstag could restore those privileges, but when rule by decree came to be used widely in the closing years of the Republic, the crises were produced precisely because it was impossible to get a majority decision.

The parliament of the Republic consisted of two houses, the Reichsrat and the Reichstag. The Reichsrat was made up of representatives of the *Länder* (territories), which had replaced the old states. Like the British House of Lords, it could only delay legislation. The real power lay in the

Reichstag, to which representatives were elected by secret ballot and universal suffrage, on a system of proportional representation. Although the States, under another name, had survived from the Empire, their power was greatly diminished, and the effect of the constitution was to give Germany a more centralized government than she had ever had before. Prussian influence remained strong, however, since over half the population of Germany lived in Prussia.

Written into the constitution were wide guarantees for the fundamental rights of citizens, including equality before the law, personal liberty, freedom of movement, of expression, of association, and of belief, and the right of collective bargaining. For the first time in their history, Germans were offered liberal government.

## THE KAPP PUTSCH 1920

The Weimar Constitution had enemies to the Left and to the Right. The Communist rising of 1919, on the Left, had been crushed, as we have seen, with the help of the Right. It was from the Right that the next blow came. Because the Germans had never considered the possibility of defeat in the war, they were quite unprepared for its consequences. They were horrified by the peace settlement, and the legend soon grew that the German army had not been defeated, but had been stabbed in the back by revolution at home, though an alternative, and equally attractive, explanation offered for the Allied victory was that the Germans had been tricked into laying down their arms by the offer of a peace based on the Fourteen Points. The Fourteen Points were loosely interpreted in Germany as an offer of peace leaving German possessions and strength intact. The Germans badly needed a scapegoat to blame for all their troubles and they found one in the Jews. The Jews were held responsible for the loss of the war, for the Communist risings, for disorder, and for inflation. Neither anti-semitism nor belief in the invincibility of the German army were new ideas in Germany, but they assumed greater importance as the Germans faced, or rather failed to face, their post-war problems. The Nazi Party (the National Socialists), which was formed in 1920, was but one of many groups which sprang up at this time, all holding anti-semitic and militantly nationalist views, hostile to the Versailles settlement and to the republican Government which had accepted it.

In March 1920 the first attempt to effect a nationalist counter-revolution was made in what was called the Kapp Putsch. The immediate cause was the disbandment of two marine brigades by order of the Inter-Allied Military Control Commission. Five thousand members of the brigades occupied Berlin, seized Government buildings, declared the Government (which had fled to Dresden) deposed, the National Assembly dissolved, and the Constitution null and void. A new government was proclaimed, headed by Dr Kapp and General von Lüttwitz. Elsewhere in Germany some Army leaders declared for Kapp and even those who remained loyal to the Ebert government refused to take up arms against former comrades. The Kapp Putsch was defeated not by the Army but by the workers of Berlin, who answered the Government call for a general strike. The life of Berlin was brought to a complete standstill. Kapp resigned, and later died in prison, but the officers who had taken part in the revolution were treated with great leniency.

In Bavaria, however, where the ground was well-prepared for a nationalist seizure of power, a simultaneous *putsch* succeeded and a right-wing government was set up. Munich was now the natural centre for anti-Republicans.

## REPARATIONS

In 1921 the Reparations Commission fixed the sum to be paid by Germany at £6600 million, which was to be settled by annual instalments of £100 million. After a very half-hearted attempt to begin payment, the Germans protested that they were unable to meet the demands. Accordingly, in January 1923, Poincaré, the French Prime Minister, ordered the French Army to occupy the Ruhr so that France could take from the industries and mines there what the Germans had been unable or unwilling to give.

The result of this dramatic action was a disaster of far-reaching magnitude. The German Government ordered the people of the Ruhr to undertake passive resistance and this soon led to strikes, sabotage, and localized fighting. The economic crisis, which had been Germany's excuse for stopping payments, gathered momentum, under the guidance of the government's financial advisers, and the mark became valueless. In July the rate of exchange against the U.S. dollar was 160 000 marks; by November it was 130 000 million marks. 300 paper mills and 2000 printing establishments worked 24 hour shifts to supply the Reichsbank with notes. Industrialists with large overdrafts, property owners, and speculators in foreign currency, were delighted, but the savings of the middle classes were wiped out almost overnight, and a man's wages, even if he could find a job, would purchase almost nothing. The wild inflation of 1923 produced more lasting bitterness and disillusionment in Germany than ever the events of 1918–19 had. Many members of the impoverished middle classes turned in the next few years to the Nazis for salvation. At Munich on November 8th, 1923, Hitler judged the opportunity ripe to seize power in Bavaria. The *putsch* was ill-organized and a failure, but Hitler turned the tables on his prosecutors at his trial by taking the opportunity to abuse the Government and to make himself a public figure.

In September, the Government had been forced to resign and Gustav Stresemann became Chancellor and Foreign Minister. He remained Foreign Minister until his death in 1929 and dominated German affairs in that period. He was the nearest approach to a leader the Weimar Republic produced. His first acts on taking office were to call off unconditionally the passive resistance in the Ruhr and to lift the ban on the delivery of reparations. The deadlock was broken, and in 1924 a new plan for reparations was drawn up by a committee under the leadership of an American, General Dawes. The Dawes Plan fixed neither the final sum to be paid nor the length of time to be allowed for payment, but merely laid down the principle of graded instalments, which would increase as Germany's capacity to pay increased. The French now withdrew from the Ruhr, and the Government, which had claimed to be powerless to halt the inflation, all the time that it had hoped reparations might be cancelled, miraculously revalued the mark and stabilized the currency, under the direction of Dr Schacht, who was later to serve Hitler well. Germany entered a boom period, but it was an ill-founded prosperity, based not on increased trade and production, but upon vast loans from America. Germany paid her debts by borrowing money.

## LOCARNO

After the 1920 elections the Social Democrats never again enjoyed an overall majority in the Reichstag, and in 1923 the democratic parties of the Left were forced to join forces with Stresemann's middle-class People's Party. The Communists were out to destroy the Social Democrats at all costs and it was their failure to vote with the socialists in 1925, when Ebert died, which brought about the election to the Presidency of the right wing Field Marshal Hindenburg. The hero of Tannenburg was now seventy-seven years of age and he proved an admirable tool in the hands of those who wished to destroy the Republic.

Nevertheless, 1925 marked the beginning of a period of improved relations between Germany and her ex-enemies. Real hope emerged for a lasting peace, with the signing of the Treaty of Locarno. Apart from the Treaty of Rapallo (1922) between Germany and Russia, which shocked the Western Powers—as it was meant to—Locarno was the first treaty signed voluntarily by Germany since the war. The frontier of France and Germany as established by the Treaty of Versailles was recognized as permanent by both countries, and Britain and Italy guaranteed each country against aggression by the other. Treaties were also drawn up by France and Germany with Czechoslovakia and Poland for the mutual settlement of disputes, but Stresemann would not recognize the Polish-German frontier as permanent and Britain would not guarantee it.

There were two main weaknesses in the Locarno settlement. It weakened the authority of Versailles by confirming some of its provisions, and, because of Britain's refusal to guarantee the frontiers of Eastern Europe, it left hope for German ambitions in that direction.

However, Locarno opened a period of some goodwill. In 1926 Germany joined the League of Nations and was given a seat on the Council. In 1928 Stresemann joined on equal terms with other Powers to sign the useless but high-sounding Kellogg-Briand pact which outlawed war. And in 1929 the Young Plan completed the work of the Dawes Plan by reducing the German reparations bill to £2000 million to be paid over fifty-nine years on a graded scale. However, in the same year the death of Stresemann and the collapse of the American stock market brought about a rapid deterioration in the international scene.

## THE END OF WEIMAR

The effects of the Wall Street crash and the trail of bankruptcies and unemployment that it left behind in the United States were felt severely by all countries which engaged in international trade. None was less well-equipped to withstand such a blow than Germany. She was existing on borrowed money, and she was powerless to meet her commitments when American and other bankers began to call in their loans. She had no means of sustaining her foreign trade, and production slumped. Unemployment rose from 2 258 000 in 1930 to over 6 000 000 in 1932. Other countries faced unemployment too. What made the situation disastrous in Germany was that it revealed the political weaknesses of the Weimar Republic. Germany was no more able to meet the political than she was the economic crisis.

In 1930 the Catholic Centre and the People's Party abandoned their coalition with the Social Democrats when the socialists supported a proposal to increase the inadequate unemployment insurance funds. From then on, no government could command a majority in the Reichstag, and Hindenburg resorted to his emergency power of ruling by decree.

Faced with economic hardship, more and more people sought desperate remedies and turned either to the Nazis or to the Communists. In the elections of 1930 the Nazis won 107 seats and the Communists 77, though the Social Democrats remained the strongest single party in the Reichstag. From 1930 to 1932 Brüning, a member of the Centre party, ruled as Chancellor under the umbrella of the presidential emergency powers, but the President no longer held the handle of the umbrella very securely. Intrigue surrounded him.

In 1932, when the elections for the presidency were due, Hindenburg was eighty-five years of age and failing mentally. He was 'all right', it was said, until about the beginning of the morning. He was nevertheless re-elected as President, though Hitler stood against him and won nearly 37 per cent of the votes cast, as against Hindenburg's 53 per cent. The man who most closely influenced Hindenburg at this stage was General von Schleicher, who represented the views of the Army. Schleicher turned against Brüning, whom he no longer regarded as useful, and persuaded the President to dismiss him and to appoint in his place, Franz von Papen, a Catholic aristocrat of some charm but no political experience. Papen was not even supported by the Centre party and in the Reichstag elections of July 1932 he failed to secure any worthwhile support. The Nazis, however, secured 230 seats and became the largest single party in the Reichstag.

Schleicher now turned against Papen, and became Chancellor himself, but Papen was not so easily dropped. He made a deal with Hitler.

While the Nazi fortunes were rising Hitler had rejected the idea of an alliance with any other group. He wanted absolute power, based on an absolute Nazi majority gained in an election. At one time it looked as if he might get it, but in the elections held in November 1932 the Nazis lost 34 seats. Papen had joined the Nationalist party, which had the support of the big industrialists. Hitler was now ready to listen to Papen, and so was Hindenburg, despite his contempt for the Nazi leader. Papen's plan was that the Nazi and Nationalist parties would join forces under Hitler as Chancellor and Papen as Vice-Chancellor. The doddering President agreed to the plan and on January 30th, 1933, Hitler took the oath to the constitution which he rapidly proceeded to destroy. Hindenburg and Papen visualized Hitler as a puppet whom they could manipulate at will, but it soon became clear exactly who was pulling the strings.

## THE FAILURE OF WEIMAR

The most important fact about the Weimar republic is that it failed, and it is not difficult to see why. It was born out of a humiliating defeat in which, by its acceptance of office from the Kaiser's government, and by its signature of the Versailles Treaty, it was closely implicated. It had been attacked with considerable success from right and left since its beginning. The Germans were unused to democratic procedures and they had little chance of learning them when many of the politicians from the Communists to the Nazis opposed the system fundamentally. Even these difficulties might have been overcome had the Republicans produced a vigorous leader, but none was forthcoming.

From its earliest days the Republic was forced to lean for support on its enemies. In many respects the old Empire carried on in thin disguise. The teaching profession remained in the same hands and the young were brought up to despise the new system of government. The civil service remained unchanged and ruled very largely independently of the legislature. Judges tended to deal more leniently in cases of public disorders with right wing groups than with those of the left. Above all, the Army retained its traditionally powerful, independent position. That position was used to aid Hitler in destroying the Weimar Republic.

# 16  Hitler

Adolf Hitler was born in Austria in 1889. His father, who was known for most of his life by his mother's name of Schicklgrüber, was a minor government official in the Habsburg Empire. He died when Hitler was thirteen years old. Hitler's mother, who was Alois Schicklgrüber's third wife, died only six years later, in 1908, but she had a decisive influence on his upbringing, spoiling him, pampering him, and flattering his dreams. After unsuccessful attempts to become a student of art or architecture, he eked out a precarious existence in Vienna until 1913, when he crossed the frontier into Germany and went to live in Munich. In the First World War he served in the German Army, became a corporal, was wounded, gassed, and awarded the Iron Cross (1st Class) for gallantry. There can be no doubt that he was an unusually brave and patriotic soldier.

He was in hospital recovering from gas wounds when the war ended. The news of the armistice and the revolutionary talk of his fellow soldiers made a profound impression on him. The cause in which he had so passionately believed seemed to him to have been betrayed. When he was discharged from hospital, he found himself, like so many of his comrades, unemployed, and like them he drifted into the semi-military, semi-political life of the Freikorps (illegal military organizations).

In Munich in 1919 he joined, as Party Member No. 7, the German Workers' Party which a year later adopted the title of the National Socialist German Workers' Party. After the unsuccessful *putsch* of 1923 (see p. 137) Hitler was imprisoned, in some comfort, in Landsberg prison, where he remained, dictating *Mein Kampf* [1] to his friend, Rudolph Hess, until December 1924.

In the years that followed, Hitler built up the party organization, centring it on himself. The party had its own newspapers and its own private army, known as the S.A.,[2] an important part of their duties being street fighting and the breaking up of the meetings of political opponents. It was however, the political and economic crisis of 1930–2 that brought the Nazis in numbers to the Reichstag, and Hitler, who was by now a member of the Reichstag, to the Chancellery (see p. 140).

When Hitler became Chancellor in January 1933, the Nazis, although the largest single party in the Reichstag, had not an absolute majority. The parties which might have opposed them were hopelessly divided, but even so Hitler insisted on immediate elections. He offered no programme, apart from opposition to the chief rival parties, the Social Democrats and the Catholic Centre. His right-hand man, Göring, as the Prussian Minister of

---

[1] 'My Struggle'. A ranting, repetitive diatribe against the Jews and Communists, part biography, part political testament, in which he outlined his plans and hopes.

[2] *Sturm Abteilung:* Storm-Troopers. Called the Brown-shirts, from their uniforms.

the Interior, reinforced the regular police by 50 000 men from the S.A. and the S.S.,[1] and on February 27th the Reichstag building was destroyed by fire. The Nazis immediately blamed this on the Communists, and President Hindenburg signed a decree suspending the liberties guaranteed under the Weimar Constitution. Even so, and with Nazi storm-troopers marching the streets, the party achieved only 43·9 per cent of the votes at the election. With the Nationalist Party, the Nazis now had a bare majority, but that was all they needed.

The legal basis of Hitler's régime was the Enabling Law (Law for removing the Distress of the People and Reich). This law effectively destroyed the Weimar Constitution by strictly constitutional means. Changes in the Constitution required a two-thirds majority in the Reichstag before they could become effective. However, those Communist deputies who had not already been arrested dared not turn up to vote, and the emergency powers proclaimed on February 28th gave Hitler the power to make enough arrests to ensure the necessary majority. The Law gave the new Government three supreme powers. First, the Government was given power for four years to pass laws without the Reichstag. Secondly, it was given the power to depart from the constitution and to conclude treaties with foreign powers. Thirdly, all new laws were to be drafted by the Chancellor, and were to come into effect the day after their publication. Only the Social Democrats voted against this measure.

Hitler lost no time in using his dictatorial powers to consolidate his position. State Diets were abolished and their powers transferred to the central government. Nazis were appointed to all key positions. Trade union offices were raided by S.A. and S.S. troops, officials were arrested, beaten, and thrown into concentration camps, and all unions and employers' organizations merged into the German Labour Front. All political parties except the Nazi party were abolished if they had not already dissolved themselves. By the summer of 1933 Hitler was sole master of a Government in which Papen, who had hoped to be the power behind the scenes, was merely tolerated. In the summer and autumn of 1933 the Government deliberately encouraged the S.A. and the S.S. to pay off old scores and to tyrannize the public. Nevertheless, the plebiscite of November 1933, in which 96·3 per cent of the voters signified their approval of Hitler's measures, should not be discounted. Violence and success were attractive, particularly to the young.

Once he had obtained power, Hitler was no longer interested in revolution. But many of his followers, particularly in the S.A., wanted a social revolution to follow the political one. At the very least they expected to be rewarded with soft government jobs. The S.A., primarily drawn from the working class, students, and tradesmen, had been useful for street fighting and thuggery, but they were too ill-disciplined and too independent in thought to be anything but an embarrassment to Hitler in power. The rival organization, the S.S., an élite drawn mainly from the middle class,

[1] *Schutzstaffel*. Originally a *corps d'élite* of the Nazi party.

disciplined, efficient, and implicitly obedient to the *Führer* (leader) was far better able to serve Hitler's new requirements.

The only organization capable of weakening Hitler's position was the Army, which had maintained its traditionally independent role throughout the Weimar régime, and had allowed Hitler into power in 1933. Hitler had the Army on his side, and he wanted to keep it there against the day when Hindenburg should die. The S.A. wanted to replace, or at least to dominate, the Army. Nothing would have been more disastrous for Hitler's purposes.

Until the summer of 1934 Hitler tried to compromise with the S.A. Röhm, Chief of Staff of the S.A., was given a Cabinet post. Members of the S.A. or of the party who had suffered sickness or injury in the political struggle were to receive pensions or grants from the State. The showdown came on June 30th, 1934, 'The Night of the Long Knives'. Röhm and perhaps as many as 400 others were murdered. The S.A. menace was crushed. Hitler had made a complete break with his old comrades. He had reinforced the loyalty of the S.S. and the Army. No more was heard of the social revolution.

In August Hindenburg died and Hitler declared himself President, Chancellor and Supreme Commander-in-Chief. Army officers and men took the oath of allegiance to Hitler personally. In the plebiscite which followed, 89·93 per cent approved his action in a poll of 95·7 per cent.

Having established himself in power Hitler left the detailed running of the country to his subordinates. He laid down the general lines of policy and he took the ultimate responsibility for all that was done, but he became more and more preoccupied with foreign affairs. Men like Göring, Goebbels, Himmler and Ley had considerable freedom of action in their own departments, and Hitler deliberately allowed rivalries to develop between them. Hitler was interested in power; administration and reform he left to others.

NAZI PHILOSOPHY

Hitler came to power with no programme save that of gaining and maintaining power, and he never developed one, but the whole Nazi movement was riddled with a jumble of pseudo-scientific claptrap which is spoken of as the Nazi Philosophy. The cornerstone of this was the race theory. The Nazis divided mankind into two groups, the Aryans (or Nordic race) who were the master-race, and the rest, who were slave-races. The Germans, they asserted, were Aryans, and destined to rule the world. The ideal Aryan physical type was tall, blond and beautiful. It was a pity that so few of the Nazi leaders resembled this ideal. Goebbels, who directed propaganda, was dwarfish, dark and crippled. Göring was blond but immensely fat. Hess, Hitler's second-in-command, was swarthy, and nicknamed 'The Egyptian'. Streicher, the Jew-baiter, looked very Jewish. Hitler's hair was dark. But inconsistencies never troubled the Nazi leaders. This Nordic race of supermen was held to be the product of the unalterable facts of Blood and Soil (*Blut und Boden*). The only system of government worthy of this race was one by which the interests of each individual were surrendered to those of the *Volk* (the community). The interests of the *Volk* were determined by the *Führer* (the leader). All that was required of the Germans by the Nazis was blind, unquestioning obedience.

### THE JEWS

The full fury of Nazi race-hatred was directed against the Jews, who, the Nazis alleged, were defiling the Aryan race. The Jews were blamed for every misfortune that overtook, or had ever overtaken, Germany. Many Germans who were not members of the Nazi party were not sorry to see the Jews removed from the important jobs, which they held out of all proportion to their numbers. Something like 50 per cent of all the doctors and lawyers in Berlin, and many university teachers, were Jewish, and so were the controllers of some of the largest newspapers. Jew-baiting, organized by Julius Streicher, began seriously in 1935, and by the Nuremberg Laws of that year Jews were deprived of all civil rights and driven from countless jobs. Some could escape abroad, but many had to remain, to endure persecution and eventual death in the gas-chambers.

### YOUTH

The Nazis attached great importance to the Youth Movement. In 1926 the *Hitler Youth* had been formed for boys between the ages of fourteen and eighteen. Two years later a corresponding girl's organization was formed, together with one for boys from ten to fourteen. By the end of 1934 the *Hitler Youth* numbered 6 000 000 boys, and had absorbed all other organizations. Great emphasis was placed on physical fitness, but the Youth Movement was also used as a means by which the rising generations could be indoctrinated with Nazi teaching. The young people learned quickly that their first and only duty was to obey the Führer. Boys graduated from the Hitler Youth to six months' compulsory Labour Service, followed by two years in the Army. After that they might join the S.A. or the S.S.

Intellectual activity was sneered at by good Nazis. Critical thought was obviously dangerous. Education became a vehicle for State propaganda, which was ably directed by Goebbels, who used every trick of the trade in wireless broadcasts, speeches and writings. Censorship clamped down on the free expression of opinion, and Germany became hypnotized by the Party line. Text-books were rewritten to conform to it. Literature, the Theatre, Films, Music and Art were all bound by the Nazi strait-jacket, and the secret police (the Gestapo), under Himmler, kept the strait-jacket firmly in place.

THE CHURCHES

Inevitably, the Nazis came into conflict with the Churches. They found one willing ally in Pastor Ludwig Müller, who became Evangelical Bishop of the German Reich in 1933. Müller set about reconciling Nazi teaching with Christianity. Where they clashed, Christianity was amended. Some of the Protestant clergy, however, rallied behind the ex-submarine commander, Pastor Niemöller, to resist this subordination of the Church to the State. In 1938 Niemöller was sent to a concentration camp.

The Roman Catholic Church presented Hitler with greater problems, but in 1933 he signed a concordat with the Pope, by which it was agreed that priests should abstain from political activities and that Hitler should not interfere in Catholic life. But Nazi control of education and all youth movements did interfere with Catholic life, and ill-feeling persisted.

ECONOMIC LIFE

Hitler had come to power in an economic crisis, and his first problem was to show that he had an answer to it. 'History,' he said, 'will not judge us according to whether we have removed and imprisoned the largest number of economists, but according to whether we have succeeded in providing work.'

Hitler did reduce unemployment, though by highly artificial means. Many of the unemployed found jobs in the huge Nazi bureaucracy and in organizations such as the Hitler Youth. Others were drafted into compulsory labour service, living in camps like soldiers, and receiving a little pocket-money for wages. Some were thrown into concentration camps. Vacancies were created by conscription into the Army, and by the persecution of the Jews. In many cases, employers were forced to retain redundant workers.

Strikes and industrial unrest disappeared because they were forbidden. A sort of super-trade-union, known as the Labour Front, was set up in 1934 under Dr Ley. Both employers and employees joined it, and were regarded as the officers and other ranks respectively of Industry. Like soldiers, they were to serve the state together, not against each other. One of the most popular departments of the Labour Front was the 'Strength through Joy' office, which provided sporting and recreational facilities, as well as ludicrously cheap holidays, for the lowest-paid workers.

Superficially, the Nazis provided the Germans with much of what they wanted. Food prices and rents were controlled, and health services centralized and extended. Slums were cleared and great Motor Roads (*Autobahnen*) were built, though with a strategic purpose in mind. Given the power over life and property that the Nazis had, it was no great problem to finance their projects. They could readily obtain credit from Germans. Their difficulty, and it was fundamental, was how to obtain credit from foreign countries. Without imports Germany must slowly collapse, yet she had no money to pay for imports.

## AUTARKY

The solution to this problem was sought by the ingenious Dr Schacht. His schemes were so complicated that they defy analysis. It has been asserted that there were 237 exchange rates for the mark for different purposes. But his aim was quite simple—to restrict imports and to boost exports. That is the aim of every country. The problem is how to achieve it, particularly at a time of world depression. One of Schacht's methods was to accept deliveries of food and raw materials from other countries and then refuse to pay cash for them. Instead he offered armaments in exchange. The countries could either accept or go without, and once they had accepted German arms, they were bound in future to purchase German ammunition. Another method was to block foreign credit accounts, so that foreigners were forced to spend their money in Germany, either by importing German goods or else by undertaking such things as building programmes.

Desperate efforts were made to make Germany independent of foreign imports. This plan for economic self-sufficiency was known as *Autarky*. Synthetic (*ersatz*) rubber and wool were manufactured in large quantities, though they were less good than the real thing, and much more expensive. Experiments were carried on to produce petrol from coal. In 1936 Göring's optimistic Four Year Plan aimed to make Germany independent of imported raw materials in four years. It is little wonder that Dr Schacht's was one of the foremost voices demanding living-space (*Lebensraum*) for Germany. This meant, in effect, that in order to be great Germany must expand to control and exploit a large area of Eastern Europe.

Such self-sufficiency, though in fact impossible to achieve, was important if Germany was to feel militarily strong. The whole economy of the Nazis was geared to war from the moment they came to power. The social and material benefits which some Germans may have enjoyed were merely part of the means by which the Nazi leaders were to become powerful in a powerful State. The idea that the Nazis did Germany a great deal of good and only spoilt their work by being so aggressive towards other nations is fundamental nonsense. Hitler's régime and the whole Nazi programme could succeed only if Germany were in a position to control or subjugate other countries. In spite of Schacht's ingenuity and his statistics, Germany's financial troubles were not solved by the Nazis. Indeed, rearmament added greatly to them. The reckoning could not be long delayed. Hitler could not survive a severe economic crisis. With or without war, he needed foreign conquests. Nazi policy, at home and abroad, was indivisible.

## FOREIGN POLICY

The first objective of Hitler's foreign policy was to remove the limitations which had been placed on Germany by the Versailles settlement. Reparations had already been abandoned, but the restrictions on Germany's armed forces still applied, and the Rhineland was still a demilitarized zone. Moreover, the Germans had never forgotten the lands taken from them by that peace treaty—the Saar, Alsace-Lorraine, Danzig and the Polish lands, Memel, Slesvig-North, Eupen, Malmédy, and the colonies, though of these Hitler was only seriously concerned with the Saar and the Eastern lands.

## REARMAMENT

Hitler's first step was rearmament. He could carry out an ambitious foreign policy only by having behind him greater military power. Rearmament was, of course, a flagrant breach of Versailles, but the signatories of that treaty were now far from united, and Hitler outmanoeuvred them politically. He began by appealing to them to disarm. Germany, he pointed out in his speeches, had no arms. She wanted peace. Why did not the other powers disarm too? If they would not, then Germany must provide protection for herself. In October 1933 Germany walked out of the Disarmament Conference and out of the League.

His next step was to sign a non-aggression Pact with Poland. This was a brilliant stroke, and Hitler was very proud of it. Of all the possessions lost by Germany in 1919, the lands Poland had taken were the most bitterly resented. Stresemann had been prepared, at Locarno, to accept Germany's Western frontiers but not her Eastern. Poland was an ally of France, but the Polish Government was becoming less happy about her position between Russia and Germany, and less convinced of the value of the French alliance. Friendship with Germany seemed to offer her greater security. The advantage to Hitler was that this agreement helped to weaken the French position.

In the summer of 1934, Hitler suffered a setback. With his connivance the Nazis in Austria assassinated Dollfuss, the Austrian Chancellor, and attempted to seize power. The rising was put down by the Austrian authorities, but Mussolini was ready to help them if they needed it. Hitler had hurriedly to dissociate himself from the whole affair. Papen was sent to Vienna to calm the Austrians. Germany was not yet strong enough to face opposition.

In January 1935 a plebiscite held in the Saar resulted in a 90 per cent vote for a return of that territory to Germany. This step, though provided for in the treaty, was hailed by the Nazis as their first victorious attack on the Versailles settlement. Two months later, however, they really did strike at the treaty's provisions.

In March 1935 the German Government reintroduced conscription and announced its intention of building up a peacetime army of 36 divisions (550 000 men). France, a few days earlier, had doubled the period of service and reduced the age of enlistment to make up for the low birth rate between 1914 and 1918, and Britain had announced increased expenditure on arms. Hitler used this as the excuse for his action. The Western powers had again been outmanoeuvred diplomatically.

At Stresa, Britain, France and Italy joined in condemning German action and the so-called Stresa front was formed. The League condemned Germany and set up a committee to consider what steps should be taken the *next* time a state endangered peace by repudiating its obligations. France signed a pact of mutual assistance with Russia, and a similar pact was signed between Czechoslovakia and Russia. Hitler, in his turn, now offered separate non-aggression pacts with all his neighbours except Lithuania. But the solidarity which seemed to be growing against Hitler was shattered by the Anglo-German Naval treaty of June 1935. By this, Germany agreed to build not more than 35 per cent of Britain's naval strength, though she could build up to 100 per cent of the submarine strength of the British Commonwealth. This was an open acceptance by Britain of Germany's right to rearm. As an act of policy it was selfish and shortsighted. France, not unnaturally, was dumbfounded. The Stresa Front collapsed. At the party rally at Nuremberg in September, the annual occasion for superb and hypnotic theatrical display, units of the new German Army paraded in the stadium for the first time.

### THE OCCUPATION OF THE RHINELAND

Hitler was further strengthened by the attitude of Britain and France to the Abyssinian war. By imposing sanctions on Italy, they made an enemy of Mussolini and robbed themselves of a possible ally against Hitler, and by refusing to enforce sanctions effectively they ruined their own prestige and that of the League. Even so, it was with considerable daring that Hitler marched into the Rhineland and renounced Locarno in March 1936. His generals were very nervous about the operation, which was carried out with limited forces. Only three battalions actually crossed the Rhine. But again Britain and France only protested. In the Reichstag elections which were held immediately afterwards, 98·8 per cent of the German electors supported the Führer's action in a 99 per cent poll. Even allowing for the police-state methods of electioneering, there can be little doubt that the German people appreciated bold action and success.

### THE ROME-BERLIN AXIS AND THE ANTI-COMINTERN PACT

Hitler's second objective was to incorporate into the Reich those Germans in the lands which had formed part of the old Austro-Hungarian Empire and which had been excluded from Bismarck's Empire, namely Austria and the Sudeten lands of Czechoslovakia. His first step was to conclude in July 1936 an agreement with Austria governing Austro-German relations. He used this in the next two years to exert increasing pressure on the Austrian Government. Mussolini was now ready to give his blessing to increased German influence in Austria.

A week later Civil War broke out in Spain. Hitler, who never sent forces on the scale that Mussolini did, had only one interest in Spain—to prolong the war as long as possible. The war diverted the attention of the Western Powers at a vital time. And as it diverted, so it divided. France, although threatened with a third Fascist Power on her frontiers, was bitterly divided, while Germany and Italy drew closer together. In October 1936 the vague, but important, alliance was signed between them which they termed the Rome-Berlin Axis. Hitler now tried to gain an alliance with Britain.

Hitler had a curious mixture of envy and respect for Britain, mainly because she was evidently so successful. He had no quarrel with Britain, who was not a Continental Power, and he could never understand why Britain was not content to give him a free hand in Europe, especially Eastern Europe. This problem alternately annoyed and perplexed him.

However, in August 1936 he sent a leading member of the party, Ribbentrop, as Ambassador to London to urge that Britain should stand with Germany against Communism, their common foe. The need for unity against Communism was an argument he used frequently after the outbreak of the Spanish Civil War, and it carried some weight in both Britain and France, though it was with Japan that he signed the Anti-Comintern Pact in November.

Meanwhile in August the Olympic Games had been held in Berlin, and representatives from all over the world had witnessed the glories of the New Order.[1] In September the Nuremberg Rally was the most spectacular yet. Unemployment had fallen, production had increased. More important in German eyes, the nation had regained its dignity. National Socialism was a distinct success.

In September 1937 Mussolini, whom Hitler admired tremendously, visited Germany, and in November signed the Anti-Comintern Pact. Earlier that year, Neville Chamberlain had replaced Stanley Baldwin as Prime Minister of Britain, and cast himself in the role of peacemaker. Hitler was now ready to take bold action.

The last outpost of independent power in Germany collapsed in February 1938, when Hitler announced to the Cabinet that he had appointed himself Commander-in-Chief of the *Wehrmacht*,[2] and that he had abolished the post of War Minister. The Army, which had for so long occupied such a dangerously independent position in German affairs, was now fully under his personal control. This was also the occasion of the last meeting of the German Cabinet of the Third Reich.

## THE ANSCHLUSS

In February 1938 Hitler summoned the Austrian Chancellor Schuschnigg and forced him to agree to make great concessions to the Nazis in Austria, and to appoint the prominent Austrian Nazi, Seyss-Inquart,

---

[1] The outstanding performances of the American negro, Jesse Owens, somewhat marred the proceedings from the Nazi point of view!

[2] The Armed Forces as opposed to the *Reichswehr* (the Army), of which he was already Commander-in-Chief.

Minister of the Interior. In the next few weeks Hitler brought such pressure to bear on Austria, by threats of invasions and civil war, that the President dismissed Schuschnigg and appointed Seyss-Inquart as his successor. Acting on instructions, the Nazi puppet then appealed to Germany to enter Austria to restore order. On March 12th the waiting German troops crossed the frontier and Austria was annexed to Germany —a move known as the *Anschluss* (union).

In the West this aggression was easily excused. After all, the Austrians were Germans, and this annexation was a perfectly logical application of the nationalist principle which Wilson had upheld at Versailles. Schuschnigg was regarded as a Fascist in left-wing circles in the West. Hitler defended his action by asserting that he had saved Austria from becoming another Spain.

*Map 16. The Expansion of Hitler's Germany*

### CZECHOSLOVAKIA

Nor was opinion sufficiently roused against Hitler by his next move— against Czechoslovakia. The Sudeten Germans had presented a minority problem in the state ever since its foundation. Following the Austrian pattern, the Nazis in the Sudetenland staged big demonstrations and protested loudly about alleged persecution by the Czech government.

Britain was so far convinced as to urge the Czechs to make every possible concession to the Germans, while warning Germany of the possibility of general war if Germany should attack Czechoslovakia. France and Russia reaffirmed their support of Czechoslovakia. Hitler suffered a temporary set-back from this united opposition, and for this he never forgave the Czechs—he determined to destroy the country utterly.

Neville Chamberlain determined to avoid war if at all possible. Twice he flew to meet Hitler. But deadlock was reached. Britain and France prepared for war. In Germany neither the generals nor the public were in favour of a war. Hitler was saved from embarrassment by the intervention of Mussolini, who proposed a Four-Power Conference at Munich. Neither the Russians nor the Czechs were invited. On September 30th agreement was reached, and Britain and France were left to communicate the dismemberment terms to the Czechs. The next day German troops marched into the Sudetenland. President Benes went into exile. Poland and Hungary joined in the grab for land, and the Prague Government was forced to grant virtual independence to Slovakia and Ruthenia.

The Czechs had been deserted, in spite of guarantees. Hitler, who had climbed down in May when faced with opposition on the Sudeten issue, had in September, although unsupported by his General Staff and his people, secured the triumph of fetching the Prime Minister of Great Britain to Germany, to accept on behalf of the Czechs a humiliating death sentence. Just before he went to Munich, Chamberlain said in a broadcast: 'How horrible, fantastic, incredible it is that we should be digging trenches and trying on gas masks here because of a quarrel in a faraway country between people of whom we know nothing.' In fairness to Chamberlain it must be said that he expressed the views of many people in this country and elsewhere. Before his final flight to Hitler, Chamberlain made a speech to the Commons describing his efforts to avert war. While he was speaking a message was handed to him. He broke off to announce that Hitler had invited him to a conference in Munich the following morning. He abandoned his speech and left the House to the accompaniment of tumultuous applause. The whole episode expressed the mood of the country—or so it seemed to Chamberlain then. The rapturous reception his announcement received confirmed him in his belief that he must return from Munich with peace—at any price. The relief felt in Britain and France at the news from Munich is not recorded as irrevocably as the words of the British Premier. But that relief was soon replaced by disillusionment.

In March 1939, under renewed Nazi pressure both inside and outside his country, the new President of Czechoslovakia, Hacha, placed the fate of his country in Hitler's hands, and German troops crossed the frontier. Bohemia, Moravia and Slovakia were brought under German 'protection', and Ruthenia was abandoned to the Hungarians. The Western Powers had witnessed the fruits of appeasement.

## LITHUANIA, MEMEL AND DANZIG

Immediately after the occupation of Prague, Hitler presented an ultimatum to Lithuania and occupied Memelland. The Poles, Germany's much-vaunted ally, were alarmed, since they had not been informed about German plans against Lithuania, or Czechoslovakia.

Danzig was Hitler's next objective, but he wanted to secure it without making an enemy of Poland, if it were possible. He demanded Danzig and a road and railway over the Corridor. The Poles rejected these demands, and Great Britain with France gave assurances to Poland.

Hitler was again temporarily checked. He denounced the Anglo-German naval treaty of 1935 and signed non-aggression pacts with Lithuania, Latvia and Estonia, and on March 21st signed the Pact of Steel with Mussolini. But his most striking move was to negotiate with Russia. During the summer of 1939, Britain and France were trying to reach agreement with Russia, but in May, Litvinov, who favoured an alliance with the West, was dismissed in favour of Molotov. Hitler was convinced that if he could sign a treaty with Russia, Britain and France would not drive their support of the Poles to a general war.

In May Russo-German talks began, and in July the German press campaign against Poland was renewed. On August 22nd Britain reaffirmed her guarantees to Poland and began to call up reservists. Chamberlain was determined to leave no doubt in the Führer's mind about the British attitude. But Hitler's experience of British and French action left him with considerable doubt. On August 24th the Russo-German Non-Aggression Pact was signed, with its secret clauses agreeing to the dismemberment of Poland.

Mussolini urged Hitler to settle the Polish issue peaceably. He declared that he was not yet ready for a general war. Momentarily Hitler held up the invasion plans. But on September 1st, following carefully staged frontier incidents, German troops marched into Poland. Hitler still believed that after Poland had fallen Britain and France would accept the fact. Their past behaviour gave him good grounds for thinking so. But on September 3rd both Britain and France declared war against Germany, and there began six years of fighting which was to engulf the world and was to reduce to ruins the Third Reich, which Hitler had boasted would last for a thousand years.

Hitler gave the German people six years of peace and six of war. He brought untold misery upon them as well as upon the people of other lands. He ruled by tyranny, based on violence and brutality. He exploited those aspects of human nature which civilized countries suppress. How did he manage to fool the German people into giving him full powers? How did he manage to keep on fooling them? The answer is complex, but certain facts are clear. He was supported by many people in 1932 because he abused the politicians who were failing to solve Germany's economic problems. He aroused their hopes for a revival of Germany's greatness and prosperity.

He offered them their self-respect, which they had lost, or so he told them, at Versailles. He was backed financially by the industrialists because they wanted a politician with a popular following who could ally with them against the Communists. He was backed by the Army because they thought that through him they could expel the Weimar politicians, destroy the Versailles settlement, and control the destinies of a strong Germany. Both the industrialists and the Army thought they could control Hitler. When they discovered their error, it was too late. They had given him full powers. Moreover, until 1942 he was a success. Neither the industrialists nor the Army had any quarrel with his general policy. Only after his military failures did the Army, the only group in Germany which could have got rid of Hitler after 1933, become restless.

# 17    The Second World War

## THE CAUSES OF THE WAR

Historians have not found the causes of the Second World War such a fruitful subject for investigation as the causes of the First World War. Hitler had disregarded treaties and even his own undertakings and had committed brazen aggression against his neighbours. It is possible to argue that had the United States joined the League, had Britain and France acted more closely together, or had the Weimar Republic been nursed in its infancy by the victorious powers, Hitler might never have attained and maintained power in Germany. But although these arguments—and many others—may help us to explain how the war might have been prevented, they in no way reduce the responsibility of Hitler and his supporters for the actual outbreak.

Amongst British historians A. J. P. Taylor has raised a dissenting voice.[1] In a highly readable book he has argued that Hitler had no plans for war, other than those that are prepared by any General Staff, and that he did not prepare for war. According to Mr Taylor, Hitler wildly exaggerated the scale of Germany's pre-war armaments and deceived Britain and France into thinking that Germany was stronger than they were. Hitler's aim to make his country powerful was no different from the aims of other leaders then or now. At the time, European leaders, particularly those of Britain and France, were, through fear of war and through anxiety to be just and conciliatory to Germany, following a policy of appeasement. In this situation, all that Hitler had to do was to make vague noises of dissatisfaction and wait for foreign statesmen to rush to him with offers of land and

[1] *The Origins of the Second World War* (1961, with added Foreword 'Second Thoughts' 1963).

concessions. In every crisis up to that over Danzig in 1939 they did so, and, according to Taylor, they were prepared right up to the last minute to do another deal, this time at the expense of the Poles. Careless diplomacy, coupled with the stubbornness of the Poles, brought Britain and France to war with Germany—by accident.

Fascinating and provocative as Mr Taylor's thesis is, most historians remain unconvinced by it.[1] Hitler did not want war. If he could expand the power and dominion of Germany without fighting he was happy to do so. But he was prepared to push his policies to the brink of war and beyond if necessary. He was not prepared for a long war, but then he had no reason to suppose that he would have to embark on one.

It is sometimes maintained that the Nazi-Soviet pact of 1939, by giving Hitler security in the east, tempted him to defy Britain and France. But the U.S.S.R. was unlikely to attack Germany, pact or no pact, before Germany, Britain and France had weakened themselves in combat. Nor was it likely that Hitler would have been deterred for long, even if the U.S.S.R., Britain and France had made a common stand in the defence of Poland—a most unlikely event. Hitler's whole policy was expansionist, and he stood or fell on its success or failure.

THE 'PHONEY WAR'

Hitler's conquest of Poland was achieved with terrifying, though scarcely surprising, rapidity. Although both Britain and France had declared war on Germany, they were in no position to help their ally. When the Russians marched in from the east on September 17th, the Poles were faced with a war on two fronts against overwhelming odds. By the end of the month Hitler and Stalin were able to divide the spoils.

After this dramatic and terrible curtain-raiser there followed a complete anticlimax lending some support to one aspect of A. J. P. Taylor's thesis. Neither Britain and France on the one hand, nor Germany on the other, seriously waged war against each other (except at sea) during the entire winter of 1939–40. Apart from the separate Russo-Finnish War (see p. 127) there was no major fighting either on land or in the air throughout the whole of this period which was aptly named 'the phoney war'. Having been prepared to face terrible aerial bombardment with high explosive and poison gas, and lightning blows from columns of tanks and armoured cars, the people of Britain and France found that they had braced themselves needlessly. The German generals, who did not share Hitler's great confidence in victory, had no wish to take the offensive. Having conquered Poland, they wanted a compromise peace with Britain and France. Hitler ordered the attack in the west to begin in November, but by pleading technical difficulties and bad weather conditions, the generals were able to secure successive postponements.

[1] See 'Some Origins of the Second World War', T. W. Mason, *Past and Present*, No. 29 (Dec. 1964).

**Stalin.** Marshal Stalin and members of his staff arrive for the Potsdam conference (see p. 170). The guard of honour is British.

**Communism without Russia.** A wartime photo of Marshal Tito (extreme right), the Yugoslav Communist leader, and some of his 'partisans' (see p. 177).

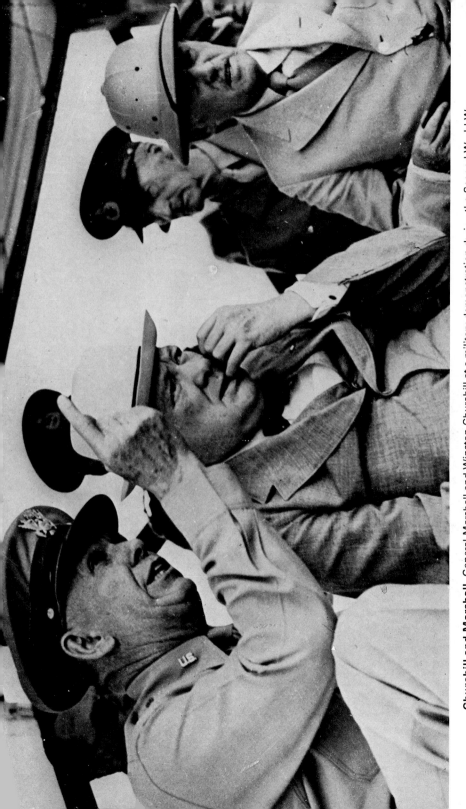

**Churchill and Marshall.** General Marshall and Winston Churchill at a military demonstration during the Second World War.

**Roosevelt.** The President was a polio victim and could not walk without assistance. It is worth reflecting on the fact that he overcame the handicap of the disease to become one of the world's greatest statesmen.

The Hungarian rising in 1956 (see p. 184). A Russian officer, reaching for his revolver, advances menacingly on the photographer.

Khrushchev and Vice-President (later President) Richard Nixon
debating in the American model kitchen at a trade fair in Moscow
(see p. 185).

President Kennedy at the Berlin Wall (see p.185).

*Left* Mendès-France, French politician and reformer (see p.188). *Below* Harold Macmillan, British Prime Minister 1957-63, later much taunted with the phrase 'You've never had it so good' that he had used in the prosperous early years of his ministry (see also footnote, p. 201).

The 'phoney war', however, had a softening effect on morale and on the sense of urgency in Britain and France. Both countries were ill-prepared, mentally as well as materially, when the blows eventually came. People really began to believe that the war would be over by Christmas. Some maintained that the Maginot line, the massive French fortifications which ran from Switzerland to Luxembourg (though regrettably not to the Channel), and their German counterpart, the Siegfried line, would reduce the land fighting to a stalemate just as the trenches had in the First World War. Germany could then be brought to her knees by blockade. Butter might prove more useful than guns. People in Britain and France, aware of the privations the Germans had been forced to endure in peace-time, had little regard for the ability of Germany to survive a long struggle economically. As the awaited attack failed to materialize, some even doubted German military strength. A popular song of the time ran: 'We're gonna hang out our washing on the Siegfried Line—if the Siegfried Line's still there!' As it happened, the Maginot line might better have been put to such use.

Disillusionment came abruptly. In April 1940 Hitler invaded and conquered Denmark and Norway. Britain was awakened from its slumbers. In a dramatic scene during a two-day debate in the House of Commons, one Conservative M.P., Leo Amery, demanded the resignation of the Prime Minister, Neville Chamberlain, with the words Oliver Cromwell had used towards the Rump Parliament; 'You have sat too long here for any good you have been doing. Depart, I say, and let us have done with you. In the name of God, go!' Chamberlain went, and his place was taken by Winston Churchill, who had been an outspoken critic of Britain's pre-war foreign policy. Churchill, offering nothing but 'blood and toil and tears and sweat', inspired the nation with a sense of urgency combined with confidence in ultimate victory. Never was Britain in greater need of great leadership.

THE FALL OF FRANCE

On May 10th, the day Churchill became Prime Minister, Hitler invaded Holland and Belgium. Holland was almost undefended and paratroopers, dive-bombers, and armoured columns were able to spread confusion and terror everywhere. On May 14th the Dutch army surrendered and Queen Wilhelmina and her government fled to Britain. The defence of Belgium lasted but a fortnight longer. The British Expeditionary Force, accompanied by French troops, had crossed into Belgium shortly after the invasion, only to find themselves cut off from the main French forces by a German thrust at Sedan which quickly penetrated to the Channel coast near Abbeville. On May 28th King Leopold of the Belgians capitulated, but by then the military situation was hopeless, and already the evacuation of troops through Dunkirk had begun. Between May 27th and June 4th some 250 000 British and 100 000 French and allied troops were transported across a mill-pond sea from the shell- and bomb-shattered beaches to the safety of England. Hundreds of small craft joined with the Royal Navy and the Merchant Marine in this immense undertaking, and the amateur appearance they gave to the operation, combined with its success, tempted many to regard the 'miracle of Dunkirk' almost as a victory. Certainly thousands of men had been saved to fight again, though their arms and equipment, guns and vehicles, remained abandoned on the Continent. But the withdrawal from Belgium was no victory. It was a major disaster made less disastrous than it might have been.

Map 17. France in 1940

Fighting continued in France, but the Germans could do much as they liked. On June 10th, Mussolini, deciding that the situation was favourable for him to risk his forces, invaded southern France, though he was in fact able to make very little headway. Paul Reynaud, the French Prime Minister, urged his cabinet to continue the fight, if necessary from the colonies. Winston Churchill flew to France with the remarkable proposal for the creation of a united British and French nation. But the peace party in the French Cabinet became dominant and, with the greater part of their army's equipment lost, reason appeared to be on their side. Reynaud resigned, to be replaced by the eighty-four-year-old hero of Verdun, Marshal Pétain. On June 22nd the French signed an armistice with the Germans in the same railway coach at the same spot in the forest of Compiègne where in 1918 Marshal Foch had dictated the armistice terms to the defeated Germans. Hitler had a fine sense of history.

## VICHY FRANCE

By the terms of the armistice German troops were to occupy a large area of France stretching along the Channel and Atlantic coasts and including Paris. The Navy was to be disarmed in French ports. France was to pay the costs of the German occupation, and French prisoners of war, some 1½ million men, were to remain in German hands.

Pétain's government moved to Vichy, where it remained until its collapse in 1944. Although the Vichy régime established the façade of a Fascist state, with a single party dictatorship, anti-semitic laws, massed youth displays and the like, it was not a mere puppet government of the type established in other occupied countries. It retained, for instance, control over the French Fleet and overseas territories, and until November 1942, when the Germans occupied the whole of France, it was allowed to maintain an army of 100 000 men.

The Vichy government was formed in 1940 because it seemed, to those who regarded Hitler's rapid victory as inevitable, the best bargain that could be made in a hopeless situation. But as the war continued, and particularly in the period when Admiral Darlan was the dominant member of the government (February 1941–April 1942), the Vichy régime came to represent the ideal of those elements, persistent in fluctuating strength since 1789, which desired order and authority. Vichy has been called 'the revenge of the anti-Dreyfusards'. Even when the slippery Laval returned to power in 1942 and German control and exactions increased, Vichy did not willingly collaborate with Hitler until, perhaps, the beginning of 1944.

But not all Frenchmen looked, even reluctantly, to Marshal Pétain for leadership. In London, in June 1940, General de Gaulle formed the Free French Movement to continue the struggle against Germany. Later de Gaulle assumed power as the head of the Free French government.

## THE BATTLE OF BRITAIN

Hitler was very reluctant to invade Britain after the fall of France. He found it difficult to believe that the British could be so stupid as to make him undertake such an operation. He had made himself master of Poland in a month, and of western Europe in just over two months. What need had Britain and her Commonwealth of further demonstrations of his military might? Hitler's next objective was Russia. He looked for peace with Britain, as he had after the defeat of Poland, but again he looked in vain. Churchill was not interested in peace with Hitler, and in the dark days of 1940, Churchill spoke for Britain.

Hitler therefore had to plan for the invasion of Britain. His first requirement was air control over the Channel, and to secure this he had to destroy the Royal Air Force. Throughout August great daylight raids took place on air-fields and on London. In the skies over southern England dog-fights took place daily between the German raiders and 'the few'—those R.A.F.

fighter pilots of whom Churchill said: 'Never in the field of human conflict was so much owed by so many to so few.'

By mid-September, the Battle of Britain, as this stuggle was called, had been won by the R.A.F. German losses in aircraft were mounting and the R.A.F. had not been destroyed. Hitler indefinitely postponed his invasion plan, and the *Luftwaffe*, the German air force, switched its operations to night attacks on London and large industrial cities. Britain had won a precious breathing space—time to manufacture the weapons of war which could one day meet the challenge of Germany on terms of equality. Britain's survival, however, depended greatly on the ability of the Royal Navy to keep open the supply routes across the Atlantic. German U-boats, operating from an immense stretch of coastline, were taking a heavy toll of shipping.

### THE BALKANS AND NORTH AFRICA

Although Mussolini's excursion into France had brought him little reward, he hoped for better luck in North Africa and in the Balkans. In September 1940 Italian forces from Libya invaded Egypt, and in October Mussolini attacked Greece from Albania. Both campaigns demonstrated the utter incompetence of the Fascist armies. The British forces in Egypt were able to drive the Italians back to Benghazi, while the Greeks invaded Albania. By May 1941 British forces from the Sudan and Kenya had over-run Mussolini's East African Empire of Eritrea, Italian Somaliland and Abyssinia.

Hitler, however, came to the rescue of his Axis partner. In 1940 he had brought Hungary (with its food) and Rumania (with its oil) under German control. In March 1941 Bulgaria, too, became part of the German New Order and in the following month German troops invaded Yugoslavia and Greece. British troops, sent from North Africa to aid the Greeks, were quickly driven from the mainland and from Crete, where they made a last stand.

The diversion in Greece caused the British to fall back into Egypt, though a garrison was left in Tobruk. German forces arrived in Libya early in 1941 and they were able to invade Egypt, but Tobruk managed to hold out until relieved by a fresh British advance in November.

### THE INVASION OF RUSSIA

On June 22nd, 1941, Hitler launched 'Operation Barbarossa'—the invasion of Russia.[1] The decision to attack in the east was made by Hitler personally and his reasons for doing so are not entirely clear. He had

---

[1] Six weeks earlier Rudolf Hess, having secretly flown from Germany, landed by parachute near Glasgow on a personal mission to negotiate peace with Britain. Hitler was furious, Stalin suspicious, and Churchill embarrassed. Hess was imprisoned.

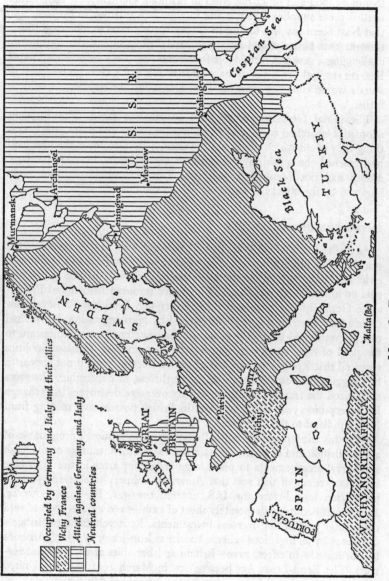

Map 18. Europe in 1942

Occupied by Germany and Italy and their allies

Vichy France

Allied against Germany and Italy

Neutral countries

always, of course, opposed Communism, and its destruction was fundamental to his ideas. Furthermore, under the Nazi New Order, Russia was to supply food and other materials to maintain Germany. In 1941 Hitler needed these supplies urgently and in abundance. It was in the east, too, that Nazi Germany was to find its 'living space'. Even so, one might have thought that Hitler would have preferred Britain out of the way before challenging a new and formidable foe. Almost certainly he underestimated Russian strength, and it is probable that he felt that a German conquest of Russia would convince even the British that further resistance would be futile.

The initial German advance into Russia was rapid. The Russians adopted a 'scorched earth' policy, falling back after first destroying everything they could which might aid the enemy. By December the Germans had reached the outskirts of Leningrad and Moscow, but the Russians' armies had not been destroyed, and German communications were harassed by the attacks of partisans behind the lines.

ENTER THE UNITED STATES

As in the First World War, most Americans wanted to keep out of the war, but they did not want the Germans to win. Congress had abandoned strict neutrality early in the war by authorizing the sale of arms to belligerents on a 'cash and carry' basis. This move favoured Britain and France, since Germany was unable to do any carrying. President Roosevelt saw clearly that America was itself threatened by Nazi aggression, but he had to tread warily. Although the events of 1940 awakened many Americans to the peril of their situation, 1940 was an election year. Domestic politics required that Roosevelt, who was up for re-election, should not appear to be dragging his country into war. Nevertheless, in September, Congress authorized the transfer to Britain of fifty over-age destroyers in exchange for ninety-nine-year leases on bases in British possessions, ranging from Newfoundland to the Caribbean.

After his triumph at the polls, Roosevelt set in motion a programme of aid for Britain and her allies. Britain had taken full advantage of the 'cash and carry' arrangements to place large orders for arms in the U.S. One important result of this was that American industry was geared to war-production long before the U.S. entered the war. By 1941, however, Britain was becoming desperately short of cash—even though she had sold the greater part of her overseas investments. Roosevelt came to Britain's assistance by an ingenious scheme known as lend-lease, by which America lent or leased—in effect, gave—Britain and her allies arms, food and services. The Lend-Lease Act became law in March 1941, and the United States became what Roosevelt termed the 'arsenal of democracy'.

In August 1941 Roosevelt and Churchill met on board H.M.S. *Prince of Wales* in mid-Atlantic and drew up a document known as the Atlantic Charter which set out the basic principles for the eventual peace settlement.

There should be no territorial aggrandizement; peoples should be free to choose their own form of government; all peoples should have freedom from war, from fear, and from want; and the use of force as an instrument of international relations should be abandoned. The Atlantic Charter was designed to show Americans, as well as the people in the enemy countries, that the Allied peace aims were just and worthy.

It was not Germany, however, but Japan which brought the United States into the Second World War. The fighting in Europe gave Japan a splendid opportunity to extend her dominion in the Far East while the European colonial powers were immobilized or distracted. On December 7th, 1941, while Japanese diplomats were in Washington discussing their country's differences with the United States, Japanese aircraft operating from carriers launched a surprise attack on the American naval base at Pearl Harbour in Hawaii. Eight battleships, three cruisers, and three destroyers were either destroyed or seriously damaged. The United States declared war on Japan on the following day. Three days later, Germany and Italy—rather gratuitously, but fortunately for Britain—declared war on America.

With the American Pacific Fleet crippled, Japan was able quickly to overrun much of south-east Asia. By May 1942, Malaya, Singapore, the Philippines, the Dutch East Indies, and most of Burma, including the 'Burma Road'—the supply route to China—had fallen into Japanese hands, as well as Hong Kong and numerous Pacific islands. The Japanese lightning advance was checked in June 1942 by two American naval victories in the Coral Sea and off Midway Island, but by then Japan had secured an immense area, rich in oil and minerals. Australia and India were in the front line.

NORTH AFRICA AND ITALY

Against the wishes of some of his service chiefs, Roosevelt agreed with Churchill to give the European and North African theatre of operations priority over the Pacific and it was decided to concentrate first on North Africa.

Rommel, the German commander in Libya, had, by June 1942, captured Tobruk and driven the British back to El Alamein, only fifty miles from Alexandria. This was the furthest enemy advance in North Africa. It was also the last. Supplies were poured into Egypt and a re-equipped and strengthened Eighth Army under its new commander, Montgomery, was able to strike back in October. The battle of El Alamein was of decisive importance. It was the first major defeat the Germans had suffered in the war, and it opened the way for a rapid British advance along the North African coast.

In November 1942 Anglo-American forces under Eisenhower landed in Morocco and Algeria. Admiral Darlan, commander-in-chief of all Vichy forces, left France for Algiers and ordered the French not to resist the

Allies. Darlan was an embarrassment to the Allies, though not for long. On Christmas Eve, 1942, he was assassinated. German forces were sent to Tunisia, but following the battle of the Mareth line in March 1943, the Eighth Army linked up with British, American and French forces in Algeria. The Germans were cornered around Tunis and over a quarter of a million prisoners were taken. The fighting in North Africa was over.

In July 1943 British and American troops invaded Sicily. In Rome, Mussolini was imprisoned[1] and a new government set up under Marshal Badoglio. When in September the Allies invaded southern Italy, Badoglio surrendered to the Allies and soon joined them against the Germans.

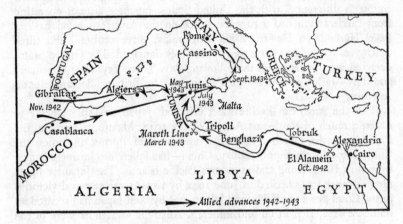

*Map 19. North Africa and Italy*

The Allied advance up through Italy was a lengthy and difficult operation. The country was ideal for defence, and the Germans were able to fight many delaying actions, notably the one at Monte Cassino. Furthermore, towards the end of 1943, the Allies began preparing for the invasion of France, and the armies in Italy no longer enjoyed priority treatment.

### RUSSIA

Meanwhile some of the bitterest fighting of the war had taken place on the Russian front. Hitler had been unable to capture either Leningrad or Moscow in 1941, and early in 1942 the Russians were able to push the Germans back a little on this part of the front. In May 1942, however, Hitler launched a new offensive in the south and penetrated deeply into the Caucasus. By September the Germans were at Stalingrad on the Volga.

---

[1] He was rescued by German paratroopers but finally, in April 1945, Italian partisans captured and shot him.

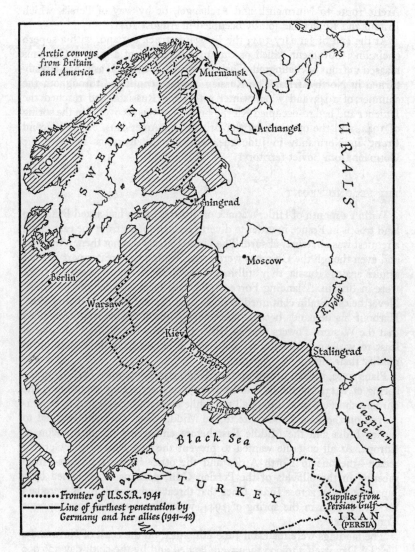

Map 20. *The Russian Front, 1941–5*

The battle for Stalingrad raged for five months and the city was reduced to ruins. The struggle was regarded as a trial of strength between Nazi Germany and Soviet Russia. The losses on both sides were terrible, but by 1943 the factories which the Russians had transferred from the war-zone to the Urals were pouring forth war materials. Added to these were the supplies sent from Britain and America under lend-lease on the perilous

Arctic route to Murmansk and Archangel, or by way of Persia, which Britain and Russia had jointly occupied in August 1941.

At the end of January 1943 the Russians struck out and, with a superb encircling movement, killed or captured the third of a million Germans massed in front of Stalingrad. The tide turned in the east, as it had already turned in North Africa. The Russian advance continued throughout the summer of 1943 and when winter set in the Russians had reached the Dnieper and had re-occupied Kiev. The Crimea was recovered in the spring of 1944, and the opening, by the British and Americans, of the 'Second Front' in Normandy in June 1944 enabled the Russians to drive the Germans from Soviet territory.

### THE SECOND FRONT

Within a month of Hitler's attack on Russia, Stalin had asked Britain to land troops in France in order to divert German forces from the east. Such a request was obviously absurd. The United States was not then in the war, and even though the Germans were concentrating the greater part of their armies against Russia, they still had more divisions in the west than there were in Britain. A landing Force would have been suicidal and pointless. Nevertheless, Stalin continued to press for a Second Front, and after Pearl Harbour his demands became more curt. Most Russians were convinced that the Western Powers wanted Hitler to destroy the Soviet Union, or at least to weaken it drastically. Subsequent events have done nothing to modify their view.

Plans were, in fact, drawn up for a landing in September 1942, or in the spring of 1943, but the difficulties were immense, among them being the chronic shortage of shipping all the while so many vessels had to be employed on the long Cape route to the Middle East. Churchill wanted to secure India and the Middle East before embarking on an invasion of Europe. At all costs he wanted to prevent the two arms of the German attack—the one in North Africa and the other in the Caucasus—from meeting in the oilfields of the Persian Gulf, perhaps to be joined by a Japanese thrust across India. Once that threat had passed, plans were laid for an invasion in the spring of 1944, with Eisenhower as the Supreme Commander.

The landings were made on June 6th, 1944, on the coast of Normandy. On 'D' Day itself 130 000 men were landed and by the sixth day 326 000 men were holding the bridgehead. Though hampered by bad weather, the build-up continued steadily. Such an operation required immense planning and technical skill. Two novel features were the 'Mulberry' harbours— prefabricated sections of harbour wall which were towed across the Channel and sunk into position—and Pluto (Pipe Line Under the Ocean) which carried fuel direct from England to the fighting area.

Fighting in Normandy was severe, but in August the Americans broke out and swung the Germans back. Paris was liberated on August 23rd, a few days after another landing had been made by American and French troops in southern France. By mid-September most of France was clear of Germans.

The advance of the Allied armies afforded relief to Londoners who, since the early days of the invasion, had been subjected to attacks from flying-bombs, officially termed V.1's, popularly known as 'doodle-bugs'. Hitler had hoped to shower these on London at the rate of a salvo of 64 every hour. In fact nothing like that number came, but fighters had to be diverted from the battle in France to combat the pilotless aircraft, and bombers were switched from strategic targets in Germany and tactical targets in Normandy to the V.1 bases in the Pas de Calais. However, the invasion plans were in no way modified.

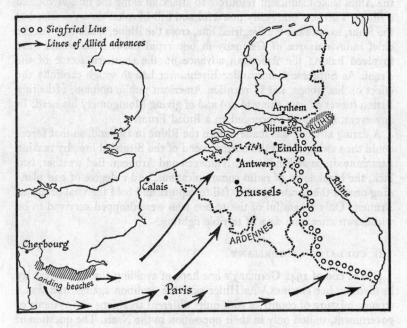

*Map 21. The Western Front, 1944–5*

Even more unnerving were the V.2's—rockets—introduced in August. No defence existed against them, and since they could not be heard approaching it was impracticable to take cover. Only the capture of the launching sites in Belgium and Holland removed their menace.

## PLANS FOR THE FINAL ASSAULT

Eisenhower, though without battle experience before the Algerian campaign and with little previous experience of commanding troops, proved his capacity for the post of Supreme Commander time and again by his skilful handling of his subordinate commanders. Montgomery, with his immense prestige, had directed the actual operations in Normandy but after the capture of Paris the command of the land forces was divided between Montgomery and two American generals, Bradley and Patton. These commanders were allowed considerable independence of action in their own areas, and the Allied strategy was then much less co-ordinated than it had been before.

As the Allies prepared for the final assault against Germany a major difference of opinion arose between Eisenhower and Montgomery. Briefly, Eisenhower, unwilling to halt any commander while he was advancing, favoured an attack on a Broad Front. Montgomery, who maintained that the Allies lacked sufficient resources to attack all along the line, advocated a Single Thrust—'one really powerful and full-blooded thrust'—aimed at the Ruhr, to outflank the Siegfried line, cross the Rhine, and knock out the chief industrial area of Germany in one rapid blow. This would have involved halting the American advance on the southern sector of the Front. As Supreme Commander Eisenhower had to weigh carefully the effect on his troops, not to mention American public opinion, of halting Patton (never an easy thing to do) and of giving Montgomery his head. In any event, the attack proceeded on a Broad Front.

A daring attempt was made to leap the Rhine in Holland, so that forces could then swing round the northern end of the Siegfried line, by making parachute drops at Eindhoven, Nijmegen and Arnhem. Bad weather, bad luck, the breakdown of radio communications, and a degree of bad planning caused the paratroopers to fail to capture and hold the vital bridge at Arnhem. Only a handful of the 10 000 who were dropped survived to be withdrawn after nine days of terrible fighting.

### THE COLLAPSE OF GERMANY

By the end of 1944 Germany's one hope of avoiding absolute defeat lay in dividing her enemies.[1] As Hitler saw, the coalition against him was a strange mixture of countries with quite different traditions and systems of government, united only in their opposition to the Nazis. The question of the Second Front had not been the only rift between the Allies. Churchill, both for political and strategic reasons, favoured an Anglo-American invasion of the Balkans from the Mediterranean. This suggestion was opposed by Stalin because he wanted Russian troops to secure that area, and by Roosevelt, partly because he wanted to keep on good terms with Stalin, and partly because he suspected that he was being asked to spend American lives to extend British influence in south-east Europe.

[1] The German army was ready to cut its losses. On July 20th, 1944, some high-ranking officers made an attempt on Hitler's life by means of a time-bomb concealed in a brief-case placed under the conference table at the Führer's headquarters. The bomb exploded but Hitler escaped with singed hair, bruises, and a ruined pair of trousers. The plotters were shot or hanged.

As the Allies neared victory, the Nazis pinned increasing faith on a negotiated peace with the British and Americans. What the Germans needed was one big offensive to persuade the western Allies that they could not achieve the unconditional surrender without a long, tough fight. This was the purpose of the Ardennes offensive in December 1944. Against a thinly-manned sector of the American line, Hitler launched a surprise attack in great strength. Fit and fanatical young Nazis, brought under arms by the reduction of the call-up age in Germany to sixteen years and trained intensively for only a few weeks, marched with crusading spirit to death or glory. But although the Germans were able to penetrate deeply into the Allied front, the further they advanced the more vulnerable they were to counter-attacks on the flanks of the bulge. Nevertheless, it was not until February 1945 that the Americans were back to the positions they had held before the offensive began.

Meanwhile on the Eastern Front the Russians were steadily advancing. In August 1944 Rumania surrendered, to be followed by Finland and Bulgaria in September. In Yugoslavia, the Communist partisans under Tito opened the way for the Russians into Hungary, which surrendered in January 1945. Poland was cleared by the beginning of February, and Vienna fell to the Russians in April.

Roosevelt, who died in April 1945, lived long enough to see Communist-dominated régimes established in eastern Europe as Churchill had predicted. On the other hand, Stalin became increasingly distrustful of his allies as Hitler withdrew more and more forces from the west to hold the Eastern Front. Politics and strategy were inextricably mixed.

On the afternoon of April 30th, with the Russians less than half a mile away, Hitler committed suicide, and his body was burned in the garden of the Chancellery. Admiral Dönitz became Hitler's successor, but his power was short-lived. On May 7th Germany surrendered unconditionally. At midnight on May 8th–9th, 1945, the war in Europe ended.

## THE JAPANESE WAR

While events were moving swiftly in Africa and Europe, bitter fighting had taken place in the Pacific. By the end of 1943 New Guinea had been recaptured, and during 1944 the Americans moved northwards from island to island. In October, at the great naval battle of Leyte, the Americans won a decisive victory which paved the way for the recapture of the Philippines, which were completely recovered by July 1945. In May 1945 the British troops fighting on the 'forgotten' front in Burma recaptured Rangoon and reopened the supply-road to China.

The war against the Japanese was brought to a dramatic end by the new terrible weapon which was to symbolize the coming age—the Atomic Bomb.[1]

---

[1] Intensive work in the production of an atomic bomb began in Britain and America in 1942. Not until November 1944 did the British and Americans know for certain that German nuclear research was years behind their own.

The profound problems raised by the decision to use the bomb against Japan have been widely debated. At the time the decision was regarded primarily in military terms. The Japanese were spread over such a large area and were so fanatical in their resistance that had the fighting continued with conventional weapons only, the war would have been long and very costly. Against this, it has been argued that the Americans should have warned the Japanese that they possessed this mighty destructive power, if necessary by demonstration in some area where it would do little harm.[1]

As it was, a uranium bomb was dropped without warning on the town of Hiroshima in the early morning of August 6th. Of the population of some quarter of a million, 60 000 were killed, and 100 000 injured. Almost the entire city was destroyed.

The U.S.S.R. had been kept in ignorance of the atomic bomb, but once the secret was out the Soviet Union hastened to declare war on Japan (August 8th) before it was too late, and Soviet troops invaded Manchuria. On the following day, a more powerful plutonium bomb was dropped on Nagasaki. The Japanese government agreed to surrender unconditionally, and the capitulation took place on board the battleship *Missouri* in Tokyo Bay on September 2nd. The war had come to a rapid and abrupt end.

## TEHERAN, YALTA AND POTSDAM

During the war three conferences were held between the heads of government of the Big Three—Britain, the United States and the U.S.S.R. It is convenient to look at these meetings together here, for the decisions taken then have had a great influence on post-war politics.

The first meeting was held in November 1943 at Teheran in Persia. It was attended by Roosevelt, Churchill and Stalin. The chief matter discussed there was the British and American plan for the Second Front. It was at this meeting that Roosevelt first tried to strike up a friendship with Stalin, playfully calling him 'Uncle Joe', and teasing Churchill in front of him. Stalin was not slow to exploit the situation.

The second, and most important, meeting was held at the Crimean resort of Yalta in February 1945. Again Roosevelt, Churchill and Stalin attended. The timing of the conference was unfortunate for the western allies, coming as it did just after the set-back they had suffered in the Ardennes, while the Red Army was winning great victories in Poland.

The Big Three arranged for a conference to be held at San Francisco in April to draft the Charter of the United Nations. They agreed that Germany, once conquered, should be divided, pending a peace settlement, into four zones, to be occupied by the United States, Russia, Britain and France. Berlin, though within the Russian zone, was to be divided into four

[1] It has, however, been asserted that at that stage the scientists could not guarantee the success of every bomb. If a demonstration had proved a fiasco, the Japanese might have continued the fight to secure a negotiated and conditional surrender.

sectors and administered jointly by the powers. France was given a voice in German affairs on Churchill's insistence and against Stalin's wishes. Churchill did not want Britain to face Russia alone, and he was not convinced that the United States would not again withdraw into isolation as she had after the First World War.

**Map 22. The Far East, 1941–5**

Stalin wanted severe reparations but Britain opposed any scheme which would make Germany dependent economically on aid from the Allies. Deadlock was resolved by leaving the actual sum to be determined by a Reparations Commission. In fact, reparations were exacted only from the Russian zone.

Another considerable difference arose over Poland. As they advanced the Russians had established at Lublin a Communist-dominated Provisional Government which was a rival to the exiled Polish Government in London. At Yalta, Britain and the U.S.A. agreed to withdraw recognition from the London Poles in return for the holding of free elections in Poland. The Russians readily agreed to this proposal, but rejected the suggestion that the elections should be supervised by representatives of the 'Big Three'. This, said Molotov, would be 'an affront to the pride and sovereignty of the independent people'!

Little agreement could be reached over the future frontiers of Poland. Russia was allowed to retain those provinces she had acquired with Nazi collaboration in 1939 and it was agreed that Poland should be compensated in the north and west at Germany's expense. But the delineation of the western frontier was to be left to the peace-makers.

Agreement was, however, reached on a matter of great importance to the United States, namely Russia's undertaking to enter the war against Japan within two or three months after the collapse of Germany. Stalin demanded as his price the return of Russia's 1905 losses and the recognition of Soviet interests in Manchuria.

The third meeting of the heads of government took place at Potsdam, a suburb of Berlin, in August 1945. Stalin was the sole survivor from the earlier meetings. Roosevelt was dead and his place was taken by President Truman. Churchill was replaced by Attlee while the conference was in progress as a result of the Labour Party's victory in the General Election.

The three powers (France was not invited) confirmed the decisions taken at Yalta about Germany. German minorities in Czechoslovakia, Hungary and Poland were to be deported to Germany. A Council of Foreign Ministers of the five Allied powers (the Big Three plus France and China) was formed to draw up peace treaties with Italy, Bulgaria, Finland, Hungary and Rumania. No agreement was reached about Poland's western frontier, but the Poles were to be allowed to administer territory up to the Oder-Neisse Line.[1]

CONCLUSION

Though the war had destroyed the vile menace of the Nazis and the Japanese imperialists, nothing could undo the misery they had caused. Millions of people had been transported to the Reich from the occupied countries to work as slaves. Those who became too old, or weak and ill, to work were murdered. Children uprooted from their homes in infancy, their parents taken from them, grew up not knowing who they were or where they came from. Jews and gypsies were systematically exterminated. Brutality became the order of the day in the enemy-occupied parts of Europe and Asia, and even some of the occupied peoples seized the chance to pay off old scores against their neighbours.

Those who survived were not always able or willing to return to their homes. With the coming of new governments in eastern Europe, many found themselves homeless and stateless. Still, years after the fighting has ceased, these people are obliged to live out aimless lives in 'displaced persons' camps.

[1] Poland and East Germany subsequently recognized this as the permanent frontier.

*Map 23. Germany: Zones of Occupation, 1945*

In the occupied countries divisions were created between those who collaborated with the enemy forces and those who joined underground resistance groups. Britain, alone of the European countries involved in the war, was spared the bitterness and the difficulties left by this problem. The task of reconstruction after the war was immense, not least in Germany and Italy where the Allies had to try to eradicate Nazism and Fascism without causing a complete breakdown in the life and work of those countries. The material damage alone was very great, but it was more easily put right than the damage done to millions of ordinary people in terms of social disruption and of physical and mental suffering. The price of liberty was high. Some paid the price without getting their liberty.

# 18  The United Nations and the Cold War

The term United Nations was first used to describe the alliance against Germany, Italy and Japan. In 1942 the twenty-six[1] nations who were fighting those powers signed the United Nations Declaration by which

[1] This number had risen to forty-five by April 1945. There were some last-minute scrambles on to the bandwaggon.

they each subscribed to the principles of the Atlantic Charter and undertook not to conclude a separate peace. It was not until November 1943 that the representatives of Britain, America, Russia and China, by the Moscow Declaration, proposed the establishment of an organization to maintain international peace and security, and the structure of that organization was not agreed upon until after the conferences at Dumbarton Oaks in 1944, and at San Francisco in 1945. Before looking at the peacetime organization, we must see how the leaders of the wartime alliance dealt with their enemies once the fighting was over.

### THE NUREMBERG TRIAL

At Nuremberg, between November 1945 and October 1946, the Nazi leaders were solemnly tried before a tribunal composed of judges from Britain, the United States, France and Russia, on charges of committing crimes against peace, war crimes and crimes against humanity. Such a trial was unique in history and many have questioned its wisdom. Some, who thought that the defendants should have been shot out of hand, regarded it as a waste of everyone's time. Others felt that the victorious powers were abusing legal traditions by formulating laws (except those concerning war crimes), and the machinery for enforcing them, after the crimes had been committed. Whatever the validity of these arguments and whatever effect the proceedings may have had on deterring future aggressors, the Nuremberg trial did at least put on public record, for those who have the stomach to read it, the appalling story of Nazi inhumanity. Of the twenty-two accused,[1] twelve were sentenced to be hanged, three (including Hess) were given life imprisonment, four (including Dönitz) were given sentences of between ten and twenty years' imprisonment, and three (including Papen and Schacht) were acquitted. Göring cheated the gallows by committing suicide in his cell. Goebbels and Himmler had, like Hitler, committed suicide before the trial began. Similar trials took place in Japan, and in both Germany and Japan special courts dealt with other cases of war crimes over the next few years.

### THE PEACE TREATIES

In accordance with the agreement at the Potsdam Conference a Council of Foreign Ministers of the five great powers drew up draft peace treaties with Italy, Bulgaria, Rumania, Hungary, and Finland. Twenty-one countries attended the Peace Conference in Paris in 1946, but the conference had power to make recommendations only, and the final texts were drawn up by the Foreign Ministers at a subsequent meeting. Essentially, these treaties were the work of the 'Big Three' and, like the Versailles terms, were not negotiated with the enemy states but dictated to them.

[1] One, Martin Bormann, the Deputy Führer after Hess, was tried in his absence. Whether he is dead or alive has not been discovered.

The only negotiating that there was took place between the victors, and the settlement was delayed by disagreements between Russia and the western powers. However, the treaties were finally signed in February 1947.

Italy ceded land on her frontiers to France and to Yugoslavia, and lost the Dodecanese Islands to Greece. Trieste was declared a free United Nations territory. Italy renounced all claims to her former colonies[1] and was required to pay reparations to Yugoslavia, Albania, Ethiopia, Greece and the U.S.S.R.

Rumania ceded Bessarabia and Northern Bukovina to Russia and Southern Dobruja to Bulgaria, Hungary ceded Transylvania to Rumania. Finland ceded Karelia and Petsamo to Russia. Rumania and Finland had to pay reparations to Russia, Bulgaria to Greece and Yugoslavia, Hungary to Czechoslovakia, Yugoslavia and Russia.

The Council of Foreign Ministers next turned its attention to the treaties with Austria and Germany, but Russia, which was happily engaged in exploiting Austria's resources—particularly oil—refused to consider the German and Austrian problems separately and no agreement could be reached about Germany. Eventually, however, in 1955 peace was signed with Austria alone upon condition that Russia received heavy reparations, including one million tons of crude oil a year for the following ten years. Austria undertook to remain permanently neutral.

## THE UNITED NATIONS

The Charter of the United Nations Organization was signed at San Francisco in June 1945 by fifty nations.[2] The Charter, like the Covenant of the League, set out the aims, the rules, and the structure of the organization. Its aims were to maintain international peace and security, to safeguard human rights, and to foster international co-operation. Members undertook to settle their international disputes by peaceful means, and to support United Nations resolutions. Two other important provisions of the Charter need to be noted: First, that members were permitted, and indeed encouraged, to make 'regional arrangements or agencies' for the maintenance of peace, provided that the Security Council was kept fully informed of them and provided that they were consistent with the purposes and principles of the United Nations; second, that the United Nations would not interfere in the internal affairs of any nation.

The United Nations was to function through six principal organs:

1. *The General Assembly* was to consist of all members, each of whom would have one vote. The Assembly would normally meet once a year,

[1] Ethiopia had been liberated in 1941. Libya was granted its independence following a U.N. resolution in 1949, and further resolutions in 1950 federated Eritrea to Ethiopia and gave Italy trusteeship over Somalia (formerly Italian Somaliland).

[2] Including one neutral country, Argentina, and three representatives from Russia —one from the U.S.S.R., one from Byelorussia, and one from the Ukraine. Russia had originally demanded separate representation for all sixteen Soviet Republics.

though special sessions might be held. It could discuss any matter lying within the scope of the Charter and could make recommendations to members or to the Security Council. It was to approve the annual budget.

2. *The Security Council* was to consist of eleven members, five of whom were to be permanent (the United States, Russia, Britain, France and China), and six of whom were to be elected by the Assembly for two years. Each member would have one vote. The Security Council would be in continuous session and it would bear the primary responsibility for the maintenance of peace and security. On any issue, however, other than a purely procedural question, no decision could be made without the approval of seven members of the Council, including all the five permanent members. The only exception to this rule would be if one of the members were a party to a dispute, in which case it must abstain from voting. This power of veto, possessed by all the major powers, came to be employed frequently in the following years to block action by the Security Council, though a resolution passed by the Assembly in November 1950, after the outbreak of the Korean War, provided that if the Security Council failed, because of the veto, to fulfil its function of maintaining peace and security, the Assembly could take action if it were approved by a two-thirds majority. Members of the Security Council could also veto the admission of new members to U.N.O., and this right, too, came to be widely employed, though a 'package deal' in 1955 brought in sixteen new members, some of whom were supported by the western powers only, and some of whom were supported only by the U.S.S.R.

3. *The Economic and Social Council* was to be responsible to the Assembly for supervising U.N. work in economic, social, cultural, educational, health, and similar matters. This Council established numerous commissions on such matters as Transport and Communications, Human Rights, Drugs, and Population, and it also supervised and co-ordinated the work of the specialized agencies, e.g. the United Nations Educational, Scientific, and Cultural Organization (UNESCO), the Food and Agricultural Organization (FAO), the International Civil Aviation Organization (ICAO), the International Labour Organization (ILO), the International Trade Organization (ITO), the World Health Organization (WHO), the Universal Postal Union (UPO), the International Telecommunication Union (ITU), the International Bank, and the International Monetary Fund. Some of these agencies were already in existence, others were newly created. In a special category was the United Nations International Children's Emergency Fund (UNICEF) which was created in 1946 to meet the needs of children, particularly in the war-devastated areas, and to foster the health of children generally.

4. *The Trusteeship Council* was established to supervise U.N. Trust territories. Nations granted trusteeship were to be required to prepare the peoples in those territories for self-government, and to submit annual reports to the U.N. The Council could receive petitions from the peoples in the territories and could visit those territories.

5. *The International Court of Justice* established at the Hague was to consist of fifteen judges selected by the Security Council and the General Assembly. Members of the U.N. could not be bound to use the Court or to accept its decisions, but if both parties to a dispute agreed to the case's going before the Court they would have to accept the Court's ruling.

6. *The Secretariat* was to consist of a Secretary-General appointed for a term of five years, and his staff.

In its aims and structure the U.N.O. bears a marked resemblance to the League of Nations. Had the U.S.A. and the U.S.S.R. been members of the League it might even have survived in name. The chief changes to be noticed are the enhanced position of the great powers and of the Security Council, the replacement of the unanimity rule in the League by a two-thirds majority rule in the U.N. Assembly, and the powers given to the Trusteeship Council to receive petitions and to visit territories. Another difference is that the Charter of the U.N., unlike the Covenant of the League, was not written into the peace treaties. Like the League, however, the United Nations depended for success on the goodwill of its member-states and their readiness to fulfil their obligations. The United Nations had a better start than the League because the most powerful nations in the world were all members, but the workings of the organization were soon to be severely hampered by the rivalry of those powers.

## THE COLD WAR

The Second World War brought about a great change in the balance of power in the world. America, the only country to finance the war out of production, emerged as easily the strongest power. What is more, she had manufactured, and used, atomic bombs. Only Britain shared the secret of their construction. Britain herself had been gravely weakened economically by the war and, although still a great power, was no longer in a position of even apparent supremacy. France was weaker still, both economically and, since she had been defeated, politically. Germany and Japan, which had occupied such dominating positions in Europe and the Far East, had disappeared as powers. China, which with the defeat of the Japanese became engulfed in civil war, had yet to emerge as a strong nation. Soviet Russia, on the other hand, emerged as a dominant power for the first time. Although the U.S.S.R. had been devastated, her industrial power, the foundations of which had been laid before the war, had grown from infancy to maturity during the course of the fighting. Her task of reconstruction was undoubtedly great, but as a victor she was able to make good at least some of her material losses by seizing goods and machinery as reparations from her defeated enemies. Politically, the U.S.S.R. emerged in control of the greater part of eastern Europe, and elsewhere the ravages of war seemed likely to have left a fertile seed-bed for the growth of Communism, particularly as in many places Communists had played a leading part in the resistance movements.

Rivalry between the United States and the U.S.S.R., with the division of nations into those of the West and those of the East, has become such an accepted feature of the post-war world that it is sometimes difficult to realize that such a situation was not readily apparent when the war ended. As we have seen, the Allied leaders had their disagreements in the war and there were disputes over the peace treaties. The structure of U.N.O. also occasioned divergences of opinion. But these were not regarded as fundamental divisions. Few people in Britain and America would, in 1945, have thought it possible that within a year or two their countries would be on better terms with Germans, Italians and Japanese than with Russians, Poles and Czechs. When Churchill made a speech at Fulton in the United States in 1946 in which he spoke of an 'iron curtain' having fallen across Europe and urged Anglo-American unity, he was widely regarded as a warmonger. Nevertheless, the divisions between the ex-Allies grew and there developed between them a system of diplomatic and economic manoeuvring designed to weaken their opponents' position and to strengthen their own, without actually going to war. This high-level shadow boxing was called the Cold War.

A good example of the way the Cold War was to be conducted occurred over Persia very soon after the war. Britain and Russia had jointly occupied Persia in 1941, and even before the war ended Russia tried to exact—with menaces—an oil concession from the Persian government. Failing to get immediate satisfaction, the Russians began to encourage one of the occupied provinces to establish its independence from the rest of Persia, and they prevented government troops from entering the area.[1] The matter came before the Security Council in 1946, but in May of that year Soviet forces withdrew from Persia, having been promised an oil concession. When this agreement came before the Persian National Assembly for ratification in 1947 it was rejected. A few days earlier America had been given the exclusive right to send military advisers to Persia. Russia also tried, at the end of the war, to bring pressure to bear on Turkey to permit Soviet forces to garrison the Straits. These incidents may be regarded either as examples of Russia's traditional urge towards an outlet to the sea in warm water, or as attempts to extend Communist domination to the Middle East with its vital oil. In either event, America had taken over Britain's traditional role of preventing Russian penetration to the south.

The real division between Russia and the West came, however, in 1947 over Greece. British troops had gone to Greece in 1944 to put down a civil war between the rival Communist and monarchist resistance groups. As a result of elections held in 1946 the royalists formed a government and a plebiscite declared in favour of the return of the King. Civil war then broke out again, Greece complained to the Security Council, and an investigation showed that the Communists were receiving aid from Yugoslavia, Albania and Bulgaria. Russia refused to accept this finding and attributed the

---

[1] A method not unlike that by which the United States acquired the Canal Zone in 1903. See p. 195.

disorders to the undoubtedly vindictive policies of the Greek government and the social distress of the country. Britain, unable to bear alone the cost of maintaining her troops in Greece in these circumstances appealed for help from the United States. President Truman responded by asking Congress to grant $400 million in military and economic aid for Greece and Turkey. In doing so, he declared that 'it must be the policy of the United States to support free peoples who are resisting attempted subjugation by armed minorities or outside pressure'. Civil war continued in Greece until 1949 and was brought to an end largely because the expulsion of Yugoslavia[1] from the Soviet bloc in 1948 cut the rebels off from their supplies. But the 'Truman Doctrine', as the President's Declaration was called, marked a momentous step in American foreign policy. It marked America's acceptance of the leadership of the free world and it also marked the beginning of the policy of containment—that is, of preventing further encroachment by the Communists.

The Truman Doctrine was quickly followed by the Marshall Plan (see p. 11). This offer of American aid was officially open to all European countries, though it is difficult to imagine that Congress would have agreed to finance any Soviet-controlled states. In any case, the Soviet Union and its satellites boycotted the discussions after the first meeting, called by Britain and France to consider the plan. Czechoslovakia at first accepted an invitation to the second meeting but then withdrew under Soviet pressure. The Czechoslovak Communists, fearing that because of their rejection of so much material aid, they would lose their majority in the coalition government after the elections which were due in 1948, carried out a *coup d'état* early in that year. The stifling of democratic life in Czechoslovakia was one of the most tragic of many tragic episodes after the war. It shocked those with doubts into a full realization of Stalin's ambition to extend the considerable area over which he already had dominion. It should nevertheless be noted that the Communist seizure of power would have been made more difficult had it not been for the support given to the Communist leaders by some non-Communists. Czechs could hardly be expected to forget Munich. They did not naturally look to the western powers for protection.

Russia replied to what she regarded as America's economic domination of Europe by establishing the Cominform (Communist Information Bureau) to co-ordinate the activities of the Communist parties of Bulgaria, Czechoslovakia, France, Hungary, Italy, Poland, Rumania, Yugoslavia and the U.S.S.R. To sabotage the Marshall Plan industrial unrest was fomented in Western Europe.

[1] Tito, the President of Yugoslavia, and ex-leader of the Communist partisans in the war, had won his country's independence largely on his own efforts and he saw no reason why he should be subservient to Moscow.

SPARKS IN THE COLD WAR

*The Berlin Blockade 1948–9.* By the beginning of 1948 the Iron Curtain
had undeniably fallen across Europe. The western powers put into operation a scheme for the economic rehabilitation of their zones of Germany
and their sector of Berlin by introducing a currency reform and by making
available Marshall Aid. The Soviet authorities, who had been extracting
food and materials from their zone, became alarmed by the course of events
in the western zones and introduced new traffic regulations which effectively
blockaded the western sector of Berlin, isolated as it was in the Russian
zone. Here was a test-case. If the western powers allowed themselves to be
bullied out of Berlin, where would Soviet encroachment end? The western
powers accordingly organized a massive and costly air-lift which kept
Berlin supplied for nearly a year until the Russians lifted the blockade in
May 1949. This trial of strength took place without fighting, though in the
early stages of the blockade the Cold War certainly appeared to be getting
dangerously warm. The division of Germany was, however, reinforced. In
May 1949 France, Britain and America established in Western Germany
the German Federal Republic, while in October the German Democratic
Republic was created in the Russian zone. Both republics became independent sovereign states, in the eyes of their sponsors at least, in 1955.

*The Korean War 1950–3.* The victory of the Chinese Communists over
Chiang-Kai-Shek's crumbling Nationalist régime in 1949 and the establishment of the Chinese People's Republic carried the Cold War dramatically into the Far East. Although the 'Big Three' had all supported Chiang-
Kai-Shek during the war, none was as heavily committed to him as
America. When the Nationalists were forced to withdraw from the mainland to the island of Formosa, both the Soviet Union and Britain transferred their recognition to the Communist People's government, but the
United States did not, and it has persistently refused to do so ever since.[1]

An absurd position was created on the Security Council, where the
Nationalist delegate remained a permanent member with the right of veto.
Russia, in protest at the exclusion of Communist China from the U.N.,
walked out of the Security Council and this left the way clear for the U.N.
to take military action when fighting broke out in Korea.

By the Cairo Agreement of 1943 between China, Britain and the U.S.A.
Korea was to become independent after Japan's defeat. When the war
ended Korea was temporarily occupied by Soviet troops north of the 38th
parallel and south of that line by American troops. As in Germany, no
agreement could be reached about setting up a new government. As a
result a Communist government was established in North Korea, and in
South Korea a right-wing government was set up under Syngman Rhee,
an American-educated Korean nationalist who had for long been recog-

[1] In the summer of 1971 the U.S.A. opened diplomatic relations with Peking,
and indicated that she would not oppose China's admission to the U.N. when the
next application was made.

nized by Korean exiles as their national leader. The South Korean government, which had been elected under the supervision of a U.N. commission (which was denied access to North Korea), was recognized by the General Assembly, though it was not admitted to the U.N. In December 1948 Soviet forces were withdrawn from Korea, to be followed in the following June by the American forces, with the exception of an advisory mission.

On June 25th, 1950, North Korean forces invaded South Korea. The circumstances of the attack will probably never be known. It has been asserted that the South Koreans provoked an incident, relying on the Americans to come to their aid and then to help them crush the North Koreans. If they did, they certainly needed to rely on outside rescue for they were woefully unprepared to meet the onslaught from the north.

A resolution of the Security Council, from which Russia, it will be remembered, had voluntarily withdrawn temporarily, called for a cease-fire and for the withdrawal of the North Korean forces to the north of the 38th parallel. President Truman followed this up by ordering U.S. forces to implement the U.N. resolution. Other members of the U.N. gave support, too, though the Americans bore by far the greatest burden of the fighting and the expense. The temptation to bomb China, which sent considerable aid to the North Koreans in war material and in 'volunteers', was very great, but it was resisted. Fighting reached a stalemate in 1951 and truce talks were begun, but it was not until July 1953, after the death of Stalin—and after the election of Eisenhower[1] as President of the United States—that an armistice was signed.

By the armistice terms Korea was divided again along roughly the same line that had existed before. The policy of America was one of containment only. The Korean war was limited to a local incident, though the country was devastated and the sufferings of the Korean people, of whom perhaps as many as three million were killed, were pitiful. Like the Berlin Blockade, the Korean war made the position of the rivals more rigid. On the one hand stood Communist China, North Korea and the Soviet Union, on the other Nationalist China, South Korea and the United States. But between them the events in Berlin and Korea underlined the determination of the United States to halt the march of Communism in the west and in the east. In the 1960's as in the 1950's, this was to prove an expensive and thankless burden.

The U.S. forces had fought in Korea under the U.N. flag, but the U.N.O. was clearly unable to provide security either to the U.S. or to the nations of Western Europe which felt themselves vulnerable to a Soviet attack. At that time, before the development of long-range ICBM's, the U.S.A. needed a firm foothold in Europe if it was to be able to make an effective counter-threat to the U.S.S.R. The nations of Western Europe, for their part, wanted the U.S.A. firmly committed to their defence. They remembered only too well the isolationist policies which had kept the U.S.

[1] He had promised the war-weary American people that if elected he would do all in his power to reach a settlement.

disengaged from European affairs from 1919 until December 1941, with tragic results. All concerned had good reasons to look for agreement on regional security.

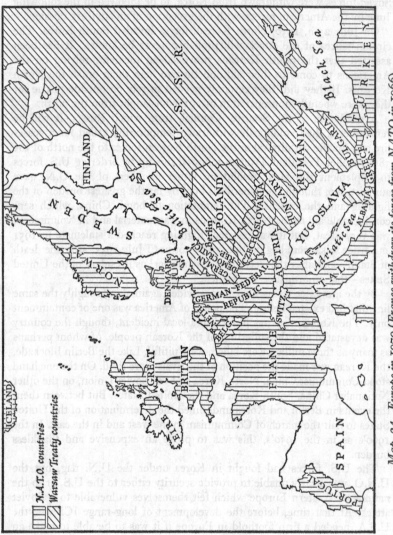

*Map 24. Europe in 1970 (France withdrew its forces from NATO in 1966)*

REGIONAL SECURITY

In March 1948 the nations of Western Europe (Britain, France, Belgium, Luxemburg and the Netherlands) signed the Brussels Treaty for joint defence against aggression in Europe. This organization was expanded in 1949 into the North Atlantic Treaty Organization (NATO), which comprised the Brussels Treaty signatories plus Canada, Denmark, Iceland, Italy, Norway, Portugal and the United States. Greece and Turkey joined NATO in 1952 and the Federal German Republic in 1955. Similar steps were taken to provide security in the Pacific by the Pacific Security Pact of 1951 signed by Australia, New Zealand and the U.S.A., which led to the creation of the South East Asia Treaty Organization (SEATO) made up of Australia, New Zealand, Pakistan, the Philippines, Thailand, Britain, France, and the United States.

Added to these were the various economic agreements, which have been referred to elsewhere, and the Council of Europe[1] set up in 1949 to discuss all matters of common concern, except defence.

Russia, which had already soon after the war concluded alliances with its satellites, replied to these western organizations by creating in 1955 the Warsaw Treaty Organization which integrated the armed forces of Albania, Bulgaria, Czechoslovakia, the German Democratic Republic, Hungary, Poland, Rumania, and the U.S.S.R.

THE END OF THE STALIN ERA

The death of Stalin brought hopes of an end to the Cold War. In part these hopes were realized, but the world got no nearer the general peace and security which it is the function of the U.N. to promote and maintain. Divisions remained, but gradually attitudes changed as American and Russian technologists made the destruction of life on earth a real possibility. Rifts occurred both in the Communist and in the non-Communist blocs, and new conflicts arose in South-East Asia, in Africa, and in the Middle East in which East-West divisions were by no means clear-cut. It was in these new situations that the U.N. developed, by trial and error, its peace-keeping rôle.

[1] Its membership in 1957 comprised the Brussels Treaty powers, Denmark, the Irish Republic, Italy, Norway, Sweden, Greece, Turkey, Iceland, the German Federal Republic and Austria.

# 19   Coexistence and Confrontation

## THE KHRUSHCHEV ERA

Under Stalin the Soviet Union had been engaged in a struggle to survive politically, economically, and militarily. His death in 1953 marked the end of a long era in Russian history. But even before his death the circumstances which had caused Stalin to be as suspicious of his friends as of his enemies, both at home and abroad, were changing significantly. By 1953, the Soviet Union had successfully manufactured a hydrogen bomb. Although the U.S.A. remained well ahead in its stock-pile of nuclear weapons and in its ability to deliver them to enemy targets, nevertheless Russian foreign policy became based more on self-assurance and less on fear. Russian leaders, although alert to any dangers, were inclined to believe that the U.S.A. dare not risk an attack on the Soviet Union. A major step had been taken towards the creation of what has been called *the balance of terror*. Since both major powers had so much to lose from war against each other, they became more conciliatory towards each other. The Russian leader who initiated this change of mood in foreign and domestic affairs was Nikita Khrushchev.

Stalin had occupied such a dominant position that his death inevitably brought a prolonged struggle for power in Soviet politics. There were many in the Soviet hierarchy who wanted to abolish one-man rule and to re-establish collective leadership, with the Party as the chief instrument of power. For a while, it looked as if they might succeed. From the man-oeuvres following Stalin's death, Malenkov emerged as Prime Minister, and Khrushchev as First Secretary of the Communist Party. When Malenkov was removed from office in 1955, he was replaced by Bulganin, and for the next three years Bulganin and Khrushchev operated ostensibly as joint rulers. It was not until 1958 that Khrushchev, having survived an attempt by Malenkov to bring about his downfall the previous year, felt strong enough to take office as Prime Minister while still remaining First Secretary. He was then supreme in the Soviet Union until his sudden dismissal in October 1964.

Khrushchev was born in the province of Kursk, close to the Ukraine, in 1894. His father was a poor peasant who eked out a meagre living by going each winter to work in the coalfields of the Donets basin. In 1908, the whole family moved to that industrial region, and Khrushchev became first a herdsboy, and then an apprentice fitter at a German-owned engineering works. His minor rôle in a strike in 1912 cost him his job, but he was able to find work as a mechanic in a French-owned mining company. The inhuman living and working conditions he witnessed daily during this period of his life made a permanent impression on his political thinking. In 1918, after the Revolution, he joined the Communist Party, and then in 1922 he was able to go to Technical College, where he seized the opportunity to add to the very limited education he had received as a boy. He rose rapidly in the Party, became Secretary of the Moscow District Party Committee, and by 1939 he was a full member of the Politburo (see pp. 119 and 123). During the war Khrushchev was head of the Ukranian Communist Party, and he conducted the ruthless purges of anti-Stalinists which took place in the Ukraine after the German retreat. Yet, although his entire political career up to that point had been under Stalin's leadership, a greater contrast to Stalin could scarcely be imagined.

Whereas Stalin was cold, taciturn, and remote, Khrushchev was amusing, talkative, and quick-witted, with a fast line in repartee. As he was not slow to point out to Western diplomats, his lack of early formal education had not left him uninformed or lacking in mental agility. One of the chief aims of his home policy was to increase farm production which had so far failed to respond to Soviet planning. He was ready to give farm workers advice on how to grow better crops, but more important, he gave farms greater freedom from central control. He also encouraged officials to be honest about production figures, which had been persistently falsified through fear under the Stalin régime. Output did increase, though in 1963 poor harvests forced the U.S.S.R. into the humiliating position of having to import grain from North America. The greater freedom granted to agriculture was matched in industry, which was increasingly directed towards producing consumer goods for the Russian people and for export, rather than capital goods and arms.

## DE-STALINIZATION

One of the earliest indications of the beginning of liberalization in the Soviet régime came in June 1953, when Beria, the hated head of the secret police and one of the chief instruments of Stalin's terror, was arrested and later summarily shot after a special session of the Presidium. But it was not until February 1956 that the key event occurred. At the 20th Congress of the Soviet Communist Party, Khrushchev made a sensational speech, lasting six hours, in which he detailed and denounced the crimes committed under Stalin's orders. Although the speech was made in a secret session of the Congress, its details were soon widely known. He also accused Stalin of anti-socialist behaviour in that he had sought his own personal glorification (the cult of personality) rather than sticking to the principle of collective responsibility in government. This speech triggered off a series of acts of de-Stalinization. Stalin's body was removed from the Mausoleum in Moscow, statues of Stalin were torn down, portraits removed, and Stalingrad (see pp. 162–3), which had symbolized Russia's victory over the Germans in the battlefield, was renamed Volgograd. Observers in the West viewed these events favourably. Some forecast that now that the U.S.S.R. had transformed itself into a strong industrial power and now that the people were beginning to enjoy the benefits of consumer goods, the revolutionary aspects of Communism would disappear and the Soviet

Union would become more and more like every other rich 20th century state. After all, uncontrolled free enterprise existed nowhere in the capitalist West. Governments everywhere exercised considerable influence and direction over all aspects of economic and social life. Other observers were content merely to welcome the prospect of 'peaceful coexistence' which Khrushchev had indicated was the Soviet Union's aim in foreign policy. One of the key resolutions of the 20th Congress declared that World Communism would no longer be brought about, as Lenin and Stalin believed, by a series of inevitable wars. Some countries it declared might reach Communism by non-violent or parliamentary means.

De-Stalinization produced immediate repercussions in the Soviet satellite states, which wanted to follow socialist policies in *alliance* with Moscow, rather than in *subservience* to it. Khrushchev's efforts to restore friendly relations with Tito's Yugoslavia, which as early as 1948 had successfully defied Stalin and broken from Soviet domination while remaining a Communist state, seemed to suggest to other satellite states that national communism paid off. In 1956 there was a rising in Poland. Bulganin and Khrushchev hastened to Warsaw and decided to accept the new leader Wladyslaw Gomulka. The Polish Communist Party was then permitted to follow an independent policy at home while following Russian direction in foreign policy. A few days later, however, a rising took place in Hungary. The new Prime Minister, Imre Nagy, withdrew Hungary from the Warsaw Pact (see p. 181) and proclaimed the country's neutrality. This was altogether too much for the Russians. On November 4th Russian tanks moved in, crushed the rising, and installed Janos Kadar as Prime Minister. Had Khrushchev allowed the Hungarians to follow an independent foreign policy, the other Soviet satellites in Eastern Europe would have demanded equal freedom, and the Soviet position in Europe would have been weakened. It is doubtful if Khrushchev could have survived such a disaster and those who favoured a return to Stalinist policies might have re-emerged triumphant. As it was both Poland and Hungary enjoyed greater internal freedom after 1956. The Western Powers were fully distracted during the Hungarian rising by the Suez Affair.[1] The Security Council of the United Nations was prevented from taking any action in response to the Hungarian appeal for help by the veto of the U.S.S.R., but it was clear that the U.S.A. was not prepared to take any steps to prevent the Russians from reasserting their control over Hungary. Few people, on either side, wished to see the precarious balance of power in Europe disturbed.[2]

## SUMMIT MEETING

The Russian launching of the first Inter-Continental Ballistic Missile in August 1957, followed by the first earth satellite (the sputnik) in October,

[1] The Anglo-French attack on Egypt in 1956 which followed the nationalization of the Suez Canal.
[2] Reaction to the Soviet invasion of Czechoslovakia in August 1968 was similar.

shocked the U.S. profoundly and led to an intensification of its own space programme, together with a critical examination of its educational system. Although the U.S. was not anxious to remain at an apparent disadvantage, both sides were anxious for a relaxation of tension—a détente. Following a visit by Vice-President Richard Nixon to Moscow,[1] Khrushchev visited President Eisenhower in the U.S. and presented a plan for disarmament to the General Assembly of the United Nations. A meeting—called a summit meeting[2] because it brought the leaders of the Powers together— between Eisenhower, Khrushchev, Macmillan (British Prime Minister), and de Gaulle (President of France) was arranged to be held in Paris in May 1960.

On May 1st, however, an American U2 reconnaissance aircraft was shot down over Russia. The pilot, Gary Powers, was captured and charged with spying. Khrushchev refused to begin the conference until Eisenhower apologized, and this Eisenhower refused to do. Reconnaissance flights over Russia between U.S. bases in Norway and Pakistan by high-flying U2 aircraft had been taking place for some time. It is not known whether Khrushchev deliberately sabotaged the talks under pressure from his own generals or to placate the Chinese, or whether the incident was merely an untimely accident. In any event the attempted détente had to be postponed.

BERLIN AND CUBA

In June 1961, six months after his inauguration as President of the U.S.A., Eisenhower's successor, John F. Kennedy, met Khrushchev in Vienna, but the political situation remained tense. A fresh crisis centred on Berlin. Although the frontier between East Germany and West Germany was strictly guarded, East Germans could move into the Russian sector of Berlin, and from there they could move freely into the Western sectors.[3] At the rate of a thousand a day, East Germans were using the city as an escape route from the gloom and misery of the German Democratic Republic to the brighter promise of the West. West Berlin was, as it were, a glittering shop window of the West, set in the midst of the most wretched of the Russian satellite countries. All the while free movement was permitted between the Russian sector and the rest of Berlin many East Germans were tempted to do more than window gaze. On the night of 12th–13th August a wall was built between the two sectors. The flow of refugees was effectively halted. Henceforth those who attempted flight did so at the risk, and frequently the cost, of their lives. The Wall became a tourist attraction for visitors to West Berlin, and it remains a grim monument to democracy as understood in the Democratic Republic.

[1] Nixon and Khruschev had a forthright, and widely televised, debate on the respective merits of communism and capitalism when they met in the American model kitchen at a trade fair.

[2] The first Summit Conference was held at Geneva in July 1955 and was attended by Bulganin, Khrushchev, Eisenhower, Eden (Britain), and Fauré (France).

[3] See p. 168.

Kennedy's first year in office had begun badly. In April he had permitted a group of Cuban exiles to make a foolhardy and disastrously unsuccessful attempt to invade Cuba and overthrow Fidel Castro. This episode—the Bay of Pigs—brought Cuba and the U.S.S.R. closer together and tempted Khrushchev to make a daring move to outmanoeuvre the U.S.A. In mid-October, aerial reconnaissance by U.S. aircraft revealed that the Russians were building bases in Cuba both for defensive ground-to-air missiles and for offensive ground-to-ground missiles. The whole defensive strategy of the U.S.A. was placed in jeopardy. Kennedy decided on a show-down. He demanded that the Russians remove their nuclear bases from Cuba. While the world waited to see if this was to be the occasion of nuclear war between the U.S.A. and the U.S.S.R., Kennedy drew up his plan for action. As Russian ships carrying more nuclear missiles made their way across the Atlantic, the U.S. Navy was moved to blockade Cuba. Khrushchev reckoned that the American President meant business. The Russian ships slackened speed and then, to everyone's relief, turned for home. Khrushchev had withdrawn from the brink, the bases were dismantled, and the Russian weapons already on the island were removed.

## TEST BAN TREATY

In April 1961 the Soviet astronaut Yuri Gagarin had been the first man in space—ten months before the American John Glen accomplished this feat. The effect of the apparent Soviet superiority over the Americans in missile technology, however, had been to intensify the efforts of the U.S.A. The expense, and to some extent the futility, of the race, coupled with increasing world-wide fears of the health risks of fall out from nuclear test explosions, led to negotiations which culminated in the Nuclear Test Ban Treaty. This treaty, signed in Moscow in July 1963 by the U.S.A., the U.S.S.R., Britain, and a number of other countries, banned the testing of nuclear weapons in space, in the atmosphere, and in the water. It did not ban underground tests. Although signatories could withdraw from the agreement if they judged that their special interests warranted it, in fact the Treaty has been adhered to. Two major nations which did not sign the treaty, and which have tested nuclear weapons in the atmosphere since 1963, were China and France.

## FRANCE. THE FOURTH REPUBLIC 1946–1958

De Gaulle, who had kept alive the spirit of Free France throughout the war, returned to his country in 1944 a national hero. He formed a new French government and, following a referendum in October 1945, a Constituent Assembly was formed to draw up a constitution to replace that of the defeated and discredited Third Republic. A year later, after another referendum (a favourite instrument of de Gaulle's), the new constitution was adopted and the Fourth Republic came into existence.

General de Gaulle greatly enjoyed moving freely among crowds wherever he went, though no doubt his bodyguards were not quite so relaxed!

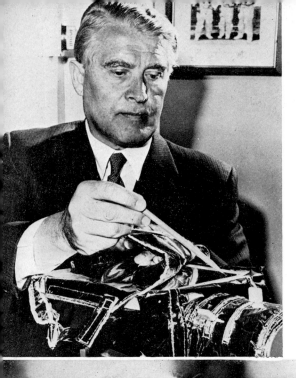

*Left* Werner von Braun, the German rocket engineer who built the V2 weapons launched against Britain in 1944 (see p. 165). After the war he went to the U.S.A. and played a leading part in the development of rockets for the Space Research programme. *Below* General de Gaulle and Dr. Adenauer, post-war leaders of France and West Germany, who achieved a remarkable reconciliation between their two countries.

Geoffrey Rippon, M.P. (left) who led the team which, in 1970-71, successfully negotiated terms for Britain's entry to the European Community. He is seen leaving the conference building with M. Maurice Schumann, the French Foreign Minister (no relation to M. Robert Schuman, architect of the E.C.S.C).

Edward Heath, who was Britain's chief negotiator when she first sought admission to the European Community in 1961. A keen yachtsman, he won the Sydney to Hobart race just before becoming Prime Minister in 1970.

Unhappily, the chief characteristic of the Third Republic—weak and unstable governments—was inherited by the Fourth. Even before the new constitution was adopted, de Gaulle himself, in January 1946, resigned and left political life for the time being. Altogether between the liberation of Paris in August 1944 and the end of the Fourth Republic in October 1958, no fewer than 26 Cabinets were formed in France. The longest surviving of these lasted for 16 months, the shortest for 3 days. The average was $5\frac{1}{2}$ months.

The problems which none of these governments was strong enough to grapple with were inflation, with wages lagging behind prices, weakness in foreign affairs, and the break-up of the French colonial empire.

## INDO-CHINA WAR 1946–1954

At the end of the Second World War, France, like other European colonial powers, faced the difficult task of re-establishing its authority over those areas of its Empire which had been involved in the fighting. The problem was most acute in the Far East where the French, like the British and the Dutch, had been ignominiously routed by an Asian people, the Japanese. After the British and (Nationalist) Chinese occupation forces left, the future of Indo-China became a matter of negotiation between the French and Ho Chi-Minh, leader of the Communist liberation movement, the Viet-Minh [1]

It seemed likely that agreement would be reached on the basis of virtual independence for North Vietnam under Ho Chi-Minh. But certain local commanders and officials, disliking the drift of events, decided to reassert French control by a show of force. In November 1946, French naval vessels bombarded Haiphong, killing 6000 people. Reprisals against Europeans by the Viet-Minh in Hanoi led to full-scale war which dragged on until 1954. The war cost the French dearly in men, money and in military prestige. After Mao Tse-Tung's victory over the Nationalist Chinese and the establishment of the People's Republic in 1949, Ho Chi-Minh was able to receive military aid from the Chinese Communists. As the United States was to discover later, it was impossible to defeat the Vietnamese guerrillas in the field, and yet unthinkable to withdraw from the contest. The French made one final bold bid for victory. A large force of paratroopers, the greater part of which consisted of anti-Communist Vietnamese soldiers, was landed at Dien Bien Phu deep in enemy held territory. They hoped to attract large numbers of enemy troops whom they could then destroy. The plan was similar in thought to that of the Germans at Verdun in 1917 (see page 136). For six months the French troops held out and received reinforcements, but defeat was inevitable, and in May 1954 they surrendered.

[1] This was later superseded by the N.L.F. (National Liberation Front). Viet-Cong is an American label meaning Vietnamese Communists.

## MENDÈS-FRANCE

Dien Bien Phu forced the French people to accept the fact that it was impossible to recreate a pre-war colonial empire, or anything like it. Pierre Mendès-France, who took office as Prime Minister pledged to end the war in Indo-China in weeks, was well placed to guide France through the agonizing experience of facing up to reality. For years he had been warning the French people that a policy of avoiding difficult decisions, whether they were economic, social, or political, could only end in disaster. The Geneva Conference, under the co-chairmanship of Britain and the U.S.S.R., negotiated the settlement terms. North Vietnam became an independent state with Ho Chi-Minh as its President. South Vietnam became independent under Bao Dai,[1] the former Emperor of Annam whom the French had supported against Ho Chi-Minh in 1946. Cambodia and Laos were granted independence and declared neutral.

Mendès-France was Prime Minister for only seven months but his importance was considerable, quite apart from his major achievement of ending the Indo-China War. Steps were taken to avoid further entanglements in Tunisia and Morocco, and both protectorates gained their independence in 1956. The economic reforms he proposed met with opposition and led to his defeat, but he had managed in a short space of time to rid a number of Frenchmen of apathy and to persuade many that with dynamic leadership France could again be great, prosperous, and significant.

Not everyone in France viewed the prospect of change with pleasure, and after the fall of Mendès-France in 1955, there followed a period of reaction which manifested itself in the 1956 election in the short-lived but interesting phenomenon of Poujadism. Pierre Poujade, a provincial shopkeeper, spoke for the rural and small-town France. Encouraged by the success of his Association for the Defence of Shopkeepers and Artisans, which argued that small businessmen needed to practise tax evasion to survive, Poujade entered national politics and appealed to a wide variety of people who were disgruntled and distrustful of politicians and the authorities. In 1956 his party won over 50 seats in the Assembly and polled almost three million votes. Poujade had not the powers of leadership, and his party had no coherent policy. Its rapid collapse in the following years was predictable, but the movement once again demonstrated the problems facing any constructive leader in the Republic.

## ALGERIA

Although Tunisia and Morocco achieved independence relatively painlessly, Algeria presented altogether a different problem. Whereas they were French protectorates only, Algeria was constitutionally a part of France. Furthermore a million *colons*, French settlers and descendants of

---

[1] He was deposed after a referendum in 1955.

settlers, had made their homes in Algeria. These men and their families were understandably reluctant to hand over their power to Algerian nationalists. Equally understandably, the Algerians were increasingly opposed to remaining subservient to the French *colons*. A revolt broke out in Algeria in 1954 and it grew into a bitter and costly struggle which appalled the world as news leaked out of the terrible tortures inflicted and atrocities committed by both sides. The morale of the French Army, which had suffered a series of defeats from 1940 to 1954, was low, and this partly accounted for the determination of the officers to produce victory by whatever means they had. But victory eluded them and the drain on French economic resources became crippling. One way or another, the war had to end, but the Fourth Republic had no leader strong enough to take effective action without plunging the nation into civil war.

The Army felt that it was being let down by the politicians and that the time had come for strong leadership. Fearing that the French government might start negotiating with the rebels, the diehards organized a demonstration outside the government building in Algiers. A Committee of Public Safety was formed and a similar *coup d'état* was staged in Corsica. With his country on the threshold of civil war, the President of France asked de Gaulle to emerge from retirement and become Prime Minister.

## DE GAULLE AND THE FIFTH REPUBLIC

On June 1st, 1958, de Gaulle once more became Prime Minister. His first task was to present a new constitution to the country. This constitution, drafted largely by Michel Debré, the Minister of Justice, reduced the powers of the Assembly in law-making and in overthrowing Cabinets. At the same time, it increased the power of the President to take independent action. Only a strong government could solve the problems facing France, and the new constitution was designed to give France strong government. In a referendum, 80% voted in its favour.

De Gaulle took office for a seven year term as President and Michel Debré became his first Prime Minister. De Gaulle acted swiftly to prevent the Algerian revolt from spreading through Africa. He offered all the French overseas territories (Algeria was not included) one of four choices: (1) they could become independent immediately and leave the French Community. (2) They could become integral parts of France itself. (3) They could continue the partially autonomous status they held under the Fourth Republic. (4) They could proceed to full autonomy as self-governing states within the French Community. Only French Guinea chose independence.

De Gaulle had no immediate solution to the Algerian problem. In September 1959, he offered the Algerians full self-determination after four years if they would stop fighting. But the rebels were in no mood for parley, and the *colons* were not ready to surrender. Many of the latter had looked to de Gaulle to reassert French authority, and they tried to force his hand by demonstrations when he looked like wavering. The truth is that de Gaulle had few specific policies. He was convinced that it was his destiny to make France great once more. His actions in any given situation were governed by that belief. The Algerian war was a terrible embarrassment to France and a drain on her resources. Not until it ended could de Gaulle get on with his real mission. Accordingly, after protracted negotiations, agreement was reached with the F.L.N. (Front de Libération Nationale) and peace signed in March 1962. Algeria became independent. The majority of the colonists went to France.

In the next few years de Gaulle's government was an undoubted success. Aided by devaluation and a currency reform, France flourished economically. Industry, particularly the new growth industries like electronics, chemicals, plastics, and machine tools, expanded dramatically. Exports boomed. Oil and natural gas flowed from the Sahara. Politically, France enjoyed stability. Diplomatically, de Gaulle asserted his rôle as an independent World statesman. He cultivated close relationships with Dr Adenauer, Chancellor of the German Federal Republic from 1949 to 1963, and in 1963 negotiated a Treaty of Franco-German Co-operation. At a time when British Governments were accustomed to abuse and criticism from the leaders of their former colonial territories, de Gaulle was treated deferentially by the French Community. He recognized the government of Communist China and visited the U.S.S.R. He believed that Europe would be free only if it could stand equally beside both the U.S.A. and the U.S.S.R.

In 1960, France exploded its own atomic bomb, and in the same year de Gaulle gave notice to the U.S.A. to withdraw its air forces from France. In 1966, he withdrew French forces from NATO and the NATO Headquarters had to leave Paris. He was critical of Britain's apparently willing subservience to the U.S.A. in matters of defence, and it was this more than anything which led him to veto Britain's entry into the Common Market (see p. 13).

It was all a far cry from the Fourth Republic, or the Third for that matter. De Gaulle made his mistakes. He created a diplomatic scandal when, on a state visit to Canada in 1967, he appeared to give support to the Quebec separatists by ending a speech with the words 'Vive le Québec libre'. But for all of his first term as President, and for much of his second term which began in 1965, he personified the greatness of France.

His first major setback came in May 1968 when a student rebellion followed by widespread strikes brought his Government almost to its knees. Although de Gaulle was able to rally support for a while, the country rejected him in a referendum in April 1969, and he resigned.

He was a remarkable man, and a great national statesman in the old tradition. By his own standards, however, he is likely to be judged a failure. French industry is no less dominated by American business than that of other Western European countries. Neither France nor Europe can defend itself against serious attack without American support. The problems of Europe have become too great to be solved by leadership alone.

# 20 The United States of America

In 1870 the United States was still an infant power, a predominantly agricultural country with only a quarter of its population living in towns. Most of the vast area between the Mississippi Valley and the west coast was then not yet organized into states, though the Atlantic and the Pacific had just—in 1869—been linked by trans-continental railways. The tremendous growth in industry and big business was only just beginning. In 1950 the United States was the richest and most powerful country in the world. No history of Europe between these years can avoid reference to America and its rise to world power.

The two most important things to remember about America are first, that it is very big, and second, that it is separated from all other great powers by two large oceans. These facts could be used to explain much of its history. Its size helps to explain its wealth and its system of government, while its geographical isolation in part explains why until recently Americans were tempted to practise political isolation.

In some ways one of the chief obstacles in the way of British people seeking a closer understanding of Americans is that both nations speak English. This has led Englishmen, at times, to expect Americans to behave and to think like themselves and to be surprised when they do not. In fact, of course, not only has America developed along its own individual lines since colonial days, but also many American citizens have no links with Britain at all. Their ancestors are more likely to have come from villages near Naples or Warsaw than from Stratford-on-Avon. It is true, nevertheless, that there are marked similarities between many American and British traditions, but it should be recognized that they are similar—not the same.

## THE GOVERNMENT

Few things show more clearly the similarities and the differences between Britain and the United States than their respective systems of government. Unlike Britain, America has a written constitution, that is to say a document which sets out how the country shall be governed and what duties and powers the various branches of government shall have. The United States is a federation. Each individual state has its own government which has considerable powers over its own internal affairs. The federal government deals with inter-state matters and with foreign affairs, though over the years the trend has been for federal powers to expand at the expense of the states. The head of the federal government is the President, who is the chief of the executive. His powers, which were defined in 1787, it must be remembered, are greater than those enjoyed by most other heads of states in the 20th century. He conducts foreign affairs and makes (or declines to make) all treaties. He is the Commander-in-Chief of the armed services, and he can veto any bill passed by the legislature. Only a two-thirds majority vote in both houses of Congress—a difficult thing to get—can override his veto. Presidents are elected every four years—on the first Tuesday after the first Monday in November—by popular vote. If the President dies in office (as Roosevelt did in 1945), he is succeeded by the Vice-President for the remainder of the four year term. Neither the President nor any members of his Cabinet are members of the legislature.

The federal legislature, Congress, consists of two houses, the Senate which contains two representatives from each state regardless of size, and the House of Representatives, whose members are elected on a population basis. Bills may begin in either house but they have to pass both and then they must be signed by the President before they become law. The members of the House of Representatives (usually known as Congressmen) are elected every two years along with a third of the Senators, who serve for six years. It therefore can, and sometimes does, happen that a President finds himself half way through his term of office facing a hostile majority in one or other—or both—houses of Congress. This happened to Wilson in 1919, to Hoover in 1931, and to Truman in 1947.

A hostile Congress can frustrate a President's actions absolutely, since the House of Representatives has the sole right to introduce bills for raising revenue, and the Senate has the sole right to approve all treaties and to confirm the appointment of members of the President's Cabinet. Full-blooded war between President and Congress rarely occurs, however, since neither side wishes to scuttle the nation. For good or for ill, the President, Senators, and Congressmen are in office for fixed terms and they generally contrive to work together. The only ways to remove a President of the United States from office are by impeachment or by assassination. Of the two, assassination has proved the more successful. Only one attempt at impreachment has been made, and that failed. Four Presidents have been assassinated. Nevertheless, it is clear that the President is not always in such a strong position to implement his policy as executive leaders in other countries are to implement theirs. Wilson failed to get the Treaty of Versailles, which he had personally negotiated, through the Senate. Truman succeeded in getting the Marshall Aid Plan through in 1948 largely because of American fears of Communism in Italy.

The United States works a two-party system. Consequently there is some temptation in Britain either to regard the Republicans and the Democrats as being equivalent to the Conservative and the Labour parties, or else, since these labels obviously do not fit, to abandon all attempt to distinguish between them. It is true that neither of the two chief American parties advocates any fundamental change in society or in the way the country is run. The differences therefore tend to be on specific issues, many of which are of regional interest only. Often on national issues the differences are of emphasis only. The vastness of the country and the variety of regional interests make it impossible for two parties to adopt narrow policies which will be consistent for the whole nation. A Republican in one part of the country may be more liberal than a Democrat in another part, while being more conservative than a Democrat elsewhere.

Certain parts of the country have traditional allegiances, like the 'deep South', for instance, which has usually given solid support to the Democrats, who there embody the principle of white supremacy. But such areas do not exercise a decisive influence on elections, and no party can take their allegiance for granted. Although the Republican party has strong associations with big business, it is impossible to make a division between the two parties on class lines. There are too many exceptions. In the 1930's and 1940's, the Democratic party was associated with Roosevelt's New Deal—a programme of national reconstruction after the slump which embodied an unprecedented degree of government direction in the economic life of the country. Some Americans regard New Dealers as little better than Socialists, though few New Dealers would agree with this view, and not all Democrats are New Dealers. The labour unions are ready to support any candidate who supports their interests. In that way they receive the attention of both parties, and they have friends in power no matter which party wins. Both parties have their radical and conservative wings and because of the divergence of views amongst their members, neither party can exercise rigid control over the way Senators and Congressmen vote. Most issues find the parties divided.

The Republican and Democratic parties, then, mean different things to different people in different places at different times, but this is not to say that the differences are unreal. As far as the workings of the American political system are concerned, the continued existence of two great parties means that neither can afford to neglect the varied and varying wishes of the electorate. This is the way the people get the government they want.

Perhaps after all this the differences between the British and American systems of government may appear to swamp any similarities there might be. But a close examination of the two, which it would be out of place to pursue here, will reveal the broadly similar ways in which both countries strive after representative and responsible government. The American constitution was, after all, based on what were considered the best aspects of British government, which, in the 18th century at least, was the most envied in the world.

## FOREIGN AFFAIRS

One of the basic traditions of American foreign policy has been isolationism. This has meant isolation from European affairs. Isolationism grew partly from a genuine desire on the part of immigrants to shake the dust of Europe from their feet. The children of immigrants, wishing to emphasize their Americanization, often sought to dissociate themselves from their European background. But a more important reason for the growth of the tradition of isolation was that during the greater part of the 19th century the United States was too weak, too busy expanding on the North American continent, and too busy exploiting its own resources, to bother greatly about what was happening elsewhere. America was allowed to go its own way primarily because the European powers were too preoccupied with their own affairs. The growing wealth of the United States and its distance from the other continents tempted most Americans to believe that if European powers would keep out of the Americas then the United States could hold aloof from international affairs.

The basic principle of American foreign policy in the 19th century was contained in the Monroe Doctrine of 1823 which declared that no new colonies should be established by any European power in the Americas and that any interference in the affairs of the Latin-American states would be regarded by the United States as an unfriendly act. This doctrine had British support and without the backing of the British Navy it would have been meaningless—then and for many years to come. Few Americans realized, however, the extent to which their own safety depended on Britain's survival as a friendly power. That is why they continued to pursue isolationist policies long after they had become not merely selfish, but dangerous.

The national faith in isolation was in no way weakened by American participation in the First World War. If anything it was strengthened. The United States entered the war ostensibly to uphold another traditional doctrine, that of 'freedom of the seas'—a doctrine which upset Anglo-American relations at the beginning of the war (see p. 83). Less specifically, the Americans fought to make the world safe for democracy. Few Americans regarded the war as a war to protect themselves. They came to save Europe from itself, and having done so went home. The problems of peace and post-war settlement quickly confirmed Americans in the belief that European politics were best left alone. It was in this mood that the United States declined to join the League. So anxious were the Americans not to be dragged into another war, that between 1935 and 1937, as the European situation deteriorated, a series of Neutrality Laws were enacted which prohibited loans, credits, or the shipment of arms to belligerents, forbade American merchant ships to be armed or to sail in belligerent waters, and forbade Americans to travel on ships of belligerent nations. Although a law of November 1939 permitted the sale of arms on a 'cash and carry' basis and although Roosevelt did everything in his power to aid Britain short of going to war, only direct aggression against the United States itself brought the nation into the Second World War.

It was significant that the attack which brought the United States into the war in 1941 came from across the Pacific. If Americans traditionally turned their backs on Europe, their eyes traditionally faced west. Throughout the first part of the 19th century Americans leapt westwards from the original states on the eastern seaboard until they had engulfed, by purchase and by war, a broad belt of land across the continent. In 1867 Alaska was purchased from Russia, and Midway Island in the Pacific was annexed. It was an American, Commodore Perry, who in 1853 had opened up Japan to foreign trade and contact. In a brief flurry of imperialistic fervour at the end of the century, the United States went to war with Spain in 1898, and as result of a few weeks' fighting found itself the temporarily proud, though later embarrassed, possessor of subject peoples in the Philippines and Puerto Rico. In 1903 a convenient and bloodless revolution was engineered in the Panama Isthmus, which was then part of Colombia, and United States marines were landed with uncanny rapidity to prevent Colombian forces from suppressing the rising. The United States purchased forthwith from the newly declared Panama Republic a ten mile strip across the isthmus for the construction of a canal. The opening of the Panama Canal in 1914 gave her the sea link she needed between the two oceans which surrounded her.

The United States extended its influence in the Caribbean in the early years of this century, chiefly by financial domination, but in the late 20's a new policy of friendship and co-operation with Latin America, known as the Good Neighbour Policy, was inaugurated. Whatever the faults of South American governments, the United States has remained determined that they shall suffer no interference from outside.

Across the Pacific the crumbling of the Chinese Empire at the end of the 19th century and the rush of Japan and the European powers to establish themselves there filled Americans with apprehension. The American Secretary of State propounded the 'Open Door' policy, which called upon the powers who were entering China to keep the trade of that country open for all nations. Though this policy was not, in later years, accepted by Japan, America continued and continues to take a close interest in Chinese affairs.

## THE UNITED STATES AS A WORLD POWER

The economic growth of the United States and the part that country has played in reconstruction after the Second World War has been described in Chapter 1. All that is necessary here is to note the great change that has taken place since 1945 in America's political position in the world. Isolation is now almost a meaningless term. In an age when intercontinental ballistic missiles can be sent across the Arctic route to cities on the American continent, not even the illusion of geographical isolation remains. Pearl Harbour, in any case, demonstrated finally that oceans provide little security in themselves. The intense American involvement in South East Asia since 1945 has been based quite as much on historical and geographical facts as on ideological fears.

With the passing of isolationism, other pillars of American foreign policy, such as the principles of 'the Freedom of the Seas' and of neutrality, have gone too. The 'Open Door' policy in China has ceased to be applicable since the establishment of the Chinese People's Republic.

The immensely strong position the United States occupied at the end of the Second World War and the dominant part it was called upon to play in the ensuing Cold War, left no doubt in the minds of Americans of their power and their commensurate responsibilities. The United States has embarked on a new policy of aid, co-operation, and leadership.

Governments and people of the U.S.A. have learned that involvement in World Affairs attracts as much criticism, hostility, and bitterness as isolationism did. Even giving economic aid is full of pitfalls. Money meant to build roads and power stations to eradicate poverty can end up paying for better uniforms and bigger armies. In the 25 years since the war, the U.S.A. has learned to identify many of the problems of being a World Power, without coming up with many of the solutions to them. But it has shown no sign of abdicating its responsibilities. Isolationism is no longer a practicable policy.

# 21　Colonial Developments

Colonialism was distinctly old-fashioned in the middle years of the 19th century. Men like Gladstone and Bismarck, both of whom regarded Empires as things best got rid of or left alone, represented a view which was widespread in Europe. Yet the period from 1870 to 1914 witnessed such a feverish scramble on the part of European powers to acquire colonies that it has been named 'the age of imperialism'.

Why did this sudden change take place? An early explanation, and one dear to subsequent Communist writers, was in terms of what is called economic imperialism. The argument was that, because of the unequal distribution of wealth in the big producing countries of Europe, the capitalist classes were accumulating in the last decades of the century wealth which they could not re-invest. Therefore they sought new areas for investment. This argument has many times been refuted. It is too simple, and it ignores too many troublesome facts. Many countries, for example, were able to invest heavily in South America and Russia without asserting any political control. Again, other countries, like France and Russia, without having surplus capital, were anxious to expand.

There is no simple explanation for imperialism which will cover all countries on all occasions. Undoubtedly the economic urge was there, for, as well as offering opportunities for investment, colonies could supply raw materials and markets for goods. The need for new markets became important as successive countries raised tariff barriers to protect their own industries. Defence was another factor. After the race for colonies had begun, it became important to acquire naval bases and coaling stations before one's enemies seized them. But perhaps the greatest factor, to begin with at least, was the existence of individuals and groups of people with a strong will to colonize, whether they were statesmen, soldiers, traders or missionaries. It was significant that the older colonial countries, like Britain and France, played a leading part in this new movement, while Germany, even allowing for the fact that she was not unified until 1870, was a latecomer in the race. Once the race had begun, prestige became important. This was a major factor in the case of both the German and Italian empires, but even there strategy played a part. There was, indeed, nothing simple about imperialism. As one historian has written: 'It was not just that trade followed the flag, but that the flag accompanied the botanist and buccaneer, the Bible and the bureaucrat, along with the banker and the businessman.'[1]

### THE GRAB FOR AFRICA

In 1870 the greater part of Africa was uncolonized and almost unknown. By the end of the century the continent was almost entirely in the hands of European countries. First off the mark in the race was King Leopold II of the Belgians who took a great interest in the activities of Livingstone, Stanley and the other African explorers who in the 1850's, 60's and 70's made great journeys into the continent. Stanley, who reported vividly on the riches of the Congo basin, was invited to Brussels and there in 1878 the 'International Association of the Congo' was formed. This led the French to strike south into what later became French Equatorial Africa, while Britain extended her control in Egypt, and both Italy and Germany converged on Africa for the first time.

When Britain recognized the Portuguese claim to both banks of the mouth of the Congo—a claim that was historical rather than actual—Leopold became alarmed and sought support from France and Germany. As a result all the powers concerned in Africa were invited to the Berlin Conference (1884-85) and a common policy was drawn up. By the Treaty of Berlin of 1885 the powers agreed to suppress the slave trade and slavery, to permit free trade and to foster the well-being of the natives. They further agreed that, in future, claims would be recognized when powers had established effective control and had informed the other Conference powers. Most of the Congo Basin was to go to the 'International Association of the Congo' which in 1885 became the Congo Free State

[1] David Thomson: *Europe since Napoleon*, p. 464.

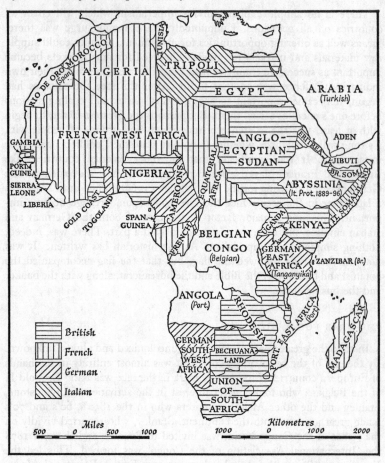

*Map 25. The Great Powers in Africa before 1914*

with Leopold as its King. After revelations of misgovernment and the exploitation of the natives, this private empire of the King became a Belgian colony—the Belgian Congo—in 1908.

Having agreed the rules of the race (though they were not always observed), the powers set off, and in the next few years, mainly through the agency of chartered companies, they spread themselves over the map of Africa. Less amicably they also turned their eyes to the east.

## CHINA

In the 1880's and 90's, Britain, France, Germany, Holland and America shared out the Pacific islands, but the great prize after Africa was China. Although the Portuguese, the Dutch and the British had made some trading contact with China and Japan in the past, these two countries were able to keep themselves almost entirely secluded from Europeans until the 19th century. China, which was a fast-decaying empire, succumbed first, and after a war with Britain was forced in 1842 to cede the then barren island of Hong Kong to the British and to open five so-called Treaty ports to the trade of all nations. Following this, western penetration increased and much of the direction of Chinese affairs passed into the hands of Europeans.

Japan had been even more secluded than China and it was not until 1854 that she was opened up to foreign trade following the arrival of an American fleet under Commodore Perry. Whereas, however, the Chinese resisted and resented Western penetration at every step, the Japanese flung the door wide open in their apparent anxiety to become westernized. Japan rapidly embarked on a course which was to make her a great industrial country and a great world power. In so doing, the Japanese were chiefly concerned at first to establish themselves on a footing of equality with their powerful visitors and thus to avoid the fate of China. Japan was, in fact, soon ready to expand at the expense of her neighbour. After the Sino-Japanese war of 1894–95, China ceded to Japan Formosa, the Liaotung peninsula, including Port Arthur, recognized Korea as independent, and placed Japan on an equal footing with the western powers in China. Russia, however, stepped in, with French and German support, and secured the cancellation of all Japan's gains except Formosa. In return Russia exacted the right to carry a railway across Manchuria, a lease of Port Arthur, and the right to fortify the Liaotung peninsula. Germany, for her part, acquired the lease of the port of Kiaochow, while Britain and France— joining in the battle for Concessions—both secured other ports. When Russia, Germany, France and Britain shared out spheres of economic influence on the Chinese mainland, the United States put forward its 'Open Door' policy (see p. 195), and the powers reluctantly adhered to it. The partition of China was avoided. The only western powers to annex land in China were Russia, which had pushed steadily east and south since the Crimean War; France, which acquired Indo-China (1885–87); and Britain, which had acquired Hong-Kong; but the effect of the western penetration of China was to weaken the country without giving it the protection of colonial status.

## COLONIAL POLICIES

In considering the colonial activities of the various powers, it is worth remembering that they each regarded their colonies in a different way. There was a marked difference in this period, for instance, between the British and French colonial policies.

The French policy has always been one of 'assimilation'. French colonies were regarded as being part of France, subject to the direct control of the central government, and uniformly governed. The colonial peoples were expected to learn the French language and customs and to absorb

French culture. This policy was modified with the acquisition of new lands in Africa and Asia, because most of the new subjects were too backward to be readily assimilated. For them the policy was one of association. The most capable of the natives would still be assimilated, but the masses would merely learn enough French to enable them to go about their work. Neither of these policies, it will be noted, aimed to preserve native customs or to prepare the people for self-government. Since the colonies were part of France, self-government was out of the question. This attitude can explain the bitterness provoked in France by the loss of Indo-China and by the independence movements in North Africa after the Second World War. It also explains the absence of a colour bar either in France or in its colonies.

Britain's policy, on the other hand, has essentially been to educate the natives to the point where they can govern themselves. The worst features of native societies—slavery and cannibalism, for example—have been eradicated, but where possible the structure of these societies and their customs have been preserved, and the authority of the chiefs respected. It has thus been much easier for Britain to relinquish her control of her colonies as they reached maturity. The system of colonial rule laid down for the Mandated Territories of the League of Nations and for their successors, the Trusteeship Territories of the United Nations, has long been established British practice.

### THE DECLINE OF COLONIALISM

The Second World War hastened the decline of colonial empires. In the Far East the control of the European powers was broken by the Japanese occupation of the colonies, and, in the case of Holland and France, by the German occupation of the mother countries. Once the ties were broken they were not easily restored. In 1945 the former Dutch East Indies declared themselves independent under the name of Indonesia, and their position was recognized in 1949. France carried the burden of war against the nationalists in Indo-China, but had to withdraw in 1954. In 1947 Britain handed over power in India to the two new states of India and Pakistan.

Burma and Ceylon became independent in 1948, and Burma left the Commonwealth. In Africa, Ghana (formerly the Gold Coast) led the way to independence in 1957, to be followed by some dozen other former British Colonies in the next decade. Most of these new countries chose to remain within the British Commonwealth, though increasingly they chose Republican status. All were admitted to the United Nations. In the same period, Malaya, Singapore, and the major islands in the West Indies also achieved independence.

In 1958, all the former French African colonies except Guinea joined the French Community and remained closely linked with France in financial, technical, and economic matters.

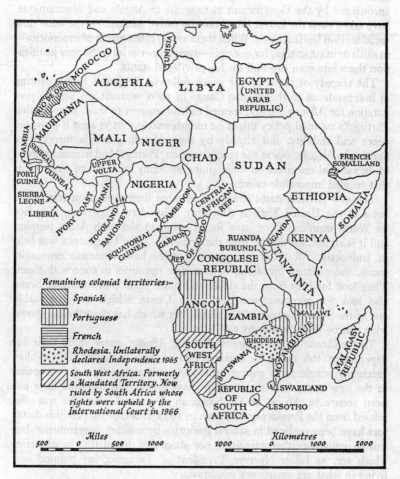

*Map 26. Independent African States, 1971*

Portugal alone of the major colonial powers resisted 'the wind of change'[1] Since 1951, the Portuguese colonies have been legally regarded as overseas provinces of Portugal itself. Portuguese peasants and artisans, encouraged by the Government to emigrate to Angola and Mocambique, have taken even the lowest jobs from the native African. At the same time racial tension has increased. When there are no other marks of superiority—in skills or in education, for example—racial superiority is the only justification the white man can find for his privileged status.

The tragedy of the civil war which followed Belgium's hasty granting of independence to the Belgian Congo in 1960, without any serious preparation for African control, seemed to lend support to those who felt that Portugal's colonial policy might be unfashionable, but at least it provided peace and stability. But already by then African guerrilla forces were fighting in Angola, and as the 1960's wore on, Portugal had to commit more of its national resources on maintaining an Army in Africa to wage a war that seemed impossible to win.

The new African states command between them over a quarter of the votes in the United Nations Assembly. They have a growing influence on World opinion. They have found common ties with Asian peoples, and it is significant that in 1955 the first Afro-Asian Conference was held in Indonesia. All these emergent countries have immense economic, social, and political problems, and too few resources to cope with them. They look for help from the richer and more developed countries. Some also look for guidance and help from China, which is recognizably one of the poor countries of the world, but which has nevertheless shown what can be done largely by self-help.

The evidence so far suggests that the African states value their independence too much to become tied to any particular Power-bloc. Internally, single party government is the rule rather than the exception in the new states, and dictatorships have arisen, but dictators have not been secure in Africa, as Dr Nkrumah discovered when he was dismissed from the Presidency of Ghana in 1966. It is true that civilian dictators have been replaced in several countries by military governments, but this is perhaps neither surprising nor altogether disquieting in countries which are, as Julius Nyerere, President of Tanzania, has pointed out, living in what are emergency conditions.

What is certain is that just as events in Europe vitally affected Africa in the last quarter of the 19th century, so events in Africa, in the last quarter of the 20th century, will vitally affect Europe.

[1] In a speech delivered before the South African Parliament in 1960, Mr Harold Macmillan, then Prime Minister of Britain, referred to African nationalism as 'the wind of change blowing through the continent'.

*Map 27. E.E.C. and E.F.T.A. Countries, 1971*

# Biographical Notes

ADENAUER, Dr. Konrad (1876–1967)
Born in Cologne. Studied law at Munich, Freiburg, and Bonn. Chief Burgomaster of Cologne 1917–1933. Dismissed by Nazis in March 1933. Reinstated as Chief Burgomaster by Americans 1945. Dismissed by British 1945. Formed Christian Democratic Union. First Chancellor of Federal Republic 1949. Established E.C.S.C. 1951. Resigned Chancellorship 1963. Retired from Chairmanship of C.D.U. 1966.

ANDRASSY, Count Gyula (1823–90)
One of the leaders of the 1848 revolution in Hungary. Fled the country and was hanged in effigy. Granted an amnesty in 1857 and became the first constitutional Prime Minister of Hungary in 1867. Foreign Minister of Austria-Hungary 1871–79.

ATTLEE, Clement (1883–1967)
Educated at Haileybury and University College, Oxford. Became a social worker and then a lecturer at the London School of Economics. Served in Gallipoli, Mesopotamia, and France (1914–19) and reached the rank of major. Entered parliament in 1922 and became Leader of the Labour Party in 1935. Deputy Prime Minister in the Coalition Government 1942–45. Prime Minister 1945–51. Created Earl 1955.

BETHMANN-HOLLWEG, Theobald von (1856–1921)
German Chancellor 1909–17. Resigned following a dispute with Hindenburg and Ludendorff.

BISMARCK, Otto von (1815–98) see pp. 27 ff.

CASTRO, Fidel (1927–    )
Educated at Jesuit School at Santiago and Havana, and at Havana University. Rebelled against Batista régime 1953. Sentenced to 15 years' imprisonment. Granted amnesty 1956. Exiled in Mexico. Raised rebellion in Cuba 1956. Became Prime Minister when Batista fled 1959.

CHAMBERLAIN, Joseph (1836–1914)
Son of a Birmingham screw manufacturer, he first worked for his father's firm and then entered local politics and became Mayor of Birmingham (1873–76). Became a Liberal M.P. 1876, but opposed Home Rule for Ireland and became leader of the Liberal Unionists. He also favoured Tariff Reform (the abandonment of Free Trade) and friendship towards Germany. Colonial Secretary 1895–1903.

CHAMBERLAIN, Neville (1869–1940)
Son of Joseph Chamberlain. Educated at Rugby. Member of Birmingham City Council 1911 and Lord Mayor 1915–16. Entered parliament as a Conservative 1918. Chancellor of the Exchequer 1923. Prime Minister 1937–40.

CHURCHILL, Sir Winston (1874–1965)

Educated at Harrow and Sandhurst. Between 1895 and 1898 he fought in Cuba, India and the Sudan. War correspondent in Boer War. Captured by the Boers but escaped. Conservative M.P. 1900. Later joined Liberal party and became First Lord of the Admiralty 1911. Resigned after failure of Gallipoli campaign 1915 and went on active service in France. Appointed Minister of Munitions 1916, Chancellor of the Exchequer 1924–29. Rejoined Conservatives 1925. Strongly criticized the Baldwin and Chamberlain government for failing to take strong measures against the threat from Germany. Became First Lord of the Admiralty on the outbreak of war in 1939 and was Prime Minister 1940–45 and 1951–55. Knighted in 1953, having refused a peerage.

CLEMENCEAU, Georges (1841–1929)

Began his political career while still a medical student. Mayor of Montmartre 1870. Elected to National Assembly 1871. Prime Minister 1906–9, 1917–20. Chairman of Versailles Peace Conference 1919.

DE GAULLE, Charles (1890–1970)

Fought in First World War under Pétain (q.v.). Captured by Germans. Served on Weygand's staff in Polish-Soviet war (1920–21). Fervent believer in tanks and motorized forces. Formed Free French in London 1940. Head of French Provisional Government 1945–46. Became Prime Minister in 1958 on the fall of the Fourth Republic. President of the Fifth Republic 1959–1969.

DELCASSÉ, Théophile (1852–1923)

French Foreign Minister 1898–1905. Played a leading part in securing the *Entente* with Britain 1904. Ambassador to St. Petersburg 1913–14. Foreign Minister 1914–15.

DISRAELI, Benjamin (1804–81)

Of Spanish Jewish descent but joined Anglican Church 1817. Conservative M.P. 1837, Prime Minister 1868, 1874–80. Created Earl of Beaconsfield 1876. He pursued a vigorous Imperial policy. Author of several novels.

EDEN, Anthony (1897–    )

Educated at Eton and Christ Church, Oxford. Entered parliament 1923 as a Conservative M.P. Foreign Secretary 1935–38 and 1951–55. Prime Minister 1955–January 1957. Created 1st Viscount Avon 1961.

EBERT, Friedrich (1870–1925)

Son of a cobbler. Leader of the German Social Democrats. First President of the Weimar Republic.

EISENHOWER, Dwight David (1890–1969)

Born in Texas. Served under General Patton in First World War. Held various administrative appointments in the army between the wars. C-in-C Allied troops in North African invasion 1942. Supreme

Commander in Normandy 1944. Supreme Commander NATO forces in Europe 1950. President of the United States 1952. Re-elected 1956.

FRANCO, Francisco (1892–    )
Son of a naval officer. Educated at a military academy. Rose to the rank of general by the age of thirty. Became director of a military academy which was closed by the Republican Government in 1931. Army Chief of Staff 1935. Organized Moroccan troops in nationalist rebellion 1936. Declared himself Head of State (*Caudillo*) 1938.

GAMBETTA, Léon (1838–82)
French Radical lawyer. Minister of the Interior 1870 and organizer of the defence of Paris. Leading politician in the early years of the Third Republic, though he was P.M. for ten weeks only (Nov. 1881–Jan. 1882). Advocated active colonial policy. Died mysteriously in a shooting accident.

GLADSTONE, William Ewart (1809–98)
Educated at Eton and Christ Church, Oxford. Began his political career as a Conservative but later became leader of the Liberal party. Prime Minister 1868–70, 1880–85, 1886, and 1892–94. He favoured Free Trade and Home Rule for Ireland. He disliked Imperialism and the Turkish Empire in Europe.

GOEBBELS, Paul Josef (1897–1945)
Granted degree of doctor of philosophy at Heidelberg University 1920. Joined Nazi party 1922. Member of the Reichstag 1930. Became Nazi Minister for Propaganda. Committed suicide 1945.

GÖRING, Herman (1893–1946)
Served in German airforce in First World War. Organized Nazi S.A. Wounded in 1923 putsch. Member of the Reichstag 1928. Became Prussian Minister-President under Hitler and also held other ministerial posts. Committed suicide 1946.

HESS, Rudolph (1894–    )
Born in Alexandria, Egypt. Joined Nazis 1921. Helped Hitler to write *Mein Kampf*. Named as deputy Führer. Flew to Scotland with peace proposals 1941. Life sentence at Nuremberg 1945.

HIMMLER, Heinrich (1900–45)
Organized Nazi S.S. Chief of Bavarian Police 1933. Chief of German National Police 1936. Minister of the Interior 1943. Chief of all troops in Germany 1944 (after the Army Plot). Committed suicide 1945.

HINDENBURG, Paul von (1847–1934)
German Army officer. Pupil of Schlieffen. Placed on retired list 1911. Recalled as C-in-C Eastern Front 1914. Supreme Commander 1916. President of the Weimar Republic 1925. Re-elected 1932.

HITLER, Adolf (1889–1945) see pp. 141 ff.

HO-CHI-MINH (1890–1969)
Vietnamese political leader. Founder member of French Communist

Party 1920. Met Lenin and Trotsky in Moscow 1922. Involved in revolution in China 1925–27. Imprisoned for political activities in Hong Kong 1931. President of Democratic Republic of Vietnam 1945. President and Prime Minister of North Vietnam 1954–55. Remained President until his death in 1969.

KAMENEV, Lev (1883–1936)
Real name was Rosenfeld. Banished to Siberia for anti-war activity. Took part in October revolution 1917. Formed triumvirate with Stalin and Zinoviev after Lenin's death. Married Trotsky's sister. Confessed to all charges at 1936 trial. Executed.

KEMAL, Atatürk (1881–1938)
Turkish soldier and statesman. Leading Young Turk. Commanded Turkish defence forces at Gallipoli 1915, and later fought in Palestine. Organized Nationalist Party 1919 and rejected peace treaty. President of Turkish Republic 1923–38.

KENNEDY, John Fitzgerald (1917–1963)
Born in Boston, Mass., son of millionaire Joseph Kennedy (U.S. ambassador to Britain 1940). Educated at London School of Economics and Harvard. Served in U.S. Navy during Second World War. Democratic Party Senator for Massachusetts 1952. Elected President of U.S.A. November 1960. Assassinated in Dallas, Texas 1963.

KERENSKY, Alexander (1881–1970)
Studied law at St. Petersburg. Member of Fourth Duma. Minister of Justice in Provisional Government 1917. Replaced Lvov as head of Provisional Government. Fled after Bolshevik revolution first to Paris and later to America where he became a law lecturer.

KHRUSHCHEV, Nikita (1894–    )
See pp. 182–186.

KITCHENER, Horatio Herbert (1850–1916)
British soldier. 1884 served in Nile expedition that attempted to relieve Gordon at Khartoum. 1898 at Fashoda. Gov. of Sudan 1899. Commander against Boers 1900. Secretary of State for War 1914. Planned for a long war. Drowned on the way to Russia 1916.

LAVAL, Pierre (1883–1945)
Began political career as a socialist lawyer specializing in trade union cases. Moved steadily to the right between the wars. Foreign Secretary 1934. Prime Minister 1935–36. Played leading part in Vichy régime. Executed 1945.

LENIN, Vladimir (1870–1924) see pp. 45, 115–18.

LLOYD GEORGE, David (1863–1945)
Born in Manchester. Began as a solicitor; then in 1890 entered parliament as Liberal member for Caernarvon, a seat he held for fifty-four years. As President of the Board of Trade 1905 and as Chancellor of

the Exchequer 1908 he was a leading Radical reformer. Prime Minister 1916–22. Created Earl 1945.

MACMILLAN, (Maurice) Harold (1894–   )
Educated at Eton and Balliol College, Oxford. Entered parliament as a Conservative M.P. 1924. Minister Resident with Allied H.Q. in North-West Africa 1942–45. Prime Minister 1957–1963.

MAO-TSE-TUNG (1893–   )
Teacher and Trade Union official in China in 1920s. Joined Communist Party 1921. Fought General Chiang-Kai-Shek's Nationalist Government 1945–49. Chairman of the People's Republic and of the Chinese Communist Party 1949–1959. Mao stepped down as Head of State but he remained in effective control.

MARSHALL, George (1880–1959)
American soldier and diplomat. Chief of Staff U.S. Army 1939–45. Retired from Army 1945 but was immediately sent as President Truman's special representative to China to negotiate between Chinese Nationalists and Communists. Appointed Secretary of State 1947 and introduced the European Recovery Programme (Marshall Plan).

MARX, Karl (1818–83) see pp. 44–45.

MONTGOMERY, Bernard. Viscount of Alamein (1887–   )
Educated at St. Paul's and Sandhurst. Eighth Army Commander 1942. C-in-C Armies in N. France 1944. C.I.G.S. 1946–48.

MUSSOLINI, Benito (1883–1945) see pp. 130–33.

NIXON, Richard Milhous (1913–   )
U.S. politician. Republican party Congressman 1947–51. Senator from California 1951–53. Vice-President of U.S.A. 1953–61. President 1969–   .

NKRUMAH, Dr. Kwame (1909–   )
Educated at Pennsylvania University, U.S.A., London School of Economics, and Gray's Inn, London. Formed Convention People's Party in Gold Coast (Ghana) 1949. Imprisoned. Released to become Leader of Government Business in the Assembly. Prime Minister of Gold Coast 1952–57, of Ghana 1957–60, and President of Ghana 1960–66. Overthrown by a military coup. Retired to exile.

PAPEN, Franz von (1879–1969)
Military attaché and spy in U.S.A. 1915. Served on Prussian diet 1921–32. German Chancellor 1932. Vice-Chancellor under Hitler 1933. Ambassador to Austria 1934, and to Turkey 1939–44. Acquitted at Nuremberg trial 1945.

PÉTAIN, Philippe (1856–1951)
Defender of Verdun 1916. Commander of French armies on the Western Front 1917–18. War Minister 1934. Head of Vichy government

1940–45. Sentenced to death 1945 but pardoned by General de Gaulle. Died in exile on island off Brittany coast.

POINCARÉ, Raymond (1860–1934)
French statesman and lawyer. Became a deputy in 1887 and first held office 1893. Prime Minister after Agadir crisis 1912. President of the Republic 1913–20. Recalled as Prime Minister 1922 during reparations crisis. Prime Minister again 1926–29.

ROOSEVELT, Franklin Delano (1882–1945)
Assistant Secretary of the Navy 1913–20. Governor of New York 1929–33. President of the United States 1933–45. Introduced the New Deal—the recovery programme after the slump.

STALIN, Joseph (1879–1953) see pp. 119ff.

STRESEMANN, Gustav (1878–1929)
Formed German People's Party 1918. Chancellor and Foreign Minister 1923–29. Nobel Peace Prize 1926.

THIERS, Louis Adolphe (1797–1877)
Prime Minister of France under Louis Philippe 1836–40. Arrested by Louis Napoleon 1851. President of the Third Republic 1871–73.

TITO (1892–    )
Real name Josip Broz. Fought in Austro-Hungarian army 1914–15. Imprisoned in Russia 1915–17 and took part in Bolshevik revolution. Returned to Yugoslavia and in 1928 was sentenced to five years' imprisonment as a Communist agent. Fought in International Brigade in Spain in Spanish Civil War. Organized guerrilla force in Yugoslavia after the German occupation in 1941. Prime Minister of Yugoslav Republic 1945–53. President 1953. Refused to allow Yugoslavia to become a Russian satellite state.

TROTSKY, Leon (1879–1930)
Real name Lev Bronstein. Took leading part in 1905 revolution and in Bolshevik revolution of 1917. Quarrelled with Stalin after death of Lenin. Exiled from U.S.S.R. 1929. Assassinated in Mexico.

WILSON, Woodrow (1856–1924)
Son of Presbyterian minister. Became Professor of Law and then President of Princeton University. Governor of New Jersey 1910. President of the United States 1912–20.

ZINOVIEV, Grigory (1883–1936)
Russian revolutionary. Worked closely with Lenin before Bolshevik revolution 1917. Head of Comintern 1919. Formed triumvirate with Stalin and Kamenev after Lenin's death. Confessed to all charges at his trial in 1936 and was executed.

# Index